LANGUAGE IN THE SCHOOLS

*Integrating Linguistic Knowledge
Into K–12 Teaching*

LANGUAGE IN THE SCHOOLS

Integrating Linguistic Knowledge Into K–12 Teaching

Edited by

Kristin Denham
Anne Lobeck
Western Washington University

LEA   LAWRENCE ERLBAUM ASSOCIATES, PUBLISHERS
2005   Mahwah, New Jersey   London

Lawrence Erlbaum Associates, Inc., Publishers
10 Industrial Avenue
Mahwah, New Jersey 07430
www.erlbaum.com

Cover design by Kathryn Houghtaling Lacey

Cover art by Rachel Denham.
The technique is intaglio-type etching

Library of Congress Cataloging-in-Publication Data

Language in the schools : integrating linguistic knowledge into K–12 teaching / edited by
    Kristin Denham, Anne Lobeck
        p. cm.
    Includes bibliographical references and index.
    ISBN 0-8058-4813-4 (alk. paper)
    ISBN 0-8058-4814-2 (pbk : alk. paper)
    1. Language arts. 2. English language—Study and teaching. 3. Language and education.
4. English teachers—Training of. 5. Linguistics—Study and teaching (Higher).
I. Denham, Kristin E., 1967– II. Lobeck, Anne C.

LB1576.L2973 2005
372.6—dc22   2004059124
                                                                         CIP

Printed in the United States of America
10 9 8 7 6 5 4 3 2 1

Contents

**PART II: INTEGRATING KNOWLEDGE OF LANGUAGE
INTO K–12 TEACHING**

Preface

As linguistics grows, the connections between linguistics and other disciplines become more and more evident. One area of particular interest to many linguists is how the scientific study of language can be productively applied in K–12 education in order to provide alternatives to more traditional approaches to language, approaches that are inconsistent with what we now know about language structure, variation, change, and acquisition, and language as a social tool. Collaboration between linguists and educators has begun to emerge on a national scale, producing work that aims to identify, first, what aspects of linguistic knowledge are most useful for teachers to know, and second, what kinds of activities and projects are most effective in introducing those aspects of linguistic knowledge to students. The importance of raising language awareness in the schools is reflected in the National Council of Teachers of English (NCTE)'s 1994 Position Statement on Language Study:

RESOLUTION

Resolved, that the National Council of Teachers of English appoint a committee or task force to explore effective ways of integrating language awareness into classroom instruction and teacher preparation programs, review current practices and materials related to language awareness, and prepare new materials for possible publication by NCTE. Language awareness includes examining how language varies in a range of social and cultural settings; examining how people's attitudes vary towards language across culture, class, gender, and generation; examining how oral and written language affects listeners and readers; examining how "correctness" in language reflects social– political– economic values; examining how the structure of language works from a descriptive perspective; and examining how first and second languages are acquired.

A similar commitment is reflected by the work of the Linguistic Society of America (LSA) Committee on Language in the School Curriculum, which explores ways to foster collaboration between linguists and K–12 educators through different research projects that target language education. The NCTE and the LSA have also recently made public their mutual interest in raising language awareness in the schools; members of the LSA, including LSA President, Ray Jackendoff, were invited to attend the 2003 annual NCTE meeting, where they presented a well attended panel on linguistics and education. Other excellent work in this emerging field has contributed resources for teachers that use the tools of linguistic analysis to raise awareness of language in a variety of ways, from teaching reading and writing to helping teachers identify language disorders, understand stages of language development, recognize differences in cross-cultural communication, to mention just a few (see, e.g., Andrews, 1998; Adger, Temple, Snow, & Christian, 2002; Wheeler, 1999a, 1999b). Also, several projects that encourage an understanding of dialect variation, in an effort to celebrate and support "home" language while also learning "school" language are in progress.[1]

The belief that language education is important is reflected in teacher education programs in many states that offer (and even require) linguistics courses for prospective teachers (at least for English/language arts teachers). Courses in linguistics, however, are not enough; prospective teachers also need help in learning how to apply their knowledge of language in the classroom in effective and productive ways. Given the relative youth of the field of linguistics education, however, and the relative dearth of linguistically informed materials currently available to K–12 teachers, teachers must either create their own curricula and materials, or turn to what is readily available, materials that rely on traditional methods and explanations (based, e.g., on the model of Latin grammar and prescriptive standards).

---

[1]For example, see:

John Baugh's projects at http://www.stanford.edu~jbaugh/faculty.html
Kirk Hazen's projects at http://www.as.wvu.edu/dialect/
John Rickford' s projects at http://www.stanford.edu/~rickford/
Walt Wolfram's projects at http://www.ncsu.edu/linguistics/bios/wolfram.htm

Prospective teachers, then, need resources that help them find ways to incorporate linguistic knowledge into the K–12 classroom in useful ways, and this book is intended to help fill that need. The book is intended as a text for students in teacher education programs who have a basic knowledge of linguistics, at the level of a typical introduction to linguistics course. We assume readers have a basic understanding of principles of sentence structure (syntax), word formation (morphology), sound patterns (phonetics and phonology), and sentence and word meanings (semantics), conversational principles (pragmatics), and basic knowledge of language acquisition, variation and change, and of language as a social tool. Each chapter in this book provides some specific ways that this basic linguistic knowledge can be applied and profitably used in the K–12 classroom. For example, the study of sentence structure, word formation, sound patterns, and meaning can aid in understanding and analyzing oral and written language (and sign language). Some examples include understanding and analyzing distinctions among literary genres, stylistic choices, and cultural literacies, or understanding and analyzing spelling patterns and irregularities. Knowledge of semantics, pragmatics, and discourse helps teachers identify and understand different conversational patterns, narrative structures, and discourse routines (in both oral and written language). Knowledge of language acquisition and variation can be applied in analyzing developmental patterns in writing and literacy in both first and second language readers and writers. Knowledge of language change and variation helps teachers respond to differences between academic and home speech varieties in reading, writing, and speaking. Understanding that language varies and changes systematically helps situate "standard" and "nonstandard" varieties of English in the classroom in reasoned rather than discriminatory ways. Studying language change and variation deepens our understanding of language as a dynamic system, expressed by shifts in word meaning, syntax, and pronunciation (the latter reflected in the English spelling system). Studying language as a social tool helps dispel myths and stereotypes based on language and fosters linguistic equality in an increasingly multicultural world.

It is unrealistic to think that we can include here all of the relevant ways in which linguistic knowledge can be specifically applied in the K–12 classroom, nor can we possibly discuss all of the ways in which knowledge of language is in general useful for teachers. Rather, what we can do here is contribute to the growing body of resources on linguistics and education, by taking prospective teachers beyond basic linguistics to ways in which linguistics can productively inform their teaching and raise their students' awareness of language. Part I of the book explores some of the ways in which basic linguistic knowledge can inform teachers' approaches to language issues in the multicultural, linguistically diverse classroom, and Part

II provides classroom strategies and suggestions for integrating linguistics into the K–12 classroom in various ways. Part Introductions provide an overview of the focus of each part, along with a summary of the content of each chapter. The book ends with a list of biographical sketches of each author that highlight their different contributions to linguistics and education.

ACKNOWLEDGMENTS

Editing a volume is a collaborative effort among editors, contributors, and the publisher, and is a much harder task than we ever imagined. We are grateful to a number of people for helping us complete this project. We thank our contributors for providing us with work of such high quality, and we thank our editor at Lawrence Erlbaum Associates, Naomi Silverman, and her assistant, Erica Kica, for their expert guidance and support. Thanks also to our families (Hugh, Ella, Ivy, and Jack Denham Conroy, and Charlie, Shellane, Schuyler, and Julia Jensen) for their support. We also, of course, thank each other.

REFERENCES

Adger, C. T., Snow, C. E., & Christian, D. (2002). *What teachers need to know about language.* McHenry, IL: Delta Systems Co., Inc. and The Center for Applied Linguistics (CAL).

Andrews, L. (1998). *Language exploration and awareness.* Mahwah, NJ: Lawrence Erlbaum Associates.

National Council of Teachers of English (1994). http://www.ncte.org/about/over/positions/category/lang/107490.htm

Wheeler, R. S. (Ed). (1999a). *Language alive in the classroom.* Westport, CT: Praeger.

Wheeler, R. S. (1999b). *Workings of language: From prescriptions to perspectives.* Westport, CT: Praeger.

PART

I

HOW KNOWLEDGE OF LANGUAGE CAN INFORM TEACHERS IN MULTICULTURAL, LINGUISTICALLY DIVERSE CLASSROOMS

Chapters in this section show how certain aspects of linguistic knowledge can help teachers approach a number of different language issues, especially in a multicultural, linguistically diverse classroom. Included in this section are chapters that address bilingualism, language authority and standardization, language variation, language change, creole languages, deafness and sign language, patterns of cross-cultural discourse, and diagnosis of language disorders. The information covered in these chapters is not intended to prioritize certain aspects of linguistic knowledge over other equally relevant ones, but to focus on several fairly "accessible" aspects of linguistic knowledge that have relevant applications in today's schools. The chapters assume some basic linguistic knowledge on the part of the reader, and suggest ways in which the teacher's knowledge may be extended or applied in the classroom.

In "Linguistics and Education in Multilingual America," John Baugh provides a brief survey of the history of linguistic diversity within the United States, including neglected populations such as deaf students, and the relevance of federal and state regulations pertaining to language minority students. Baugh draws on both his own personal childhood experiences as a minority language speaker, and on his years of experience as director of Stanford University's teacher education program, and shows how a greater appreciation of culture, language, and linguistics can help teachers and their students in all subject areas. Baugh affirms the importance of linguistic training to enhance teacher professionalism and the national quest to advance educational achievement for all American students.

Jin Sook Lee's chapter, "Embracing Diversity Through the Understanding of Pragmatics," identifies the core knowledge of pragmatic theories useful to teachers, and how teachers can make the connection between the theories and their practice. She discusses both the culture-specificity and universality of Grice's Conversational Maxims and the Cooperative Principle, based on cross-cultural research. The chapter also provides an overview of Speech Act Theory, discussing how different cultures perform speech acts and what factors guide the choice of strategies used. The chapter concludes with suggestions for activities on how rules of speaking can be identified and taught, allowing students and teachers to co-construct and discuss their understanding of language use.

Susan Burt and Hua Yang's chapter, "Growing Up Shifting: Immigrant Children, Their Families, and the Schools," also uses pragmatic knowledge, but to show how an awareness of pragmatic differences is crucial for teachers, especially ESL teachers, whose job is to help immigrant children and families cope with the language and culture of the host community. Specifically, their chapter examines the issue of *pragmatic failure*, or communication breakdown, in immigrant communities based on *language shift* as speakers begin to identify with mainstream rather than home language. The authors show, based on evidence from ways in which different generations of Hmong speakers perform different social/linguistic politeness practices, that knowledge of pragmatics plays a crucial role in understanding communication both within the community and between immigrant and host communities. Their ideas may be extended to other minority groups.

Kathryn Remlinger's chapter, "Language and Gender Matters in the Classroom" provides insights into ways in which gender and sexuality shape identity, and how these identities are reflected through classroom talk. Remlinger examines how linguistic features, such as meanings, turn-taking strategies, and function in discourse can help teachers understand how students use language to create various notions about gender, and how they use language, not only in gendered ways, but also in ways that influence what it means to be *girl* and *boy*, *woman* and *man*, ways that can limit participation in classroom interaction for some students. The author explains how awareness of gender identity and how it is constructed and reflected through language is central to inclusive classroom discourse.

Alicia Beckford Wassink's chapter, " 'My Teacher Says . . .': Mastery of English and the Creole Learner" presents key facts about the linguistic structure of creole languages, as well as some general facts about the sociohistorical settings in which creole languages develop and are subsequently used. Research into language arts education and language ideology in Creole-speaking regions has found that students' understandings about their language use, as well as teachers' own attitudes toward the Creole, impact the extent to which students are able to synthesize new material presented in the language arts classroom. The discussion is based on the outcomes of research conducted in Jamaica from the early 1980s to the present and the chapter broadens the scope of this discussion to North America, where the immigration of more than 100,000 new persons from the Caribbean each year contributes significantly to the changing face of the American classroom.

Jean Ann and Long Peng's chapter, "The Relevance of Linguistic Analysis to the Role of Teachers as Decision Makers" examines the relevance and importance of linguistics in teacher education. The authors argue that while knowledge of sociolinguistics and grammar is crucial for preservice and inservice teachers, an understanding of sociolinguistics and grammar is not sufficient. Linguistic instruction in teacher education must include training in linguistic analysis. Teachers must learn to think and analyze like a linguist, that is, to be able to look at language data, analyze it, and draw proper conclusions on the basis of the data. This conclusion stems from the authors' consulting work as specialists in teaching English to speakers of other languages, school visits, and discussions with elementary and secondary school teachers. One central finding that emerges from these contacts is that teachers are increasingly asked to make diagnostic decisions. These diagnostic decisions rely not infrequently on linguistic data. The ability to conduct basic linguistic analyses and interpret linguistic data is not only important, but is absolutely indispensable to accurate assessments of students' needs and the provision of appropriate services.

Lynn S. Mancini's chapter, "A Positive Sign: An Overview of the Benefits of Signing in the Classroom" examines the use of ASL in classrooms. Exposure to sign language has been shown to provide benefits to a wide variety of students. The use of American Sign Language (ASL) in the classroom permits Deaf children to learn content information in their native language, and facilitates the learning of English as a second language. Research indicates that children with special needs ranging from autism to mental retardation can improve their communication abilities when they are taught to sign; for example, hearing ESL Hmong students who were exposed to ASL outperformed their nonsigning peers on a Language Assessment Survey for English, and preschool and kindergarten children who did not have special needs and who were taught to sign earned significantly higher scores on receptive English vocabulary tests than their nonsigning peers.

Anne Lobeck's chapter, "A Critical Approach to Standard English," discusses the weaknesses of the traditional approach to grammar teaching that remains entrenched in the public schools, and offers an alternative approach to teaching grammar and Standard English that is informed by current descriptive linguistics. This approach provides students with tools of academic success, but at the same time raises language awareness, and challenges the normative approach to "good" and "bad" grammar that so often results in linguistic discrimination and stigmatization. Lobeck shows that by critically analyzing Standard English, teachers (and therefore their students) deepen their understanding of dialect, register, prescriptive versus descriptive grammar, and differences between oral and written language. Teachers and their students can then critically analyze and even challenge notions of "prejudicial" error in writing and speech.

Patricia MacGregor-Mendoza's chapter, "Bilingualism: Myths and Realities," examines a number of well-accepted public myths about bilingualism, and shows how applications of linguistics in the classroom can help dispel them. The author discusses ways in which we judge speakers with more than one language in their repertoire, and how the lack of knowledge or resistance to challenge traditional mindsets can often lead to larger misunderstandings about individuals who are speaking. Such misunderstandings can in turn lead teachers to unfairly evaluate the skills and abilities of their students. The author exposes the language attitudes that underpin myths about bilingualism, and suggests how teachers can provide environments that support and promote the development of both of a bilingual's languages. This task in turn engages both the community members and school personnel in an effort to provide abundant, well-rounded linguistic and cultural experiences.

And finally, Robert Bayley and Sandra Schecter's chapter, "Spanish Maintenance and English Literacy: Mexican-Descent Children's Spanish and English Narratives," examines both oral and written narratives of elementary students and the complex relationships among Spanish language maintenance, Spanish and English literacy, and the development of children's oral and written abilities in both languages. The authors investigate an array of features associated with children's writing in both languages, using a "teachers' assessment rubric" developed by bilingual teachers. They then comment on the results, in particular on how language proficiency is linked to the roles that Spanish and English play in the child's life, and that linguistic training strengthens teachers' cross-cultural sensitivity and understanding of "good" writing.

CHAPTER

1

Linguistics and Education
in Multilingual America

John Baugh

Long before European explorers ever set sail in search of new trade routes to India, the land that now occupies the United States flourished with hundreds of indigenous native languages. Language contact occurred among adjacent tribes, but did not reflect the status of multilingualism as we think of it in modernity. As European exploration and colonization expanded, so too did the New World mixing of global languages. The advent of the African slave trade further increased this linguistic mélange, albeit through the overt dislocation of enslaved Africans from communities where their native languages survived (see Denham, chap. 12, this volume).

The spread of European colonization and conquest eventually displaced native languages, supplanting them with the languages of dominant conquering groups and their posterity. Linguistic evolution throughout North and South America owes its existence to the political might imposed on indigenous populations that were powerless to rebuff cultural and linguistic transgressions.

The ensuing social stratification of linguistic diversity throughout North and South America shares a pattern of economic inequity that parallels corresponding fluency, or the lack of it, in the dominant language of the former European nation of conquest. The fact that most Brazilians speak Portuguese, or that most Mexicans speak Spanish, is similar—in historical terms—to the fact that the vast majority of Americans speak English. However, this pattern of linguistic domination is somewhat misleading, and masks the underlying plethora of languages that survive in subordinate relation to the corresponding dominant language.

Few people who strive to solve the educational problems of linguistically diverse students do so by contemplating the linguistic consequences of colonization, but the origin of contemporary linguistic inequality owes its existence to the inherently unequal relationships that emerged from colonization, slavery, and the emergence of socially stratified linguistic patterns.

The vast majority of U.S. citizens trace their linguistic ancestry to homelands where English was not native. As a result, the typical immigrant experience was that of someone who came to America speaking little or no English, and who subsequently did their best to master English as a secondary language. Most first-generation immigrants spoke with strong accents that were highly stigmatized, and it typically took at least three generations for a family to make a successful transition to posterity who were fluent native (American) English speakers.

This process shared some generic similarities throughout the nation, but also reflected unique characteristics depending upon the immediate circumstances where English was acquired. Those who learned English during the 1920s on the lower east side of Manhattan differed from those who learned English in Appalachia in the 1800s, and other contrasts are readily available.

Few Americans fully appreciate the unique linguistic legacy of slave descendants when compared to every other immigrant or indigenous group that resided within the United States. Whereas the typical immigrant from Europe or Asia may have arrived in the United States in poverty, speaking a language other than English, they typically did so with others who shared their mother tongue, thereby transplanting the language of "the old country" to a ghetto in America where people who shared common customs from the heritage country would coexist in close proximity as a self-selected support network; however, these immigrant communities were typically isolated from the larger English speaking populations that surrounded them.

By striking contrast, no African language—nary a one—survived the Atlantic crossing intact. It was not the case that Africans somehow forgot their mother tongue while other immigrants did not; rather, slave traders isolated slaves by language to prevent uprisings whenever possible, and by so doing they intentionally eliminated African languages as viable means of communication among the slaves.

The pidginization and creolization processes that ensued on plantations throughout the South are well attested, and the isolated Sea Islands off of the eastern coast of South Carolina and Georgia gave rise to the Gullah and Geetche dialects that reflect some of the strongest African retentions of any form of vernacular African-American language.

The history of linguistic diversity that is a hallmark in this nation of immigrants existed long before a national ethos that every child born in this country also had a birthright to a publicly funded education, and prior to 1954 that ethos was not equally available to all citizens. Since 1954 the nation has continued to struggle with matters of racial and social equity, and linguistic diversity among students exacerbates this effort.

Although educators and legislators have attempted to endorse and enforce policies that would advance English proficiency and literacy among all students, these policies have met with differential success and have often been highly politicized by efforts to admonish those who do not already possess English fluency, or to restrict and curtail the types of educational opportunities that are available to students for whom English is not native.

LINGUISTIC DIVISIONS WITHIN THE UNITED STATES

Although controversies surrounding race, gender, sexual orientation, and affirmative action in support of groups that have been historically underrepresented in higher education and the highest paying professions still exist, every U.S. resident (who is not linguistically impaired) can be classified into three basic groups:

1. Those for whom Standard English is native (SEN)[1]
2. Those for whom Standard English is not native (SENN)
3. Those for whom English is not native (ENN)[2]

Previous linguistic studies of the United States affirm that every racial or ethnic group within the nation is composed of citizens derived from all three categories. For example, if one looks at people of African ancestry we find X% = SEN, Y% = SENN, and Z% = ENN. That is to say, some people of African ancestry are native speakers of Standard English, while others are native speakers of English, albeit employing a dialect that is not standard. Still others of African ancestry have not learned English as their mother tongue (e.g., many Haitian immigrants).

---

[1]Standard English within the United States is diverse, owing to the fact that there is a national norm, typically associated with broadcast speech, and there are local provincial norms that reflect the speech of well-educated speakers of American English who reside in a particular area. Thus, the regional standard of American English in Boston differs from the regional standard in Atlanta. National norms for Standard American English are shared across the continental United States as well as Alaska and Hawaii.

[2]The Deaf should also be included within this population. English for them is usually a secondary language; very few people who are deaf should be thought of as having English as their native language.

It is partially for this reason, and others, that policies based exclusively on race tend not to fully serve their intended populations. Latinos reflect similar patterns of linguistic diversity, as do other ethnic or racial minorities. For the purpose of this discussion it is imperative that we acknowledge this linguistic diversity, particularly if we strive to address historical inequalities in society.

SOME PERSONAL REFLECTIONS ON THE QUEST
FOR SOCIAL AND EDUCATIONAL EQUALITY

The topic at hand is one that is very personal, because I attended inner-city public schools in Philadelphia and Los Angeles where the vast majority of my peers did not speak Standard English. We were often admonished or chastised for our lack of English proficiency, and occasionally teachers conveyed a sense of empathy for our linguistic plight. This empathy or criticism did not fit neatly into established sociological categories; some of the harshest critics of our English usage came at the hands of African-American teachers who decried the use of street language in the classroom. Some White student teachers, in my experience, were often more linguistically tolerant, whereas some of their peers were much less so. One Asian-American teacher, who spoke with a distinctive accent, appeared to be the most understanding, having struggled with learning English.

As a young child living in minority communities that were predominantly African American, I lived with the impression that we (i.e., Black people) had clear linguistic advantages over those who were learning English as a secondary language, but this illusion was shattered when I encountered White speakers of Standard English who would directly or indirectly ridicule my speech.

At that time I tended to associate Standard English with what Fordham and Ogbu (1985) have classified as "talking white," and African-American language usage with "talking black." My comfort level was higher with nonstandard usage; it was the language of my peers and my community. Also, those boys who embraced Standard English with enthusiasm were castigated within the Black peer group, or worse.

Like many of the informants that Ogbu (1999) described from Alameda, California, I tended to associate "proper English" with Whites, and I had difficulty reconciling the fact that if "proper English" belonged to Whites, then "improper English" belonged to us—and this was very disconcerting. If that was the case then some of the smartest people known to me spoke "improperly" and I detested any suggestion that they were inherently less intelligent than Whites who spoke Standard English.

At that time, during the 1950s and 1960s, I was unaware of early efforts by linguists, educators, and civil rights attorneys to redress long-standing racial inequalities. My experience was limited to schools and communities where few (if any) students were proficient users of Standard English, and those who aspired to do so were openly targeted for mild-to-harsh playground sanctions intended to reinforce vernacular linguistic conformity.

LINGUISTIC NEGLECT AND LANGUAGE BIAS IN EDUCATIONAL POLICIES

Brown v. Board (1954) was based on racial classification, and said nothing whatsoever about linguistic diversity. Thus, while the resulting ruling attempted to overcome barriers of racial discrimination, educational barriers based on linguistic discrimination or other linguistic differences derived from the African slave trade were neglected in that watershed decision.

Elsewhere (Baugh, 2000) I describe the legal and political consequences of this more fully as reflected by the Oakland Ebonics controversy where that school board passed a controversial resolution declaring that 28,000 African-American students within that school district were not native speakers of English, and should therefore be eligible for the same kind of bilingual education funding that was available to other students for whom English is not native.

With the advent of hindsight we now know that Oakland educators created a firestorm of linguistic and educational controversy, but the linguistic problems that they raised in 1996 have yet to be resolved, because federal, state, and local educational policies tend to be divided into different linguistic categories than those described above:

A. Title III of the No Child Left Behind (NCLB) educational act is intended to support English language learners, who are classified as "Limited English proficient."

B. Deaf students are not included within Title III as akin to other English language learners; rather, the Individuals with Disabilities Educational Act (IDEA) is intended to meet their special educational needs.

C. Students who are native speakers of English, but who lack native proficiency in Standard English have been overlooked by federal educational mandates.

Under existing laws the language and literacy needs of students who are SENN are not adequately addressed, and controversies still loom regarding the education of ENN students based on voter initiatives that are intended to restrict and control the education of English language learners.

In the latter instance we have witnessed circumstances throughout the nation where voters have overwhelmingly passed initiatives that are intended to dismantle existing bilingual education programs in favor of integrating English language learners into English dominant classrooms within one year. Ironically, the vast majority of voters who have passed these initiatives will not be subject to their mandate. In other words, because the vast majority of voters in all states are monolingual English speakers, neither they nor their children will be the objects of the constrained bilingual educational programs for which they are voting.

As one who advocates greater educational choice for all students, as well as efforts to support greater local control and authority over educational programs and policies, I would prefer to give professional educators greater flexibility with regard to the ways in which they can support their (S)ENN students toward greater proficiency in Academic English and Standard English.

At present the most pervasive Supreme Court ruling that addresses these concerns is Lau v. Nichols (1974) which confirms that students who are English Language Learners (ELL) are obliged to receive an education that accounts, in some manner, for their lack of English proficiency. Again, this ruling does not apply to slave descendants of African origin, nor does it apply to deaf students who—in most cases—are English language learners. (See Mancini, chap. 7, this volume.)

THE PARADOX OF MISPLACED RESOURCE ALLOCATION

Given my professional linguistic bias toward attempts to resolve social and educational inequities in society, I am struck by the paradox of misplaced resource allocation. Although this discussion is not devoted directly to an evaluation of affirmative action, or other attempts to help level educational playing fields, I routinely attempt to evaluate the amount of linguistic diversity that exists within a school or other complex organization before commending solutions for their particular needs, especially if those needs are intended to enhance communication among culturally and linguistically diverse constituents (such as students, or employees).

Readers of this volume will no doubt recognize that some of America's most intractable educational problems exist in inner-city or rural schools that tend to be underfunded and are often overcrowded. Frequently, inexperienced teachers in these schools are poorly equipped to know how best to manage a large classroom, to say little of a large class composed of students from very diverse backgrounds.

RELEVANCE TO TEACHING AND TEACHER EDUCATION

Having once directed a teacher education program for secondary teachers, I am mindful of the many pressures and regulations that student teachers face as they enter the teaching profession. Whereas elementary teachers are devoted to the educational well being of students across various subjects, middle school and high school teachers are subject area specialists, and must have in-depth knowledge of their specific specialization.

As previously suggested, I think education benefits from linguistic awareness. I believe that teachers are more likely to be effective if they can make educational accommodations based on the linguistic background of individual students. I am also aware of the trend to place ever increasing burdens on teachers and that is not my present objective. Indeed, one of my aspirations for this volume, and the valuable chapters that it contains, is that suggestions contained herein can help provide educators with linguistically sophisticated solutions that enhance their professionalism at the same time that their job performance becomes more effective and, perhaps, somewhat easier through a greater appreciation of how linguistics can enhance educational prospects for all students.

In this instance, recognizing the role that linguistics might play in helping to educate citizens in multilingual America, it is essential that educators and others who are concerned with the educational welfare of students give serious consideration to the prospect of competing linguistic loyalties, much like those that I encountered as a child.

Many educational mandates for language minority children are insensitive to the combination of cultural loyalty and linguistic discomfort that English language learners encounter upon entering classes that make no accommodation to their special linguistic circumstances. I disagree with those who argue that "sink or swim" immersion with no regard for student's home language circumstances is "best" for students. Although I concede that some students survive insensitive total immersion approaches to education, I think there are more effective alternatives that provide equal or greater fluency in the target language and which do so while valuing the heritage language that students bring with them to the classroom.

In the context of the current global economy, America's multilingual heritage is an underutilized asset, be it in global business transactions, or matters of national security. The philosophy of subtractive language education, that is, which subtracts the heritage language in search of English, is wrong-headed and shortsighted.

Demand for English language instruction has never been greater, and no one needs to convince English language learners of the benefits of English proficiency within the larger American society. This demand for more English instruction grows at a time when some would politicize the field, arguing that those who teach English as a second language are more concerned with their pay than they are with the educational advancement of their students.

Anyone who is familiar with English language instructors knows that this hurtful stereotype defies reality. Those who chose to enter this profession do not do so for the money, which is modest. They typically recognize the greater public need to assist non-English speakers toward greater English proficiency, and they often do so with limited resources that are inadequate to the task.

In the same spirit that the National Board for Professional Teaching Standards has raised the domestic bar for high quality professional teachers across the country, I would like to see Schools of Education offer supplementary specialization credentials (which already exist in many states) that prepare student teachers or in-service teachers with skills that are tailored to students from the full range of linguistic backgrounds outlined earlier in this chapter.

A comprehensive linguistic educational strategy is one that truly leaves no child behind by recognizing the linguistic value of their heritage language, be it standard English or otherwise, and then tailoring the corresponding education of the student to match their individualized needs. The trend toward creating environments that increase educational choices for parents, students, and educators is consistent with this philosophy. The economic challenges associated with providing flexible educational options in a cost-effective manner will be more daunting, but no less worthy. Elsewhere (Baugh 1983) I encouraged those who are concerned with the educational welfare of less fortunate students to find creative extracurricular supplements for children who do not have the same benefits as students who are able to attend schools with smaller classes and greater educational resources.

SOME (NEARLY?) INTRACTABLE BARRIERS TO SUCCESS

A combination of factors enhances the inertia of ineffective policies that inhibit the likelihood of systemic success for students who lack proficiency in Standard English in academic settings. The financial investment that is required to adequately serve such students could be substantial, that is, if the entire burden of funding for language education fell exclusively upon public educators. Indeed, it is the prospect of increased taxes to support educational programs for (language) minority students that many politicians and nonminority citizens find objectionable.

There is a long-standing myth among many native American English speakers that their non-English speaking ancestors were somehow able to pull themselves up by their own linguistic bootstraps, that is, without any additional burden on taxpayers who funded public schools that did not cater specifically to their heritage languages, but these impressions are somewhat misleading. They don't readily acknowledge the cross-generational nature of the linguistic transition from heritage languages other than English to English, nor do they fully comprehend the fact that many first generation immigrants who did not speak English were the objects of linguistic ridicule. These linguistic barbs defy racial classification, owing to the fact that nearly every immigrant group has felt the sting of linguistic prejudice, save those immigrants who arrived speaking English or whose accents were deemed charming.

Because the United States continues to attract citizens from various parts of the world, America also continues to be a multilingual nation that is composed of linguistically diverse residents. The 2000 U.S. census suggests that these trends will prevail, as immigrants continue to seek temporary-to-permanent residency here.

Some would argue that those who chose to immigrate to the United States should recognize, in advance, that English fluency is not only an asset, it is their personal responsibility and they should not expect others to pay for it. This "you're on your own" philosophy has some substantial drawbacks, not the least of which is that it does not fully utilize or view linguistic resources that immigrants bring to the United States as potential assets.

Dual language programs exist in some school districts that strive to overcome this trend, where sufficient numbers of students who are native speakers of different languages strive to work together to teach their fellow students "the other language." Although this approach has met with considerable success in some schools, it relies heavily upon sufficient numbers of students who are willing and able to engage in give-and-take language pedagogy, and often patterns of residential segregation create pockets of linguistic isolation such that many schools simply don't have the proper ratio of linguistically diverse students to support such programs.

As long as politicians are unwilling to view languages other than English as national assets, we are unlikely to witness growing investments in efforts to preserve fluency and literacy in heritage languages other than English. Those of us in fields pertaining to language education can lend support to this effort by advancing effective bilingual education programs, and by dismantling those that prove to be ineffective. In the absence of such proactive efforts, self-appointed guardians of language minority education will continue to castigate programs that strive to improve educational prospects for English language learners.

LINGUISTIC CONTRIBUTIONS TO EDUCATIONAL EQUALITY AND EXCELLENCE

Readers of this volume are witness to some of the latest direct efforts to harness linguistic science in support of education. However, some of the earliest efforts in this regard were developed through the Center for Applied Linguistics (CAL) more than thirty years ago. Charles Ferguson, who is well known for having first described the nature of Diglossia (Ferguson, 1959), founded CAL with the recognition that a greater understanding of global linguistic diversity was in the national interests, and ever since that time scholars affiliated with CAL (and other institutions of higher learning that are devoted to applied linguistics and educational linguistics) have attempted to produce research that draws upon empirical linguistic studies to affirm educational advancement for students from highly diverse backgrounds.

References to these works are readily available throughout this text and elsewhere (see Adger, Christian, & Taylor, 1999; Cleary & Linn, 1993; Darder, Torres, & Gutiérrez, 1997; Wolfram & Christian, 1989; Zentella, 1987), and readers who are unfamiliar with these studies will find a wealth of valuable information there. The more immediate observation at hand stems from the fact that these linguistic contributions typically do not calibrate easily with laws or policies that are intended to advance the education of linguistically diverse students.

Whereas the federal government has defined language minority students as those who lack English proficiency, linguists were among the first to demonstrate that many African American students encounter significant linguistic barriers on their road to academic success (Smitherman, 1981). Despite more than 40 years of linguistic research on African American language norms, federal educational statutes have never acknowledged that many African American students require special linguistic intervention and support to enhance their educational prospects.[3]

Similarly, linguists were among the first to recognize that American Sign Language (ASL) is a distinct language that should not be viewed as a dialect

---

[3]Ironically, the federal government did (temporarily) extend such recognition to speakers of Hawaiian Creole English, as reflected by a categorical federal education program that was once intended to teach Standard English as a second dialect, but for a combination of political and financial reasons that program was disbanded.

of English. These discoveries lead in turn to observations about many native ASL signers who were English language learners, albeit through a different physical modality. Rarely do people consider ASL as adding to the multilingual heritage of the United States, but it does. Moreover, linguistic contributions to the study of ASL expose weaknesses in official efforts to isolate deaf education programs in comparison to programs and policies that are intended for other English language learners.

Beyond the established linguistic studies that seek to increase our understanding of linguistically diverse students lay future needs to further support their education. At present there is a tendency to place additional burdens and programs on pre-service and in-service teachers as they attempt to cope with the myriad of problems that confront students from various backgrounds.

A productive alternative exists through efforts that are intended to ease teacher's workloads through programs and procedures that demand LESS of their precious time while enhancing their effectiveness in classrooms. Technological advances are illustrative in this regard, and they also mitigate some of the relevant concerns about funding programs that may be tailored to various heritage languages.[4]

Future efforts, such as those contained within the present volume, may lend greater support to the educational welfare of the nation by affirming the neglected linguistic assets that immigrant students and their families bring to multilingual America, and, in so doing, we may better understand ways to increase their fluency and access to Standard and Academic English while cherishing the national resources that their heritage languages contribute as direct assets in the current global economy.

REFERENCES

Adger, C., Christian, D., & Taylor, O. (Eds.). (1999). *Making the connection: Language and academic achievement among African American students: Proceedings of a conference of the Coalition on Language Diversity in Education*, Washington, DC: Center for Applied Linguistics; McHenry, IL: Delta Systems Co.

Ball, A. (1991). *Organizational patterns in the oral and written expository language of African American adolescents*. Unpublished doctoral dissertation. Stanford, CA: School of Education.

---

[4]For example, Valdés (2005) has devoted considerable attention to efforts to advance gifted and talented English language learners who serve as interpreters within their own families. Her studies are illustrative of efforts that not only redefine how language minority students are viewed, but she also provides pedagogical scaffolds that can guide educators and parents who seek to nurture effective bilingualism among their students as an asset in the future global economy. Also, Ball (1991) and Lee (1993) independently provide alternative scaffolds for African American students who strive to increase their proficiency in Standard and Academic English, and they do so in ways that do not demand excessive amounts of time on the part of classroom teachers who may be unfamiliar with African-American culture.

Baugh, J. (1983). *Black street speech: Its history, structure and survival*. Austin: University of Texas Press.

Baugh, J. (2000). *Beyond ebonics: Linguistic pride and racial prejudice*. New York: Oxford University Press.

Brown v. Board of Education. (1954). United States Supreme Court.

Cleary, L. M., & Linn, M. D. (Eds.). (1993). *Linguistics for teachers*. New York: McGraw-Hill.

Darder, A., Torres, R. D., & Gutiérrez, H. (Eds.). (1997). *Latinos and education*. London: Routledge.

Ferguson, C. (1959). Diglossia. *Word, 15*, 325–340.

Fordham, S., & Ogbu, J. (1985). Black students' school success: Coping with the burden of acting White. *The Urban Review, 18*, 176–206.

Lau v. Nichols. (1974). United States Supreme Court.

Lee, C. (1993). *Signifying as a scaffold for literary interpretations: The pedagogical implications of an African American discourse genre*. Urbana, IL: National Council of Teachers of English.

Ogbu, J. (1999). Beyond language: Ebonics, proper English and identity in a Black-American speech community. *American Educational Research Journal, 36*, 147–184.

Smitherman, G. (Ed.). (1981). *Black English and the education of Black children and youth*. Detroit, MI: Wayne State University Press.

Valdés, G. (2005). *Expanding definitions of giftedness: Young interpreters of immigrant background*. Mahwah, NJ: Lawrence Erlbaum Associates.

Wolfram, W., & Christian, D. (1989). *Dialects and education: Issues and answers*. Englewood Cliffs, NJ: Prentice-Hall.

Zentella, A. C. (1987). *Growing up bilingual: Puerto Rican children in New York*. Malden, MA: Blackwell.

2

Embracing Diversity Through the Understanding of Pragmatics

Jin Sook Lee

In today's classrooms teachers are faced with the challenge of effectively teaching and interacting with students from culturally and linguistically diverse backgrounds. The National Clearinghouse for English Language Acquisition (ERIC/CLL) reported that between 1989–2002, the national growth rate for K–12 English language learners enrolled in public schools was 105%. These children often bring to the classroom rules of speaking based on the norms of their home culture and language. The model of communicative competence needed to function effectively in their home community may not fit the expectations of the mainstream academic culture. When speakers use different rules of speaking, it opens doors to greater chances of misunderstanding and conflict.

The role of teachers working with culturally and linguistically diverse students is not easy; teachers not only need to help students acquire the pragmatic norms of the academic discourse community, but also need to validate and respect the diversity and individuality that the students possess. They must support students in developing and maintaining multiple communicative competencies in the discourse patterns used in the home and school culture.

Wong Fillmore and Snow (2000) in their report entitled "What Teachers Need to Know about Language" argued that all teachers must learn about the structure, functions, and uses of language to better deal with the challenges that culturally and linguistically diverse students bring. They identify teachers' roles as the following. As communicators, teachers must understand their own discourse patterns and possess the skills to understand those of other cultures as well as acknowledge there is none more superior than the other. As educators, teachers must play a critical role in the development of social and academic language in their students through the understanding of students' language development. As evaluators, teachers must make valid and accurate judgments about the abilities of the students and help them understand the different sources of variation in language use. As agents of socialization, teachers must facilitate the process of socialization for children from culturally and linguistically diverse families in ways that respect the children's home language and culture.

Thus, teachers need fundamental knowledge about rules of communication and about variations in discourse styles. This can be achieved through the study of pragmatic principles and theories. This chapter reviews three central principles in the study of pragmatics: the Gricean conversational maxims, principles of politeness and face, and speech act theory. The goal is to offer an overview of pragmatic principles that can inform teachers in their analytic attempts to understand how communication works in various cultures.

PRAGMATICS AND ITS RELEVANCE TO TEACHERS

Pragmatics is "the study of language from the point of view of users, especially of the choices they make, the constraints they encounter in using language in social interaction, and the effects their use of language has on other participants in the act of communication" (Crystal, 1985, p. 240). Pragmatics analyzes how language is used to perform functions and to create meaning in context. In order to fulfill the communicative functions we choose to accomplish, we select particular linguistic structures that match the surrounding context we are operating in. For example, we have access to many different expressions that can convey a request to "borrow a pencil" such as "who has a pencil?" "lend me a pencil," "I need a pencil," "may I borrow your pencil please?" etc. However, depending on the surrounding context, certain expressions can be more appropriate than others; for instance, in North American English, very close friends would probably say "I need a pencil" or "can I use your pencil" instead of "may I borrow your pencil please?" to one another, although these expressions convey the same basic request.

The relationship between the linguistic structure and the context is defined by the sociocultural norms of the particular language. In other words, different cultural and linguistic systems may have different rules governing what should be said to whom, when, where, why and how. In the Korean culture, slight bumping of the shoulders with passers-by on the street does not call for an "I'm sorry" or an "excuse me" nor is a "thank you" required to a waiter who brings you your food; whereas in the North American culture, "I'm sorry" and "thank you" would be appropriate in both instances, respectively.

Successful communication takes place when interlocutors adhere to similar pragmatic expectations of what should happen in a particular context. It is essential for teachers to learn about pragmatics so they have the basic tools to understand and identify their *own* communication styles as well as their students'. Without a critical examination of the differences and similarities between the cultural assumptions and language practices of oneself in relation to others, teachers are likely to expect their own norms of language behavior from students of different backgrounds and make misinformed judgments of students' language abilities. Only after teachers recognize what communicative resources students bring with them, can they begin to successfully help them acquire the language rules of the classroom. The following sections review three pragmatic principles that are central to understanding the basic ways in which language is used.

CONVERSATIONAL MAXIMS

As native speakers of a language, we constantly employ pragmatic strategies that allow us to play with words to achieve various communicative effects. Our language use is not random; it systematically follows certain tenets of conversational behavior. Grice (1975) laid the groundwork for the study of conversation by formulating a set of fundamental conversational maxims. He claimed that all interlocutors are expected to cooperate with one another in recognition of a common purpose to communicate, which he defines as the Cooperative Principle. Associated with this general principle are four types of individual maxims that direct the particulars of discourse. The Maxims of Quantity, Quality, Relevance, and Manner specify the rules of what should and should not be included in the conversation and how they should be said.

  (i)   Maxim of Quantity: One should give as much information as is called for, but no more information than is required.
  (ii) Maxim of Quality: One should tell the truth, and not say anything that one lacks information for.
  (iii) Maxim of Relevance or Relation: One should ask questions and provide information that is relevant to the course of conversation.
  (iv) Maxim of Manner: One should be orderly, brief, and avoid ambiguity and obscurity when speaking.

The failure to live up to these codes of conversation in itself conveys a different meaning. As creative and logical beings, based on the context, we make inferences from utterances that seem to violate the maxims. For example,

[phone rings]
John: Can you get that, Susan?
Susan: I'm in the shower.

In this case, it appears that Susan is not following the Maxim of Relevance; that is, she is not directly answering John's question. However, John assumes that Susan is obeying the Cooperative Principle and makes the connection between Susan being in the shower and therefore, not being able to answer the phone.

The foregoing examples illustrate that through intentional violation of one of the conversational maxims, speakers can produce a conversational effect known as conversational implicatures that call for hearers to make inferences based on shared knowledge between interlocutors. A conversational implicature is "something which is implied in conversation and left implicit in actual language use . . . that is captured by a certain type of regularity that cannot be captured by a simple syntactic or semantic rule" (Mey, 1993, p. 99). Due to the differences in how contexts are interpreted across cultures, teachers working with culturally and linguistically diverse students cannot automatically assume that the student will be able to make the intended inferences. Until students have been enculturated into the pragmatic norms used by the academic mainstream culture, more direct and explicit speech is needed to minimize the risks of miscommunication.

In contradiction to Grice's claim that the maxims of conversation are universal, research has shown that the interpretations of the maxims seem to vary cross-culturally (Blum-Kulka, 1991; Fraser, 1990; Keenan, 1976). For example, in the case of the maxim of quantity, unlike the North American academic community, where the primary objective of a conversation is to exchange necessary information, in the Malagasian society, speakers are expected to "provide less information than is required, even though they have access to the necessary information" for cultural reasons such as "the stigma of guilt attached to those who provide incorrect or damaging information and the reactive rarity of new information in society" (Keenan, 1976, p. 70). Thus, for the Malagasian culture the perception of what is considered enough information is determined by the degree of accuracy or the content of information.

Moreover, with regards to the maxims of relevance and manner, Cazden (1988) noted that "while there may be situational reasons for pressing children to speak relevantly and to the point, there are developmental and cultural reasons why it may be difficult for children to meet such expectations" (p. 193). According to Philips' (1983) research on the discourse patterns of the Warm Springs Native American Community, responses to a topic are often given long after the topic has already shifted to avoid direct conflict between speakers. Although adult speakers have access to linguistic strategies that allow them to introduce a comment that is not directly related to the previous utterance (i.e., by the way, going back to your point about . . . , speaking of), children do not use such discourse markers and thus, their comments are often judged to be off topic. Tannen (1981) reported an excerpt of classroom discourse in which the class had been talking about people's ages at the time of Martin Luther King's death. The following dialogue shows how after the teacher signals a shift in topic, a Black student's "belated" response to an earlier initiation was ruled out of turn by his teacher's nonverbal gestures, thus leading the student to abort his communicative attempt. What the teacher failed to recognize was that this student's response was valid in that it was adhering to the discourse patterns of his home culture that carried a different interpretation of the maxim of relevance. Because the teacher and the student held different assessments of what is acceptable as relevant to the topic and the timing of the response, a powerful teachable moment where the student was attempting to share a personally relevant experience with the class was lost.

> T: *I'm just going to start this story on Martin Luther King//*
> S: *Well, my mama was 19 when she died.*
> T: *[Touches Student's knee] (and moves on with story)*

Thus, when the teacher and students abide by different rules of speaking, it can lead students to shut down their willingness to participate or engage in communicative events. The purpose of these examples is not to give teachers a list of possible interpretations of maxims that different communities may hold, but to bring teachers to recognize variations in communicative styles and realize that the same utterance in the same context can be interpreted differently or completely misunderstood by speakers from different cultures.

POLITENESS THEORY AND FACE

Another principle of language use that is believed to underlie communication is the principle of politeness (Brown & Levinson, 1987). Although in some instances speakers intentionally use rude language, for the most part, conversation is directed under the assumption that speakers use various linguistic strategies such as indirectness, hedges, or politeness markers to strategically avoid conflict. Building upon the Cooperative Principle, politeness strategies are used to establish, maintain, and renegotiate relationships between speakers. What is considered polite and impolite varies depending on the social norms of the culture. For example, in Korea, when a teacher is reprimanding a student for misbehavior, it is considered to be impolite and disrespectful to look the teacher directly in the eye or to bombard the teacher with explanations, whereas in the United States, students are expected to look the teacher in the eye as a sign of attentiveness and are asked to provide a explanation for their behavior. Moreover, maxims of conversation may intentionally be violated to achieve politeness. For instance, the maxim of quality is often flouted to save someone from a truthful evaluation of a bad performance. If someone were to ask a teacher what he or she thought of a student's essay and the teacher's only comment was that the essay was neatly typed, the intended implicature in North American English is that the teacher does not think highly of the paper, but is trying to be polite about it, whereas in the Chinese or Korean culture, this implicature may not necessarily hold because the stylistic presentation of one's work is often a standard criteria of assessment.

In order to understand why speakers use politeness strategies to avoid conflict, we need to examine the notion of face, the positive public image that people try to portray to others; that is, "face is the negotiated public image mutually granted to each other by participants in a communicative event" (Scollon & Wong Scollon, 1995, p. 35). In general, an underlying goal in communicative interactions is for interlocutors to save face. In order to save face, when inherently face-threatening speech acts such as complaining or refusing are being performed, speakers rely on politeness strategies to minimize the risk of conflict or embarrassment that can lead to losing face.

Although the concern about face exists in all cultures, the ways in which face is assessed is culture-specific. Matsumoto (1988, 1989) reported that unlike western societies where the individual and the individual's rights are greatly emphasized, non-western collectivist societies such as the Japanese and Korean are concerned with sustaining their proper position in relation to the others in the group and his or her acceptance by the people in the group, which is the basic norm that governs all social interaction. In a similar vein, according to Liu (2001), in Asian cultures such as Chinese, Korean, and Japanese in order "to save face, one needs to be polite to maintain a good public image, but to be polite, one needs to give others' face priority when there is a conflict between one's own interests and those of others" (p. 207). This is different from the more individualistic societies such as the North American culture, where face-saving is an act of defending one's own territory from the encroachment of others rather than of establishing oneself in proper hierarchical relation to others (Matsumoto, 1988). The differences in how face is conceptualized in communicative attempts can explain why students from certain Asian backgrounds are reluctant to speak out in class or challenge the ideas presented by the teacher or other students. Chinese and Korean students, for example, are taught that in order to show respect for someone's ideas one must agree with them. Thus, to maintain both their own face and the speaker's face, they refrain from acts such as questioning the ideas of speaker in public. For many Asian second language learners, this is coupled with their insecurities about their language ability. They tend to keep silent in class to avoid being misunderstood as being impolite. They believe that by not disrupting the teacher and giving other students more opportunities to talk, it is a way for them to express politeness and to be viewed favorably (Liu, 2001, p. 207).

Each speech community develops politeness principles from which they derive certain linguistic strategies. The decisions about which strategy is used within a culture depend on how the culture assesses the following three factors: the relative power relationship between speaker and hearer often defined in terms of age, rank, wealth, education, etc.; the social distance between speaker and hearer; and the individual ranking of the particular imposition in the social context in which it is used. What is interesting is how the combination of these three factors brings about different interpretations and expectations with regard to the communicative event. For teachers, it is important to know that different cultures have different ways of expressing deference and politeness and of maintaining face. Thus, teachers need to develop an awareness of such strategies and cues to better understand the intentions of students from culturally and linguistically diverse backgrounds.

SPEECH ACT THEORY

Although the Gricean maxims and politeness theory together provide a basis for understanding how interactions work, speech act theory is better able to explain how meaning and action are related to language. When a particular utterance is used as a request to do something, we are concentrating on what that utterance means and how the listener should react to it. Because each utterance is carrying the communicative force of performing a particular act, it is called a speech act. Speech Act Theory is basically concerned with what people do with language, the communicative intentions of speakers, and the process by which they achieve the communicative goal. Teachers have a routine repertoire of speech acts that they use in class such as the speech act of instructing, requesting, explaining, greeting, and reprimanding to name a few. However, the rules that govern how, when, and why a certain speech act is performed may differ culturally. The objective of this section is to provide a general overview of what speech acts are so that teachers will have the analytic framework to identify the differences and similarities in language use.

Speech Act Theory builds on Austin's (1962) observation that in saying something, one is performing something. He states that communication is a series of communicative acts that are used systematically to accomplish particular purposes and that all utterances perform actions by having a specific force assigned to them. Austin (1962, p. 102) isolates three basic kinds of acts that are simultaneously performed by uttering something.

Locutionary act: uttering a certain sentence with a certain sense and reference, which is roughly equivalent to meaning in the traditional sense

Illocutionary act: the making of a statement, offer, promise, etc., when uttering a sentence by virtue of the conventional force associated with it

Perlocutionary act: all of the effects on the audience whether intended or unintended, brought about by means of uttering the sentence, such effects being special to the circumstance of utterance

For instance, if a teacher were to say "Johnny, would you like to come to the board?" the locutionary act would be the literal meaning of the question whether Johnny is interested in coming to the board or not; the illocutionary act would be the communicative force of the question directing Johnny to come to the board; and the perlocutionary act would be Johnny actually going up to the board or Johnny refusing to go up to the board. Speech act theory demonstrates how one could mean more than what is literally said. For students, the acquisition of the speech acts used in classroom discourse would entail recognizing the cues that identify the speech act and understanding the intended meanings of all three acts.

Searle (1969), however, proposed that the basic unit of human linguistic communication is the illocutionary act. He presents five basic kinds of actions or speech acts that one can perform in speaking:

1. Representatives which commit the speaker to the truth of the expected proposition (i.e., asserting, concluding)
2. Directives which are attempts by the speaker to get the addressee to do something (i.e., requesting, questioning)
3. Commissives which commit the speaker to some future course of action (i.e., promising, threatening, offering)

4. Expressives which express a psychological state (i.e., thanking, apologizing, complimenting, welcoming)
5. Declarations which affect immediate change in the institutional state of affairs and which tend to rely on elaborate extra-linguistic institutions (i.e., christening, declaring war)

Although Searle classified the number of basic things that one does with languages into a limited number of illocutionary acts, he suggests that one can do more than one of these at once in the same utterance. For example, by uttering "John is the best student in class," the speaker can be complimenting John's performance in class and also making an assertion about John's individual capabilities.

In addition, speech acts can be performed directly and indirectly. Direct speech acts refer to the performance of certain acts where the speaker means what he or she literally says (e.g., "Open the door!"), and indirect speech acts refer to performative acts where the speaker means more or something other than what is uttered (e.g., I am hungry → an assertion about the speaker's appetite or a request for food or a request for attention). For the purposes of a teacher, the five categories proposed by Searle may or may not be the most relevant, however, it illustrates a way for us to start thinking about the different ways in which language functions can be categorized that may be more relevant to the types of speech acts teachers use in class. For examples, by analyzing classroom discourse in a Western Australian Aboriginal school, Malcolm (1982) adopted the framework of viewing language in terms of communicative functions and developed a schema of the categories of speech acts commonly found in Western Australian Aboriginal children's lessons such as declined replying after a direct elicitation, deferred replying after a longer than normal pause, and unsolicited replying without having been nominated. The use of the decline replying speech act by students in a U.S. classroom would be considered an indication that the students are having difficulty with the content material presented or are not interested in learning, whereas in the classroom studied by Malcolm, these speech acts were appropriate and common.

Thus, it is important for K–12 teachers to investigate how they and their students use speech acts in the classroom and to identify the functions that underlie each speech act. What are the speech acts that are commonly used in the classroom? What cultural assumptions and beliefs are governing how the teacher uses speech acts and how his or her students use speech acts? Are the speech acts clearly conveyed? Who seems to be having trouble understanding the speech acts and why? These are some questions that teachers can begin asking to develop a more critical perspective on their teaching practices.

CONCLUSION

With this basic knowledge about pragmatics, how can teachers begin to learn more about the various pragmatic norms that govern their own and their students' communicative styles? In working with linguistically and culturally diverse students, the central pragmatic principles reviewed in this chapter can serve as points of departure for teachers to start a systematic analysis of students' language behaviors. For example, through vignettes about how one would perform a certain speech act given a particular context, teachers and students can explore their own assumptions and beliefs of how language is used as well as those of others within and across cultures. Analysis of the responses can bring about rich discussions on politeness strategies as well as cultural norms of what is appropriate and inappropriate in particular contexts. It can also provide a means for students to gain empowerment in knowing that the ways of their home culture are not "wrong" or "strange" or "stupid," but that they are a different set of rules than the ones used in the North American academic culture.

By explicitly teaching about variations in communicative patterns and pointing out the differences that each student may bring to the classroom, it gives teachers a focal point not only to discuss the fact that all communicative styles are valuable for different purposes, but also to help students realize and compare and contrast the differences in styles. Thus, students and teachers are encouraged to become ethnographers of language use in the various speech communities in which one participates. (For detailed discussion on pedagogical activities that model how learners and teachers can become ethnographers of language use, see Lee and McChesney, 2001).

In sum, through activities that encourage teachers and students to examine their own language use practices and those of others, they will be able to co-construct their understanding of language use to allow for an open and concrete discussion of the many different ways that communication takes place. June Jordon (1988) provided a powerful example of how she and her students in a course on African American Vernacular English (AAVE) critically examined their language use, their values, and worldviews and their positions in society by bringing their "invisible" assumptions and language rules to the surface and testing the validity of their generated assumptions and rules against those of other AAVE speakers. Such activities will offer teachers and students a way to raise their level of meta-awareness about the various pragmatic modes, to develop multiple pragmatic competencies, and to respect and understand other ways of communication that are different from their own. As we live and work in an increasingly global community, it is our goal as teachers to help students develop multiple competencies in both the pragmatic systems of their academic community and their home community by socializing students into the new ways and sharing respect for their native ways.

REFERENCES

Austin, J. (1962). *How to do things with words*. Oxford, England: Oxford University Press.

Blum-Kulka, S. (1991). Interlanguage pragmatics: The case of requests. In R. Phillipson, E. Kellerman, L. Selinker, M. Sharwood-Smith, & M. Swain (Eds.), *Foreign/second language pedagogy research* (pp. 255–272). Clevedon, UK: Multilingual Matters.

Brown, P., & Levinson, S. (1987). *Politeness: Some universals in language usage*. Cambridge, England: Cambridge University Press.

Cazden, C. (1988). *Classroom discourse: The language of teaching and learning*. Portsmouth, NH: Heinemann.

Crystal, D. (1985). *A dictionary of linguistics and phonetics*. Oxford, England: Blackwell.

Fraser, B. (1990). Perspectives on politeness. *Journal of Pragmatics, 14,* 219–236.

Grice, H. (1975). Logic and conversation. In P. Cole & J. Morgan (Eds.), *Syntax and semantics, 3.* New York: Academic Press.

Jordon, J. (1988). Nobody mean more to me than you and the future life of Willie Jordon. *Harvard Educational Review, 53*(3), 363–374.

Keenan, E. (1976). The universality of conversational postulates. *Language and Society, 5,* 67–79.

Lee, J., & McChesney, B. (2001). Discourse completion task: A teaching tool for developing sociocultural competence. *ELT Journal, 54*(2), 161–168.

Liu, J. (2001). *Asian students' classroom communication patterns in US universities*. Westport, CT: Ablex.

Malcolm, I. (1982). Speech events of the Aboriginal classroom. *International Journal of Sociology of Language, 36,* 115–134.

Matsumoto, Y. (1988). Reexamination of the universality of face. *Journal of Pragmatics, 12,* 403–426.

Matsumoto, Y. (1989). Politeness and conversational universals: Observations from Japanese. *Multilingua, 8,* 207–221.

Mey, J. (1993). *Pragmatics: An introduction*. Oxford, England: Blackwell.

Philips, S. (1983). *The invisible culture: Communication in the classroom and community on the Warm Springs Indian Reservation*. White Plains, NY: Longman.

Scollon, R., & Wong Scollon, S. (1995). *Intercultural communication*. Cambridge, MA: Blackwell.

Searle, J. (1969). *Speech acts*. Cambridge, England: Cambridge University Press.

Tannen, D. (1981). Review of H. Mehan, Learning lessons. *Language in Society, 10,* 274–278.

Wong Fillmore, L., & Snow, C. (2000). *What teachers need to know about language*. Eric Clearinghouse on Languages and Linguistics Special Report. This document can be found at website http://www.cal.org/resources/teachers/teachers.pdf

3

Growing Up Shifting: Immigrant Children, Their Families, and the Schools

Susan Meredith Burt
Hua Yang

Lillian Faderman's *I Begin My Life All Over* (1998) presents narratives by Hmong refugee immigrants from Laos, now living in the United States. In one narrative, a young gang member, Loco Vang, tells how a communication rift developed between himself and his father:

> When I go home, I know my mother cares about me a little. But I don't really talk to her. I just say, "Hi, hello." Everytime I used to help out my dad, he never showed respect to me for it. If he needed me to help him carry, I'd help him. But he never said "Thank you," or "You're welcome." So I got mad. Whenever he tells me what to do now, I don't even bother to do it. (p. 193)

Intergenerational miscommunication is a staple in most societies, but particularly painful in immigrant groups, whose members typically also struggle with feelings of alienation toward their adopted culture (Hones & Cha, 1999). Our project applies the linguistic perspective of intercultural pragmatics to understanding how pragmatic differences between English and Hmong can lead to *pragmatic failure* (Thomas, 1983), a type of communication breakdown in which the speaker's intentions are badly misunderstood. If there are pragmatic differences between host language and immigrant language, we can expect to find pragmatic failure both within the immigrant community and between the immigrant and host communities. We argue that an awareness of these pragmatic differences is crucially important for those in the schools, especially ESL teachers, whose job it is to help immigrant children and families cope with the language and culture of the host community.

Central to the linguistic experience of immigration is *language shift*, that process by which a population comes to substitute the language of its host society for its heritage language in everyday use. Language shift is now evident in Hmong communities in the United States; the elders in Hmong-American families typically speak Hmong, their children are bilingual, and the grandchildren are most comfortable in English. Differences in linguistic repertoires between family members can obviously lead to communication difficulties between generations. The perspective of intercultural pragmatics, however, leads to the hypothesis that even if members of different generations in immigrant communities manage to learn the language that speakers of the other generation are most comfortable with, there will still be communication difficulties, because members will have grown up with different expectations of how to speak in certain situations; in other words, they will have grown up with different pragmatics.

SPEECH ACT REALIZATION

One major focus of intercultural pragmatics over the last two decades has been speech act realization, the study of how speakers perform linguistic/cultural/social tasks such as requesting, refusing, complimenting, apologizing, greeting, or thanking (Blum-Kulka, House, & Kasper, 1989; Gass & Neu, 1995; Kasper & Blum-Kulka, 1993). Even advanced second-language learners, researchers have found, often have difficulties performing such speech acts in their second language, since both linguistic and cultural knowledge necessary for felicitous performance may elude them. For example, in Anglo-American interaction, appearance compliments are frequent, and may even function as greetings ("Nice sweater!"), particularly between women. An American who tries to transfer this strategy to a culture where compliments are less frequent but more consequential may find that she is being offered the sweater—not the outcome expected or intended. This mismatch between communicative intention and result is an example of how pragmatic failure (Thomas, 1983) can result from use of an inappropriate speaking strategy.

Although pragmatic differences between languages and cultures have been widely explored, most of the research has been on pragmatic differences between languages with large speaker populations, such as English, French, Spanish, German, Chinese, and Japanese (see Lee, chap. 2, this volume). However, pragmatic differences also occur when speakers of less well known languages, such as Hmong, encounter more populous language communities, such as American English-speaking communities. An understanding of these differences is clearly important for speakers of both languages involved (see Lee, chap. 2, this volume).

There is also reason to believe that pragmatic failure between generations of a single community who have different language repertoires, and thus, different pragmatic knowledge, will accompany language shift. Loco Vang's story is one example: If the young man expected thanks for helping his father with household chores, we can guess that these expectations came from exposure to Anglo-American politeness practices, where "please" and "thank you" are rehearsed even with very young children. A Hmong-American woman we know once said, "Hmong people don't thank each other enough." Her claim suggests that traditional Hmong speaking practices call for explicit thanking in fewer situations than in Anglo-American pragmatics. We can expect more stories like that of Loco Vang, if the linguistic and pragmatic backgrounds of speakers of different generations lead them to assess each other's speech as inappropriate, because they come to the interaction with different expectations.

One problem that may arise from pragmatic differences between generations in an immigration situation is that some immigrant parents feel that they are not being respected, which widens the communication gap between children and parents. As communication between generations deteriorates, children start to seek out other peers or social groups who speak like them and understand them. This need for understanding has led to teens forming gangs, a serious concern in the Hmong-American community. This concern gives particular urgency to the need to understand the pragmatics of the languages in contact in an immigration situation.

DATA COLLECTION

To test the hypothesis of pragmatic failure between generations, we arranged to interview both Hmong elders and college-age Hmong-American young adults living in a small city in Wisconsin, using for both groups a questionnaire that would elicit examples of requesting and thanking. We had our speakers tell us what they would say to ask family members to pass the rice at a family meal, and to request help while carrying groceries inside the house. Similarly, we asked speakers what they would say to family members who voluntarily helped them with these tasks. We interviewed 10 elders in Hmong, and then interviewed equal numbers of younger adults in Hmong and English, for a total of 30 interviews. Our elders ranged in age from 43 to 88 at the time of interviewing (July 2001); they all had lived in the United States between 9 and 22 years, but nevertheless rated their abilities in English as no better than fair. In contrast, our young adults, all between the ages of 18 and 25 at the time of interviews (May–June 2002), had either been born in the United States, or had immigrated at no more than 12 years of age. Thirteen of the 20 young adults felt that English was their stronger language, while four felt their Hmong was better, and three assessed their skills in both languages as equal. All 30 interviews were tape recorded and transcribed. Although we collected material on the performance of thanks as well as of requests, we concentrate here on requests.

RESULTS: EXAMPLES OF PRAGMATIC DIFFERENCES BETWEEN GENERATIONS

An examination of the results of the interviews with the elders reveals many differences between Hmong and English patterns for polite requests; a detailed account exceeds the scope of this chapter (but see Burt, 2002). However, two important areas of contrast between the generations are discussed here: differences in the use of pragmatic particles and differences in overall politeness strategies.

Politeness Particles

Hmong is particularly rich in pragmatic particles; both older and younger generation speakers include these particles in their requests. The count and distribution of these five politeness particles across the generations show both continuity and change in Hmong politeness practices.

The particles in question include, first of all, *thov*, literally, 'beg,' but often used as 'please' (Heimbach, 1980, p. 341), a particle which typically appears at the beginning of a request utterance, as in:

(1) **Thov** koj muab tais mov cev los   rau kuv.
    beg   you give bowl rice pass return to me
    "Please pass the bowl [of] rice back to me." (elder, to his mother)[1]

In contrast, three of the other four particles that appear in requests typically take sentence-final position:

---

[1]Abbreviations used in the morpheme glosses include the following:

bro	brother
cls	nominal classifier
cls-plu	plural classifier
cmpltv	completive particle
mo	mother
+pol	adds politeness
Q	question marker
soft	"softener" particle
top	topic-marking particle

(2) Niamntxawm, zaubmov nyob ntawm ko.   Koj sim cev
 sister-in-law food   stay there by-you you try hand
 los   rau kuv **seb.**
 return to me [+pol]
 "Sister-in-law, [the] food stays there by you; you try to hand it back to
 me" (elder)

(3) Hlob,   txav ze   mentsis **soj**.
 older-bro move close a-little [+pol]
 "Older brother, move [the rice] a little closer." (elder)

(4) Niam,   koj pab kuv nqa qhov no **yom**.
 mother you help me carry thing this [+pol]
 "Mother, you help me carry this thing." (elder, to her mother-in-law)

The fifth particle to appear in requests, *os*, seems to be more flexible in
its placement in the sentence, although it usually appears in sentence-final
position.

(5) Tub es,   muab mov los   rau kuv **os**.
 son [pause] give rice return to me [soft]
 "Son, give the rice back to me." (elder)

(6) Maiv Yaj, **os** koj   ib puas khoom **os**. Khoom no   koj los
 Mai Yang [soft] you [prt] are you free [soft] free [pause] you come
 pab kuv **soj. Thov** koj los   pab kuv nqa kuv cov
 help me [+pol] beg you come help me carry my [cls-plu]
 khoom no.
 package this
 "Mai Yang, you oh, are you free? [If] free, you come help me! Please come
 help me carry my packages." (elder)

Here, sentence (5) shows *os* in sentence-final position, while example (6)
shows *os* used in two places in one sentence—as well as having both *soj* and
thov in the utterance. The leading Hmong dictionary, Heimbach (1980, p. 4),
glosses *os* as "emphatic," but Wisconsin Hmong speakers speak of the particle as adding "softness" to the sentence, which seems to indicate that this
particle also probably adds politeness.

Both generations of Hmong speakers in Wisconsin use all five of these
particles, and as Table 3.1 shows, they use them with approximately equal
frequency. If we look at frequency alone, the younger generation of speakers shows continuity with the elders on this politeness practice.

However, a focus on the individual particles themselves tells a different
story. Table 3.1 shows the number of each particle used by the 10 Hmong
speakers of both age groups. A look at the frequencies of *soj* and *thov* shows
change between the generations: The elders used 17 instances of *soj*, while

TABLE 3.1
Use of Five Politeness Particles by Two Generations of Speakers

Particle	Number Used by Elders		Number Used by Young Adults	
	n	%	n	%
os	33	49	34	51
seb	6	9	3	4
soj	17	25	5	8
thov	6	9	20	30
yom	5	7	4	6
total	67	100	66	100

the young adults used only 5. For the elders, *soj* accounted for 25% of all politeness particles used, while for the young adults, it accounted for only 8%. In contrast, the elders used *thov* quite rarely, only 6 times in 140 opportunities (Vang, 1998, also notes that *thov* is traditionally used infrequently). But, given the same number of chances, the younger speakers used *thov* 20 times. For the elders, *thov* forms only 9% of the total particle count, whereas for the younger speakers, *thov* accounts for 30% of all the particles used. In other words, the younger speakers used *thov* more than three times as often as the elders.

Thus, although the overall count of particles in requests is almost the same for the two generational groups, the distribution of individual particles shows a change in usage between the generations. It is reasonable to think that *thov* is making gains in frequency under contact with *please*, based on the rough translation equivalence of the two words, since *please* usage is frequently stressed by English-speaking adults. If this is the case, the low frequency of *thov* use by the elders may indeed give younger speakers the impression that the elders are less polite than they should be, which is in accord with the impression Loco Vang had of his father. Conversely, if the elders perceive the younger speakers as overusing *thov*, this may contribute to the impression that the younger speakers are less capable of speaking Hmong correctly. Of course, either impression could lead to intergenerational communication problems.

Indirectness and Opting Out

Among the strategies available to speakers for conveying politeness in a request situation are the option of phrasing the request indirectly, and the option of not making the request at all (Brown & Levinson, 1987), sometimes known as "opting out." The Hmong elders we interviewed used both these strategies. For example, one speaker, rather than directly requesting his mother-in-law to help carry in the groceries, asked whether she had time to do so:

(7) Niamtais es,   kuv cov   khoom no   ntau ntau es
Mo-in-law [pause] my [cls-plu] package here many many [pause]
koj   puas muaj sijhawm los   pab kuv os?
you Q   have time   come help me [soft]
"Mother-in-law, I have a lot of packages. Do you have time to help me?"

Similarly, another speaker asked about her mother's willingness to give her the rice:

(8) Koj puas kam   muab qhov mov rau kuv?
you Q   willing give thing rice to   me
"Are you willing to give some rice to me?"

Altogether, three elders used this strategy, but they used it sparingly; only seven of their request utterances were indirect.

Four speakers in the younger generation used indirectness, and they produced nine utterances that could be classified as indirect, a few more than the elders did. But one younger speaker did not quite succeed at two of his attempts at indirectness; he omitted *puas*, the word that makes an utterance a question; his utterances (9) and (10), therefore, sound like statements rather than questions about the addressee's willingness to help:

(9) Tij laug, koj kam   muab cov   mov rau kuv.
older-bro you willing give [cls-plu] rice to me
"Older brother, you are willing to give the rice to me."

(10) Txiv,   koj kam   koj los   pab kuv nqa no, hnyav hynav.
Father you willing you come help me carry this heavy heavy
"Father, you are willing to come help me carry this very heavy [thing]."

Such statements, of course, might be interpreted as rude rather than polite, and so, with utterances like these, the speaker may well encounter pragmatic failure.

Another option is not to make the request at all; four elders chose this strategy of opting out of the request. Older speakers gave reasons like the following for doing so (English translations only):

(11) "[In] my country, no matter how heavy [the load], one will not enlist the help of one's mother. One knows that one's mother and father are an old couple, and one will simply carry [the load] quickly inside the house oneself."

(12) "If [food] is close [to] my father, I—he is the old one. If he is old, and I am young, I will be able to be patient and to stretch a little, since he is old."

(13) "[Even if] mother-in-law is right there, one simply carries oneself. One will not enlist [her] help. Because she is the mother-in-law, one does not want to enlist her help."

Opting out of the request emerges as a strategy particularly suited for use with older addressees; 10 of the 11 opt-out situations involved addressing mother, father, or mother-in-law.

In the younger generation of speakers, only 1 of our 10 speakers interviewed in Hmong used the opt-out strategy, and he used it five times. This younger speaker was 12 years old when he immigrated, and was far more confident of his speaking ability in Hmong than in English. In contrast, it is striking that none of the other younger speakers who were interviewed in Hmong chose to opt out of any requests. While opting out of a request is not a major strategy for the older speakers, it seems to be an important one, since it is used for older addressees. Perhaps it was younger speakers' lack of knowledge of when to opt out that caused one elder to make this remark about younger speakers:

(14) Yog tus   uas nws paubtab   lawm   mas nws
     If   someone who s/he knowledgeable [cmpltv] [top] s/he
     kuj tsis nug, yog tsis paubtab   ces lawv kuj yuav nug thiab.
     also not ask, if   not knowledgeable and they also will   ask also.
     "If one is knowledgeable, s/he will not ask; those not knowledgeable, they
     will ask."

The knowledgeable Hmong speaker knows when to opt out of the request, and young Hmong-Americans may fall short of expectations in this aspect of traditional politeness.

RESULTS: EXAMPLES OF DISAPPOINTMENT WITH YOUNGER SPEAKERS

Our interviews with Hmong elders in Wisconsin showed their disappointment with Hmong-American children who could not speak the heritage language well. Here are commentaries, in English translation, from elders on the abilities of young Hmong-Americans.

(15) "Oh, they do not know anything. They go, they arrive, they only scoop [rice], they eat quickly, and they go—they are like [that]. I haven't thought about that [whether they can speak well]. I cannot say."

(16) "The young now, I do not know how [they speak]. The young now, they simply use many American words, and they are not very capable of speaking Hmong words here. I don't know, it depends on the individual."

These speakers were somewhat cautious in their estimation of the speaking capabilities of the young. But one elder foresaw what language shift could lead to, in that the young were not learning the traditional politeness patterns:

(17) "Some young [people] today, it's like they simply learn many American words. They do not like to speak to one [in] Hmong words very much, you know? Speaking of some, they do not know. Then little by little, they will not know the rules of our Hmong rituals. Right now, your young today will not know. Because the mature young [people], if people from other clans come, they already do not know how to greet them, and they do not know anything. It is also extremely difficult."

These comments from the elders show what Loco Vang's story shows, that pragmatic as well as linguistic differences can cause intergenerational communication difficulties in immigrant communities. Younger speakers, who use *thov* more frequently than their elders, may perceive the elders' speech as inadequately polite; elders, on the other hand, may notice that younger speakers may not opt out of requests when, by traditional standards, they should. These results of our interviews suggest that differing pragmatic practices between generations in the Hmong-American community contribute to communication difficulties.

Moreover, the task of learning English is not an easy one for young Hmong-Americans and has its own serious pragmatic pitfalls. Because expectations for speech act performance can differ from language to language, as we have seen, what may "count" as polite ways to request or thank in one language may lead to pragmatic failure in another. The data from our interviews with Hmong elders show that strategies for making polite requests in Hmong differ from those strategies considered polite in English.

Hmong-American children, then, are faced with a difficult learning problem: They must learn two systems of politeness, two systems that differ in several ways. Furthermore, the adults with whom they interact may understand only one of the systems that the children are exposed to, and may thus be unsympathetic to deviations from it.

WHAT TEACHERS CAN DO

Teachers in the public schools are in a position to help children of immigrant families cope with the two linguistic systems and the two politeness systems they are trying to learn. With an understanding that different languages can have different pragmatics, ESL teachers can help children compare their first and second languages. If they do so, the students will understand the second language better and also appreciate the value of their first language. The following are activities that ESL teachers can work on with students:

1. Introduce different things Anglo-Americans say or do to show politeness. Give each student a set of note cards and write down each politeness-related phrase on a card. For example, one note card can read "Please pass the rice," while another can say "Thanks for helping me." Have students take the note cards home and discuss with their parents whether any of these politeness practices is the same in the heritage culture. If there is a shared saying or way to be polite, have students write on the opposite side of the card the way that saying would be expressed in their culture (whether this is a verbal or nonverbal expression). Share what the students found out the next day.

2. Find pictures in magazines of people being polite or doing things for other people. Have students cut out the picture and paste it on a white sheet of paper. Have students go home and discuss with their parents how the person who receives the politeness would answer in the heritage language. Have students write down the response next to the picture. The next day, share the different responses and then point out what an Anglo-American would say. Discuss similarities and differences in the responses.

3. Role-play activity #2 where students act out the different responses collected from parents. After a few examples, discuss what the students notice about each of the responses and different situations in which these responses may be appropriate.

One benefit of these exercises is that an appreciation of the heritage language will enable children to continue to talk with parents about it, as they seek out unfamiliar linguistic and pragmatic features in it. In addition, the teacher's awareness and support of the heritage language will encourage the children to maintain and use their first language. As mentioned earlier, our job is to help children understand both languages and cultures, not to make the children feel that their first language is inferior to their second.

An understanding of pragmatic differences between Hmong and English will be useful both within the Hmong-American community and outside it. If pragmatic differences cause misunderstanding between the generations in the Hmong-American community, teaching about these differences is needed. Both Hmong-Americans and Anglo-Americans also can be educated about the cultural and linguistic (as opposed to moral and personal) nature of these different politeness practices, not only so as to avert negative stereotyping, but also so that both Anglo and Hmong adults can understand the importance of teaching Hmong-American children their heritage language as well as English.

REFERENCES

Blum-Kulka, S., House, J., & Kasper, G. (Eds.). (1989). *Cross-cultural pragmatics: Requests and apologies*. Norwood, NJ: Ablex.

Brown, P., & Levinson, S. (1987). *Politeness: Some universals in language usage*. Cambridge, England: Cambridge University Press.

Burt, S. M. (2002). *Politeness strategies in Hmong requests*. Unpublished manuscript, Illinois State University.

Faderman, L. (with Xiong, G.). (1998). *I begin my life all over: The Hmong and the American immigrant experience*. Boston: Beacon Press.

Gass, S., & Neu, J. (1995). *Speech acts across cultures*. Berlin: Mouton.

Heimbach, E. (1980). *White Hmong–English dictionary*. Ithaca, NY: Southeast Asia Program Publications, Cornell University. (Original publication 1966)

Hones, D., & Cha, C. S. (1999). *Educating new Americans: Immigrant lives and learning*. Mahwah, NJ: Lawrence Erlbaum Associates.

Kasper, G., & Blum-Kulka, S. (Eds.). (1993). *Intercultural pragmatics*. Oxford, England: Oxford University Press.

Thomas, J. (1983). Cross cultural pragmatic failure. *Applied Linguistics, 4*(2), 91–112.

Vang, B. (1998). *How do Hmong children make requests?* Unpublished paper, University of Wisconsin, Oshkosh.

4

Language and Gender Matters in the Classroom

Kathryn A. Remlinger

SCHOOLED IN DIFFERENCE

Women and men use language differently. This assumption has been documented in academic research (e.g., DeFransisco, 1991; Tannen, 1994; Trudgill, 1972) and in popular media, including movies like *My Fair Lady*, *Erin Brockovich*, and *What Women Want*; self-help books such as John Grey's *Women are from Venus, Men are from Mars* and Deborah Tannen's *You Just Don't Understand*; talk shows like *Oprah!*; and fashion magazines such as *Glamour* and *YM*. From this perspective, our communication—and miscommunication—as women and men stem from our "natural" differences, which have led us to grow up in and experience separate, gendered cultures. The popularity of the "Venus and Mars" approach has been partly responsible for a growing awareness of language and gender issues in a variety of contexts: in intimate relationships, within family dynamics, in the workplace, and in the classroom.

Although the approach has fostered awareness of language and gender, it also has taken a toll on how critically we might examine language and gender and its effects on relationships, work, and classroom interaction. The approach describes gender differences and explains how women and men use language differently, but this explanation presumes that there *are* differences without examining *if* there are differences, as well as if there are similarities. The theory may explain how gendered differences exist in communication, but it fails to explain *why* these differences exist, and if in fact

41

they are solely attributable to gender.[1] Most of all, the theory avoids critically exploring how we form our gender identities, what our values and attitudes are about women and men, how language use reflects these values, and what their effects may be on the different realms of our lives, in particular on teaching and learning.

In classrooms, on TV shows, in movies, in ads, and in best-sellers we hear echoes of the idea that women and men are "basically equal"; "there aren't problems like there used to be"; "everyone has an equal opportunity"; and, "if someone wants to do something, all they have to do is to do it." The equal-but-different perspective is mirrored in the general attitude among administration, faculty, staff, and students that the school, and in particular the classroom, are gender-neutral places—that everyone has equal access to the classroom floor and to learning. However, if sexism is a "thing of the past," then why are there marked differences in the ways that teachers interact with and treat girls and boys—from the distribution of classroom equipment to teachers' responses to girls' and boys' class participation?[2] If "everyone has an equal opportunity," why do we observe gender bias in school staffing and organizational practices: pay inequities; hiring patterns; unequal emphasis and funding for boys' and girls' sports; skewed gender ratios of teachers in certain subjects like language arts, foreign languages, math, and science; and social events, student organizations, and activities such as dances and queen and king nominations that maintain sexist and heterosexist practices?[3] Because of the regularity of these practices, they are often seen as "normal," which reinforces an uncritical view of gendered practices in the school.

Together, the school and the classroom teach students lessons about being and behaving as girls and boys. These lessons include how to use language, not only in gendered ways, but also in ways that influence what it means to be girl and boy, woman and man, as well as ways to enact these identities. The way we use language is also seen as a "normal" way to categorize behaviors and practices that fall outside our definitions of girl, boy, woman, and man. For example, we have names such as tomboy and sissy

---

[1]The difference approach has been critiqued for other limitations it poses to language and gender research. For example, the approach assumes a heterosexist approach to relationships, ignores same-sex differences in conversation, reinforces bipolar and monolithic notions of what it means to be *woman* and *man*, and ignores issues of power and dominance. Several authors have written about the limitations of the theory, particularly in response to Tannen's (1990) work: Hall and Bucholtz (1995), Bergvall, Bing, and Freed (1996, in particular the introduction by Bing & Bergvall), and Bucholtz, Liang, and Sutton (1999). For an introductory overview see Talbot (1998). For critiques see Freed (1992), Cameron (1992, 1996), and Troemel-Ploetz (1991).

[2]For a recent review of this research see Corson (2001), "Gender and Discourse Norms," chap. 6. Also see Gabriel and Smithson (1992).

[3]See Kelly and Nihlen (1982) and Spender (1992) for discussion of the school as a site of gender reproduction.

for girls and boys, respectively, who behave outside what is seen as "normal" girl and boy behavior. By becoming aware of how language functions to normalize sexism and heterosexism in the classroom, we can understand what students' attitudes and values are about gender and how these ideologies may affect student participation in the classroom and consequently affect learning.

RAISING AWARENESS

The purpose of this chapter is to help raise awareness about language and gender in the classroom. The hope is that through awareness teachers can understand ways in which this dynamic exists, how it is central to shaping identity and classroom talk, as well as how this dynamic may limit participation in classroom interaction for some students. Included in the language–gender dynamic is sexuality; gender and sexuality are theoretically interconnected. Ideas about being women and men transfer in theory to assumptions about the body and the physical practice of sex (Nicholson, 1994). For example, the use of seemingly exclusive categories such as woman, man, straight, gay, and lesbian gives the impression that both gender and sexuality are neatly defined, with clear and consistent boundaries. Also, these terms often reflect a separation between gender and sexuality, a separation that reflects an uncritical approach to gender. For example, *woman* subsumes *straight woman*, and *man* subsumes *straight man*; neither gendered term allows for reference to sexualities other than heterosexual. This uniform sense of definitions and practices also represents a dominant sexual ideology that upholds the dualistic notion of either/or—either heterosexual or homosexual, either woman or man (Epstein, 1990). We can see from the vocabulary that we use to talk about gender and sexuality that notions of gender and sexuality are interdependent; particular attitudes about gender support and reinforce certain attitudes about sexuality. We later see that these attitudes can affect who participates in class, what gets said, and how class talk takes shape.

Awareness of language and gender also includes understanding the ways in which language functions to shape values, attitudes, and beliefs. For example, how do meanings associated with the terms *tomboy* and *sissy* reflect attitudes about being a girl or a boy? How do these labels restrict student behavior and identity? How do these limitations then affect how students approach classroom interaction? Through awareness teachers may understand how normative ways of perceiving gender affect not only what gets said and by whom in the classroom, but also how values and attitudes enculturate students into gendered ways of speaking and being that may affect their access to learning. Students who fit the "normal" definition may feel more free to participate in class talk because they have no fear of retribution from other students. However, students who do not fit "normal" definitions and are instead defined by names like *fag*, *slut*, or other pejorative gendered terms, may be silent for fear of harassment. Because learning depends in part on classroom interaction, those students who feel restricted may not have equal access to learning. If teachers can come to understand the interplay of language and gender, they may also come to see that the classroom is not a gender-neutral place and that access to learning is not equal among all students. Through awareness teachers may be able to affect what they do and say in the classroom and how they interact with students. Teachers may also be able to foster students' understanding of the effects of language and gender, encouraging equal access to participating in the classroom. Below I provide information for teachers on what they should know about language and gender in order to better understand the language and gender dynamic, and thus to better navigate these issues in the classroom.

FUNCTIONS OF LANGUAGE

Developing awareness about language and gender in the classroom includes understanding the various ways in which language functions. On one level, language functions to create meanings and to structure conversations. On this level, language is what makes conversations work. On another level, language is a tool used to perform identities and to shape values, attitudes, and beliefs; it is a force that maintains as well as challenges and changes existing ideologies.[4]

These functions of language overlap: Meanings and speaking strategies that we use to shape class talk often reflect ways in which students and teachers enact, or practice, gender—in other words, the way they play out who they are as women, boys, teachers, students, African Americans, teenagers, working class, Bostonian, or Midwestern, and so on.[5] Here, we're specifically interested in understanding how students "perform" gender in the classroom through talk in the context of the classroom. For example, one way to perform being a girl in the classroom, especially a "good girl," is to be quiet and to only talk when called upon. This behavior reflects not only what a girl is, but also what expected behavior is for girls in the classroom.

---

[4]The analysis relies on theory and method from critical discourse analysis (CDA). See Kress (1991), Lancaster and Taylor (1992), Fairclough (1992), van Dijk (1993a, 1993b, 1996), Fairclough and Wodak (1997), and Reisigl and Wodak (2001). For practice theory see Eckert and McConnell-Ginet (1992). For introductions to both theories see Talbot (1998). See Remlinger (1999) for discussion uniting CDA and practice theories in language and gender research.

[5]See Eckert and McConnell-Ginet (1992) for discussion of performance theory.

Similarly, values about being a boy are performed through talk. For instance, boys enacting what it means to be a boy may include changing the topic of discussion, interrupting class talk, taking long turns, acting out, or otherwise directing attention toward themselves and controlling the conversation. Although these are stereotypical behaviors, they are ways in which gender is often practiced in the classroom, and they are ways in which values and beliefs about gender are enacted and reinforced. These values and beliefs can limit how students behave in the classroom by allowing some students to dominate the class talk and relegating others to silence. Limiting classroom participation leads to limited access to learning since most learning in the classroom occurs through interaction (Nystrand & Gamoran, 1992).

Gendered language practices can emerge in class talk in a variety of ways. For example, during a discussion of grammar in a seventh-grade language arts class, a teacher might ask students for examples of adjectives. Students might respond with a variety of answers, some of which may be gendered, such as *blonde, handsome, or pretty.* The content of the discourse then shifts from a seemingly innocuous discussion of grammatical categories to one loaded with gender values about appearance. Next, I discuss other examples to demonstrate how meaning functions to constitute gender values and to practice gender identities.

MEANING MATTERS

Language functions to create identities and shape values through meanings embedded in language, what linguists call semantics. Awareness of language and gender in the classroom includes recognizing how the semantics of classroom discourse may reflect gender values, what these values are, how gender is talked about, and how the meanings serve to reinforce, challenge, or change ideologies.

Reclamations

We can examine common vocabulary of everyday student talk to see how meanings reflect gendered ideologies and how these values tend to be heterosexist. Common pejoratives include *bitch, girl, gay,* and *dog;* familiar reclamations[6] include such words as *girl, grrrl, chick,* and *dyke. Girl* as a pejorative among young adults reflects social meanings of powerlessness and immaturity. In contrast, *girl* and its variant spelling "grrrl," as reclamations

---

[6]A reclamation is a derogatory or euphemistic term that is consciously used by an oppressed group to empower themselves and to challenge the status quo.

represent empowerment, especially when the terms are used within all-female groups. The variant spelling graphically depicts the anger of the oppressed since *grrrl* has the onomatopoeic quality of a growl. Thus for some women the use of *girl* and *grrrl* to name themselves and to address other women is an act of resistance against the social construction of a femininity defined by immaturity and powerlessness. Similar to girl, *chick* is typically used to label women who fall within the normative definition of what it means to be female—in other words, within an androcentric, or male-centered, paradigm of what it means to be a woman. Because *chick* generally represents what it means to be a woman within the framework of the status quo, *chick* is commonly not perceived by either male or female students as being pejorative, although the term is often used and taken as a form of derogation. Yet *chick*, like *grrrl*, may also function as a reclamation. For example, the use of chick by the band Dixie Chicks is a reclamation. Example uses of *chick* from student discourse also reflect a reclaimed use of the term in that *chick* is often perceived as a term of solidarity and endearment when used by girls and women to address each other. Reclamations such as *grrrl* and *chick* demonstrate the possibility of social change through semantic shift, or meaning change. In addition, reclamations demonstrate that a critical approach to language and gender includes understanding multiple meanings and uses of language in context, as well as understanding how these meanings are ways in which students negotiate traditional gender roles. The above examples also demonstrate that normative ideals are supported and reinforced through vocabulary, thus speakers are socialized through the meanings embedded in language. The conscious use of reclamations by students also demonstrates that they are often aware of a gender hierarchy based on male-centered ideals.

"Neutral" Language

Gender socialization also manifests in so called "neutral" language, which in turn influences students' understanding and practices of gender identities. Neutral language is seen as generic, inoffensive, and not carrying any gender baggage, yet its meaning is embedded with gendered values. An example of neutral language is the use of *guy* and *girl* to refer to men and women, respectively. However, the terms are not neutral, nor are they equivalents: there are no comparable terms with *guy* marked female in students' vocabulary. Although, *gal* is an equivalent of *guy*, students typically do not use it. The collocation of guy and girl also reflects a gender inequality in which males develop from *boys* to *guys* to *men*, and in which females do not develop beyond being girls. The use of *girl* to label women implies that adult females have not yet developed, although their male counterparts are in the process of evolving into more mature beings, *men*. Similar to other gen-

der-marked terms such as chick, the naming practice of calling women *girls*
relegates them to a disempowered, diminutive, nonaggressive, complacent,
less mature position.

Reinforcing Gender Values

Another function of meaning is to reinforce gender values that limit ways of
describing girls and women, boys and men. Studies have shown that
women and girls tend to be described according to their appearance and
sexuality, whereas boys and men tend to be described in terms of their behavior, attitude, and intellect (McConnell-Ginet, 1989; Schulz, 1975, and
Sutton, 1995). For example, women are often described as food (cupcake,
tart, cookie, sweetie, peach, etc. See Hines, 1999) and animals (fox, dog,
cow, chick, hen, etc.). These personified metaphors reflect meanings referencing sexuality and appearance. They also entail semantic features that reflect gender asymmetries and an androcentric, or male-centered, world
view, as we also saw earlier with the seemingly neutral use of *chick*. An
androcentric value system is also reflected in terms like *slut*, *whore*, and *ho*.
These terms describe women solely in terms of their sexuality. It is also significant that these labels have no male equivalents, and thus represent a
standard of sexual propriety for women that does not exist for men.[7] Terms
referencing activities such as *tomboy* and *sissy* also reveal gendered values
that relegate and thus limit how girls and boys should act and the kinds of
activities in which they might participate. An imperative for specific ways of
being male is similarly reinforced through the use of *fag* and *gay* to label
boys who do not fit the normative notion of what it means to be a boy.[8] Although both labels are negative, *fag* is an overt reference to nonnormative
behavior, whereas *gay* is a more subtle form of heterosexism, and is also
used more frequently and more generally to describe objects and events
outside the norm, such as "your hair looks gay" or "that class is gay." Both
terms reinforce the idea that boys must be heterosexual and that they
ought to practice "typical" boy activities like playing on the football team,
rather than being a member of drama club. Of course there is nothing
wrong with being a "typical" boy; what is wrong is that boys who do not fit
this model and who are labeled with names like *sissy*, *fag*, and *queer* are of-

---

[7]For analyses of sexism in English see Schulz (1975), Spender (1980), Graddol and Swann
(1989), Kramarae and Treichler (1992, especially the introduction), and Sutton (1995).

[8]Talbot's (1998) chapter "New men and old boys" provides an overview of masculinity and
language research. Several studies examine masculinity and language, among them: Connell's
work (1987, 1995) examining masculinity in relation to sexuality; Bergvall and Remlinger's (1996)
research on masculinity and classroom discourse; Kiesling's (1997) research investigating masculinity, power, and language among fraternity members, and Cameron's (1998) study examining college students' linguistic performances of gender identity.

ten limited in how they can interact in various school settings without being harassed. In all of these examples meaning matters: it matters in terms of what values are reinforced, how students identify themselves, how they describe others, and therefore, how students participate or are excluded from participating in school. Below we will see an example of how meanings attached to labels for girls shape students' identities and values about what it means to be female.

GENDER AND RACE IN INTERACTION:
AN EXAMPLE FROM THE CLASSROOM

An example of classroom discourse demonstrates how meaning matters in the classroom by shaping identities and by creating gender values.[9] In a classroom discussion about regional dialects, the teacher asks students about names they call people in their neighborhoods. One boy answers that he and his friends call women "skeezers," which he defines as meaning "a woman who doesn't act like a lady." Two girls in the class contribute to the discussion by adding that such women are also called "sack chasers," "gold diggers," "and women who date somebody for they money."

What is interesting in this exchange is that the students give examples of derogatory, gender-marked terms for women when the teacher has asked for any words that name kinds of people in the students' neighborhoods. Furthermore, the derogatory terms reflect a negative categorization of women based on sexuality and sexual practices: What is appropriate sexual behavior for women is restraint, "proper" behavior, acting like a "lady," qualities typically not found in what one of the students describes as "a female who doesn't carry herself well." Both the boy and the girls produce highly masculine and heterosexualized ways of referring to other women, conforming to a dominant norm. Thus, the discussion functions to reinforce certain values about women (and girls) while it also limits who participates and what ideas get heard; students who do not agree with the definition and those who find the talk offensive may be silent.

This example of classroom talk also illustrates the interaction of gender and race, and how classroom discourse can sometimes subvert, rather than support, mainstream ideologies. The three students who engage in the conversation are African American, and the only African Americans in the class of 32 students. The rest of the class, including the teacher, are White. Thus, the use of *skeezer, gold digger, and sack chaser* may function to subvert the dominant "whiteness" of the conversational floor, while at the same time

---

[9]See Remlinger (2004) for detailed discussion and analysis of this example.

subvert the function of the conversation by making public supposedly private and potentially taboo subjects of sex and sexuality within the context of the classroom.[10]

We can think of other terms that reinforce similar gender values: *player, stud, skank, ho,* and so on. These particular labels also demonstrate how notions about gender are interdependent with notions of sexuality. Other gender-marked labels represent additional values about masculinity, femininity, as well as what it means to be boy, girl, woman, and man. For example, terms for boys and men, such as *dawg, superman, dude,* or *beefcake,* and those for girls and women, including *bitch, frigid, dog, cow, and hottie* all encode particular ways of perceiving gender and sexuality, ways that reinforce certain values and attitudes, as well as ways that students reinforce these values and practice gendered identities. Similarly, the too common derogatory use of *gay* among high school students to mean "stupid" reflects a heterosexist value where *gay* is inferior, bad, something that you call someone who doesn't fit the norm. It presupposes that not gay (i.e., straight, heterosexual) is superior, smart, good, and something that doesn't need to be named because it is the norm.

Teachers at any grade level will notice in classroom discourse various ways in which semantics plays a role in both shaping identity and creating gender ideologies. The implications of language and gender in the classroom are obvious: the gender values that the meanings teach; how students use language to reproduce certain ideologies; the relationship between gender and sexuality, especially an emphasis on heterosexuality; and how these values function to reinforce gender stereotypes that may limit language use, behavior, and therefore learning. Moreover, awareness of how students use language in a variety of school settings—from hallway conversations, to shouts on the playground and lunch-talk in the cafeteria to dialogue in novels, short stories, and song lyrics, as well as in classroom discourse—helps teachers to understand that language functions not only to reinforce certain attitudes and values, but also to subvert meanings and to shape alternative identities. This kind of challenge to the status quo is present both in the meanings and the structure of conversations, as the example below demonstrates.

---

[10]This reluctance to define the term may be related to in-group/out-group language use: *skeezer* and *sack chaser* as they are used here are words from African American English (AAE). The three students are AAE speakers, whereas the professor, who is asking for clarification is not. The reluctance may also be related to power relationships and politeness in the context of the classroom. In addition, these students are the only AAE speakers among the 32 students in the classroom. Hence, race, and ethnicity, in addition to gender, power, and politeness, may affect the negotiation of the conversation and of the meanings in this example.

SPEAKING OF GENDER

Gender shows up in more places than in labels that students use to shape their identities and to identify each other; it also is revealed in the ways students use language—how they engage in conversation and how gender is talked about in these conversations. In conjunction with the meanings of gendered terms, speakers use pragmatic features, or speaking strategies, to perform identity and to constitute values, in other words, to perform their genders and to talk about gender. During most instances of classroom discourse there are several speaking strategies at work, such as the ways speakers control the topic, respond to the teacher, ask questions, have side conversations, develop certain topics and others' turns, interrupt others, control and monopolize the speaking floor, and negate and silence what others have said. Speaking strategies also include ways of using language to define, explain, and affirm what is being said. How are these strategies used by students to shape not only the conversation, but also impact gender ideology? How does the structure of the conversation affect what topics are raised, silenced, or developed? How does the structure of the conversation affect who speaks, and thus whose ideas are heard and whose ideas are silenced? In what ways do the topic of conversation and speaking strategies combine to create gender values?

Interruptions are a significant factor affecting the structure of classroom discourse: They reflect power relationships among students and between students and the teacher by controlling topics and silencing speakers (and thus their topics). Teachers often use interruptions to control the conversation and to limit ideas by directing students to speak or to be quiet. Students often use interruptions with each other, and sometimes with teachers, for the same purpose. In contrast, tandem turn-taking, where pairs of speakers talk in unison or in turn, is also significant in shaping the topic and structuring the conversation. This kind of speaking strategy usually functions to support, affirm, and develop the other speaker and the topic at hand. Likewise, extended development works to help develop another speaker's ideas through explanation, definition, and affirmation of their turns (see Bergvall & Remlinger, 1996). Thus, the pragmatics of class talk reflects who participates, how they participate, whose ideas are deemed important or unimportant, and thus, the purpose the talk serves in shaping gender values.

Examples from the classroom illustrate how the pragmatics of classroom discourse function in these ways. For example, topic control is a way that students and teachers introduce, maintain, or close the topic of the conversation. The earlier example on gender and race reveals three important functions of speaking strategies: who participates in the conversation; how the conversation is structured; and what values about gender are developed and therefore reinforced. The conversation is structured by a boy in the class through his response to the teacher's question about names for people in their neighborhoods. The boy is the first person to speak after the teacher, and he uses topic control to raise the specific topic of *skeezer*. By asking for definitions and explanations to clarify the meaning, the teacher develops this topic, which the students further develop and maintain through explanation and definitions. In particular, the girls who respond develop much of the conversation through tandem turn-taking. The boy who initiates the topic often negates what the girls say by saying "no" in response to definitions and explanations they provide. The boy also ends the conversation by refusing to elaborate when the teacher asks for a synonymous term for *skeezer*. Ironically, after introducing the topic of *skeezer*, he responds, "It's not appropriate for this type of conversation."

What is significant about these turn-taking strategies is how they simultaneously function to both support and control the exchange. Unfortunately, too often analyses of language and gender are guided by traditional expectations of how women and men use language, rather than what is actually taking place in an exchange (see James & Clark, 1993). For example, based on traditional expectations of how girls use language, we might assume that the girls' talk is functioning as cooperative and supportive. Yet, what we see as cooperation on the part of the girls' turns may actually be a way for the girls to control or challenge the other speakers and their topics, especially in light of the power dynamics of the class, the teachers' apparent naïveté of the topic, and the risk that the girls would be taking in supporting a topic that denigrates women, and thus themselves. Similarly, the boy's turns seem to function to control the conversation and in doing so, they appear to create and reinforce a particular gender and sexual ideology—through initiating the specific topic of *skeezer* and in his taking of the floor, in saying there are alternative terms for women who don't "carry themselves well," by negating both the definition provided by the other students and the appropriateness of the topic for the classroom, and most interesting, in shutting down the topic by refusing to further elaborate his initial example of *skeezer*. However, we could question this analysis by asking if his silencing the topic is instead a way for him to challenge expectations of how he, as a boy, should talk about women. In our analyses of language and gender we must be vigilant of our own expectations and how these figure into our understanding of language use.

Our expectations of gendered behavior based on differences may also color our understanding of how students perform, or practice, their genders through speaking strategies. In the example above, the boy performs traditional masculinity by conforming to expectations about how boys (and men) talk about women and by controlling the conversation. The controlling function of his turns represent what Tannen (1990) calls "report talk," and what she finds typical in men's language use. In contrast, the girls practice traditional feminine behavior as they seem to collaboratively support and clarify each other's turns. Tannen calls this style "rapport talk," which she finds characteristic of women's speaking strategies. In this way, the students are performing their gendered identities. From a perspective based on difference, these identities conform to expectations of traditional and stereotypical ways of being masculine and feminine. This example shows that there is gender "difference," but that it is a difference based on the interaction of race, sexuality, gender, and power relations in a specific context, rather than a clean-cut division between two genders. In other words, gender *difference* is complex and is complicated by the setting of the talk and by the social roles of the speakers. In this particular example, we see how race and gender may interact to affect the negotiation of the floor and of the meaning of the talk. In short, the example demonstrates that the classroom is not a gender-neutral place and that students use classroom talk to shape gender identities and to create values about gender and sexuality.

CONCLUSIONS

Attention to semantic and pragmatic features of classroom talk, along with the ideological functions of discourse, allows us to see how students simultaneously negotiate meanings and the conversational floor, not only to construct a conversation, but also and more importantly, to negotiate gender values and identities. Therefore, as we examine how linguistic features, such as meanings and turn-taking strategies, function in discourse, we can understand how students use language to create various notions about gender. We can also become aware of how students practice gender through what they say and how they say it. In addition, we can appreciate that gender ideology is not a matter of difference alone, but more an effect of discourse processes and social practices that function to shape values, attitudes, and beliefs. Most of all, as we understand that the classroom is not a gender-neutral place, we can become aware of how language and gender matters in the classroom.

REFERENCES

Bergvall, V., & Remlinger, K. (1996). Reproduction, resistance, and gender in educational discourse: The role of Critical Discourse Analysis. *Discourse & Society, 7*(4), 453–479.

Bergvall, V., Bing, J., & Freed, A. (Eds.). (1996). *Rethinking language and gender research: Theory and practice*. London: Longman.

Bucholtz, M., Liang, A., & Sutton, L. (Eds.). (1999). *Reinventing identities: The gendered self in discourse*. New York: Oxford University Press.

Cameron, D. (1992). *Feminism and linguistic theory* (2nd ed.). London: Routledge.

Cameron, D. (1996). The language-gender interface: Challenging cooptation. In V. Bergvall, J. Bing, & A. Freed (Eds.), *Rethinking language and gender research: Theory and practice* (pp. 31–53). London: Longman.

Cameron, D. (1998). Performing gender identity: Young men's talk and the construction of heterosexual masculinity. In J. Coates (Ed.), *Language and gender: A reader* (pp. 270–284). Malden, MA: Blackwell.

Connell, R. (1987). *Gender and power: Society, the person and sexual politics*. Cambridge, England: Polity Press.

Connell, R. (1995). *Masculinities*. Cambridge, England: Polity Press.

Corson, D. (2001). *Language diversity in education*. Hillsdale, NJ: Lawrence Erlbaum Associates.

DeFransisco, V. (1991). The sounds of silence: How men silence women in marital relations. *Discourse & Society, 2*(4), 413–423.

Eckert, P., & McConnell-Ginet, S. (1992). Think practically and look locally: Language and gender as community-based practice. *Annual Review of Anthropology, 21,* 461–490.

Epstein, J. (1990). Either/or-neither/both: Sexual ambiguity and the ideology of gender. *Genders, 7,* 99–142.

Fairclough, N. (1992). *Discourse and social change*. Cambridge, England: Polity Press.

Fairclough, N., & Wodak, R. (1997). Critical discourse analysis. In T. van Dijk (Ed.), *Discourse as social interaction. Discourse studies: A multidisciplinary introduction, Vol. 2* (pp. 258–284). London: Sage.

Freed, A. (1992). We understand perfectly: A critique of Tannen's view of cross-sex communication. In K. Hall, M. Bucholtz, & B. Moonwoman (Eds.), *Locating power: Proceedings of the Second Berkeley Women and Language Conference*. Berkeley, CA: Berkeley Woman and Language Group.

Gabriel, S., & Smithson, I. (Eds.). (1992). *Gender in the classroom: Power and pedagogy*. Urbana: University of Illinois Press.

Graddol, D., & Swann, J. (1989). *Gender voices*. Oxford, England: Blackwell.

Hall, K., & Bucholtz, M. (Eds.). (1995). *Gender articulated: Language and the socially constructed self*. New York: Oxford University Press.

Hines, C. (1999). Rebaking the pie: The WOMAN AS DESERT metaphor. In M. Bucholtz, A. Liang, & L. Sutton (Eds.), *Reinventing identities: The gendered self in discourse* (pp. 145–162). New York: Oxford University Press.

James, D., & Clark, S. (1993). Women, men, and interruptions: A critical review. In D. Tannen (Ed.), *Gender and conversational interaction* (pp. 231–280). New York: Oxford University Press.

Kelly, G., & Nihlen, A. (1982). Schooling and the reproduction of patriarchy: Unequal workloads, unequal rewards. In M. Apple (Ed.), *Cultural and economic reproduction in American education: Essays in class, ideology, and the state* (pp. 162–180). Boston: Routledge & Kegan Paul.

Kiesling, S. (1997). Power and the language of men. In S. Johnson & U. Meinhof (Eds.), *Language and masculinity* (pp. 65–85). Oxford, England: Blackwell.

Kramarae, C., & Treichler, P. (1992). *Amazons, bluestockings, and crones: A feminist dictionary* (2nd ed.). London: Pandora Press.

Kress, G. (1991). Critical discourse analysis. *Annual Review of Applied Linguistics, 11,* 84–99.

Lancaster, L., & Taylor, R. (1992). Critical approaches to language, learning, and pedagogy: A case study. In N. Fairclough (Ed.), *Critical language awareness* (pp. 256–284). London: Longman.

McConnell-Ginet, S. (1989). The sexual reproduction of meaning: A discourse-based theory. In *Language, gender, and professional writing: Theoretical approaches and guidelines for nonsexist usage* (pp. 35–50). New York: Modern Language Association.

Nicholson, L. (1994). Interpreting gender. *Signs: Journal of Women in Culture and Society, 20*(11), 79–105.

Nystrand, M., & Gamoran, A. (1992). Student engagement: When recitation becomes conversation. In H. Waxman & H. Walberg (Eds.), *Contemporary research on teaching* (pp. 257–276). Berkeley, CA: McCutchan.

Reisigl, M., & Wodak, R. (2001). *Discourse and discrimination: Rhetorics of racism and antisemitism.* New York: Routledge.

Remlinger, K. (1999). Widening the lens of language and gender research: Integrating critical discourse analysis and cultural practice theory. *Linguistik Online.* http://viadrina.euv-frankfurt-o.de/~wjournal/english/index.html

Remlinger, K. (2004). Negotiating the classroom floor: Negotiating ideologies of gender and sexuality. In M. Lazar (Ed.), *Feminist critical discourse analysis* (pp. 114–138). New York: Palgrave/Macmillan.

Schulz, M. (1975). The semantic derogation of women. In B. Thorne & N. Henley (Eds.), *Language and sex: Difference and dominance* (pp. 64–73). Rowley, MA: Newbury House.

Spender, D. (1980). *Man made language.* London: Routledge & Kegan Paul.

Spender, D. (1992). The entry of women into the education of men. In C. Kramarae & D. Spender (Eds.), *The knowledge explosion: Generations of feminist scholarship* (pp. 235–253). New York: Teachers College Press, Athene Series.

Sutton, L. (1995). Bitches and skankly hobags. In K. Hall & M. Buckholtz (Eds.), *Gender articulated: Language and the socially constructed self* (pp. 280–296). New York: Routledge.

Talbot, M. (1998). *Language and gender: An introduction.* Cambridge, England: Polity Press.

Tannen, D. (1990). *You just don't understand: Women and men in conversation.* New York: Morrow.

Tannen, D. (1994). *Gender and discourse.* New York: Oxford University Press.

Troemel-Ploetz, S. (1991). Selling the apolitical. *Discourse & Society, 2*(4), 489–502.

Trudgill, P. (1972). Sex, covert prestige, and linguistic change in the urban British English of Norwich. *Language in Society, 1,* 179–195.

van Dijk, T. (1993a). Editor's forward to critical discourse analysis. *Discourse & Society, 4*(2), 131–132.

van Dijk, T. (1993b). Principles of critical discourse analysis. *Discourse & Society, 4*(2), 249–283.

van Dijk, T. (1996). Discourse, power, and access. In C. Rosa Caldas-Coulthard & M. Coulthard (Eds.), *Texts and practices: Readings in critical discourse analysis* (pp. 84–104). London: Routledge.

5

"My Teacher Says...," Mastery of English and the Creole Learner

Alicia Beckford Wassink

According to the 1999 Statistical Yearbook of the United States Immigration and Naturalization Service, the population of immigrants to the United States of America from the Caribbean has exceeded 100,000 in each year since 1997. However, for many North Americans, visits to resort destinations and the allure of reggae culture constitute the extent of familiarity with West Indians. Myths abound regarding these individuals and the language(s) they speak. Two specific but distinct misunderstandings, which have both clear and not so clear consequences for the classroom setting, are that creole languages are based on French, and that speech in the anglophone Caribbean amounts to a lilting accent with a few vocabulary differences from English. This chapter, written for teacher educators, speaks to the importance of providing teachers in North American K–12 classrooms with accurate information regarding creole languages (primarily English-related or anglophone creoles). The discussion is centered on a set of myths regarding creole languages that I have repeatedly encountered in my own teaching. These myths are rooted in misconceptions of two broad types: First, misconceptions regarding creole languages and their linguistic structures, and second, language ideology-related issues.

Types of knowledge necessary for dealing with these two types of misconceptions are presented in two separate sections. Following the characterization of one common language structure-related myth and one ideology-related one, a first section introduces principles of linguistic knowledge from language acquisition, syntax, sociolinguistics, creole linguistics, and phonology that will be of value to the teacher interested in learning about the linguistic structures of creole languages and the sociohistorical settings out of which they arise. The section that follows addresses crucial questions regarding attitudes toward creole languages, particularly as they are likely to emerge in the K–12 classroom. Both sections begin by presenting material that the teacher educator may wish to highlight for in-service and pre-service teachers who will be teaching students from the English-speaking Caribbean or who plan to teach about the diversity of the languages of the world as part of language arts curricula. Recommendations for teaching linguistic concepts are followed with information that creole-speaking students themselves need, and information for their non-creole speaking classmates. One advantage of grounding the presentation of linguistic material within a discussion of myths about creole languages is that, as a practical matter, teachers will learn how to recognize and respond to these myths when they emerge in the classroom. This chapter is not primarily intended to provide teachers with help in teaching specific subject areas (that is, it is not concerned with *what* is to be taught), but rather is concerned primarily with *who* is taught, and *how* to meet the needs of specific students.

MYTHS REGARDING CREOLE LANGUAGES (AND THEIR SPEAKERS)

MYTH 1: Creoles Are Shortcut Languages

While conducting linguistic fieldwork in Jamaica during the early 1990s, I had the opportunity to be the second of two speakers addressing attendees at a meeting of a local Parent Teachers' Association. The first speaker was an official in the Ministry of Education, and an immigrant to Jamaica from a northern European country. He announced a program to be piloted in the community that would apply new methods in language arts instruction to prepare primary school students for the verbal sections of the all-island secondary-school entrance examination. The official motivated the need for the new program by appealing to the parents' sense that the use of proper English was lacking in Jamaica. Everyone in Jamaica is aware, he said, that there is a sort of "shortcut talk" that people use on the island. One person speaks this shortcut to another, but (because it is an incomplete form of English) the two do not understand each other. He looked to his audience for a response. To my surprise, his pause was met with general agreement. His comment was, for me, a symbolically important beginning to my research into Jamaicans' attitudes toward this so-called shortcut language, Jamaican Creole. In subsequent individual and small-group interviews with several of these same parents, I discovered that although they were largely ambivalent as to whether they would call the *Patois* (a term referring to a vernacular or regional variety of language, and the popular term used by Jamaicans for their creole) used by most speakers in everyday interaction a "language," they overwhelmingly agreed that it is possible to use this language to say everything one might wish to say. This contradicted the comment of the official who said that speakers could not be mutually understood. In addition, speakers repeatedly told me that there are concepts that can be expressed in Patois better than in English. The apparent contradictions in this set of observations can most clearly be interpreted if one understands that the linguistic nature of creole languages is largely misunderstood (sometimes even by education professionals).

One widespread misconception, recognizable in the words of the education official above, is that West Indians use an idiosyncratic, simplified speech. Creoles are frequently misconstrued as shortcut languages because they appear to have vocabulary similar to languages in the Germanic or Romance families (such as English, French, or Spanish), but seem to have features "missing." The section that follows provides key principles from creole linguistics and sociolinguistics that are necessary for understanding the linguistic systems of creole languages. These principles, and those presented in subsequent sections, are illustrated using examples from Jamaican Creole.

NECESSARY KNOWLEDGE #1: The Sociolinguistic Setting and Linguistic Features of Creole Languages

Although the terms *pidgin* and *creole* are often used together they refer to different linguistic entities arising out of language contact, and it is important to make the distinction as clear as possible. For example, some languages whose linguistic features have led linguists to classify them as creoles have the word "pidgin" in their popular name, as does for example, Hawaiian Pidgin, which is referred to by linguists as Hawaiian Creole English. Linguists reserve the term *pidgin* for linguistic varieties that come about by prolonged use, when speakers of non-mutually intelligible languages communicate over an extended period of time, often on a limited number of topics and in a limited range of social settings. European colonial expansion and the intensification of international trade during the 16th and 17th centuries are two often-cited catalysts for the emergence of pidgin varieties worldwide. Typically, pidgins are auxiliary languages. They are structurally sparse, with limited vocabularies, little grammatical architecture (words that express relationships in a sentence, such as prepositions, articles, and words introducing embedded clauses), and chaotic sentence structure (there is no "right" way to combine words into a well-formed sentence). Abstract ideas and temporal relations (e.g., unrealized events, past vs. present times) are not encoded in the structure of a pidgin, but must be inferred from the conversational context. A *creole*, on the other hand, develops from a prior pidgin, typically after several generations of use, when pidgin-speaking parents transmit the pidgin to their children. A pidgin is thus never its speakers' (only) native language, while creole languages *are* learned natively, and must meet all the communicative needs of the speech community. The need for a creole is socially and linguistically comprehensive, so both its lexical and grammatical systems expand rapidly, enabling a full range of linguistic functions. Organization of words into sentences is rule-governed (there is a "right" way to make a well-formed sentence), and it is possible to express abstract ideas and temporal relations. All aspects of the linguistic structure of a pidgin can be traced to both or all of its parent languages. This is not true for creoles, which over time develop linguistic features that cannot be attributed to any of their input languages. The nature of the linguistic forms that surface in a creole is believed by many to be determined in part by the proportion and distribution of speakers of the creoles' parent languages in the speech community during *creolization* and in part by inborn universal features of human cognition.

Pidgins and creoles, then, are linguistic varieties that result from contact between speakers of non-mutually intelligible languages. It is not always the case that cultural contact results in *pidginization* (formation of a new linguistic form, a pidgin, that may subsequently evolve into a creole). The communication problem has also, across human history, been solved by emergent bi- or multilingualism. By some estimates, there are about 80–127 pidgin and creole varieties in the world, and about 6 million people who speak them. Historically, these varieties have developed largely in coastal areas (e.g., eastern China, West Africa, Indonesia, Melanesia), and around inland trade routes (sub-Saharan Africa), where the need for communication between different language groups was ongoing. Some nations contain more than one pidgin or creole within their borders (e.g., Surinam).

NECESSARY KNOWLEDGE #2: Linguistic Similarities and Differences Between English and One English-Related Creole

The linguistic varieties spoken in Jamaica, Haiti, Trinidad and Tobago, and Barbados, four of the Caribbean countries from which the largest number of immigrants to the United States come, are creole and not pidgin varieties. While it is true that most of the vocabulary words (or *lexical items*) in Haitian Creole come historically from French (so that French may be said to be a *lexifier* language for Haitian Creole), Haitian Creole is the only French-related creole in this list. The bulk of the vocabularies of the Jamaican,

Trinidadian, and Barbadian creoles are derived from English. Linguists have found it problematic, however, to say that these languages are "based" on their lexifier varieties, because the vocabularies often also contain forms from other *substrate* (or parent) languages, in all of the cases above, languages of various West African countries (for example, Twi, Mandingo, Ewe, and Mande).[1] There are similarities between the creoles of Jamaica, Trinidad, and Barbados, but differences also abound, sufficient to signal to native speakers which Caribbean country an interlocutor is from. For example, while the word "nyam" (meaning "eat," from the West-African language Ewe) is widely retained in the region, the word "christophene" is used in Trinidad to refer to the same food that goes by the name "cho-cho" in Jamaica and Barbados, but "chayote squash" in Mexico and the United States. Besides lexical differences such as these, there are phonological and grammatical differences that distinguish these English-lexifier creoles from each other, and from internationally recognized varieties of English. As already mentioned, anglophone creoles are popularly conceived of by some as "English with an accent." However, as speakers of these languages well know, their speech is often unintelligible to English-speaking foreigners. (It is likewise true that Haitian Creole is not intelligible to speakers of European varieties of French.) Furthermore, most speakers are able to fluently *code-switch* between their creole and English. The similarities between English and these creoles all but end with lexical forms. We now turn to examples of linguistic differences drawing on several levels of the grammar. Our examples come from Jamaican Creole, but similar types of patterns occur for other anglophone creoles. The differences lie in several areas:

1. Words that have the same sound as English words, but different meanings.
2. Words that have a different sound, but express the same meaning as English words.
3. Grammatical constructions different than those of English.
4. Intonation/syntax relations that signal different meanings than English relations.

The first two examples draw on linguistic research into creole lexical features, while the third draws on research into creole syntax, and the final example, creole phonology. Lexical differences (such as in 1 and 2 above) have been discussed at some length by linguist-educators such as, for example, Velma Pollard in, *From Jamaican Creole to Standard English: A Hand-*

---

[1]The term *substrate* has a more technical meaning. It is typically used to refer specifically to the parent languages of that contributed most of the creole's phonological and grammatical infrastructure.

book for Teachers. What follows deals instead with features that have been subjected to rather less discussion in the literature. Additional resources may be found in Pollard's book and works referenced at the end of this chapter.

Grammatical Constructions (Temporal Relations)

In Jamaican Creole syntax, temporal relationships are expressed using free words, called *preverbal markers*, that precede the unmarked verb. This differs from English, which relies on verb endings (e.g., -ed) to express tense. The unmarked Jamaican Creole verb expresses either present tense or the simple past, depending upon the relationship between the actual, real-world timing of the event under discussion and the time of utterance. The use of preverbal markers is similar to that of Ewe, one of the West African parent languages of Jamaican Creole. In a number of the anglophone creoles English auxiliary verb forms appear to have provided the *etyma* (or outer form) for preverbal markers. However, it becomes clear that the resemblance is mostly phonetic (only in sound). Note that the example also provides one instance of a lexical difference such as indicated in (2) above. *Nyam* is a Jamaican Creole form with an Ewe cognate.

Jamaican Creole	English Gloss
Mi nyam di bammy.	I eat (generic) / ate the (specific) cassava patty.
Mi a nyam di bammy.	I am (progressive) eating the cassava patty.
Mi a go nyam di bammy.	I will (future) eat the cassava patty.
Mi hafi nyam di bammy.	I must (obligation) eat the cassava patty.
Mi bin nyam di bammy.	I ate (past / past perfect) the cassava patty.
Mi bin a nyam di bammy.	I was (enduring past) eating the cassava patty.

Intonation/Syntax Relations

Intonation is a term used by phonologists to refer to a melody of the voice used to signal linguistic meaning. Often, particular patterns in the inflection, or *pitch* of the voice are used to support various types of syntactic structure. Different syntactic structures typically have unique intonational contours in American English. For example, declarative utterances typically end with falling intonation to signal that a statement is being made, whereas interrogatives end with rising intonation. The *syntactic* structure of the English declarative is also distinct from that of English interrogatives. To form questions, such as "Will Mary clean the blackboard?" which may receive a yes or no response in English, the auxiliary verb (*will*) and subject noun (*Mary*) are inverted relative to their positions in the corresponding declarative "*Mary will* clean the blackboard," a phenomenon referred to as *subject/auxiliary inversion*.

In Jamaican Creole, the difference between declaratives and yes/no interrogatives is signaled by a different relationship between the syntax and the intonation. Namely, the intonation does all the work of making the contrast. In both statements and questions, the subject noun (*Mary*) precedes the auxiliary verb (*will*). Thus, both sentences are ordered as follows: "Mary will clean di blackboard." However, the declarative exhibits falling intonation, while the interrogative exhibits rising intonation.

For both American English and Jamaican Creole, declarative "melodies" have a *final-fall*, while interrogatives have a *final-rise*. While this pitch difference means that the contrast is clearly signaled for the native creole-speaking listener, the different intonation/syntax relation may result in ambiguity for the American English listener, who expects an interrogative to additionally exhibit different syntax.

These few examples demonstrate that although there are lexical similarities between Jamaican Creole and American English, there are also differences that extend well beyond the pronunciation of words (or *accent*), to syntax, other parts of the lexicon, and phonology. Other such examples might be given to illustrate the linguistic systems of other creole languages, which share features with their parent languages, but also show points of divergence. (See "Suggested Reading" for comparative studies of creole grammars.)

ATTITUDES TOWARD CREOLES AND CONSEQUENCES FOR THE CLASSROOM

MYTH 2: Creole Languages Are Based on French

The news media publishes occasional reminders that American society is insufficiently equipped to respond to the needs of its creole-speaking populations. In November, 1999, the *Seattle Times* carried an article by Sarah Rose, Knight Ridder Newspapers, entitled "Housing pamphlets lost in the translation." The Department of Housing and Urban Development (HUD) requisitioned the translation and publication of a pamphlet intended to inform Haitian Americans living in federally subsidized housing in Florida of their rights and responsibilities as residents. Five thousand copies of the document were published using language characterized by some as an "imitation" Jamaican dialect, showing neither the syntactic nor lexical structure of Jamaican Creole, angering both Jamaicans and Haitians, who expressed concern that their government showed a gross lack of knowledge about their languages. This story also points to a lack of knowledge about where to turn for answers to linguistic questions. Apparently, at no time in this process were linguists consulted to provide information about either creole.

A more recent article entitled, "Language Barriers to Learning" (Annie Ngana-Mundeke, *Anthropology News*, April 2000), demonstrates that the blame for widespread lack of understanding about Haitian Creole resides not only with institutions, as misconceptions may also be propagated by native speakers themselves. The article tells of a 13-year-old girl, a recent immigrant from Haiti, who told her teacher that she spoke French at home with her parents. The teacher attempted to communicate with the child using French, but became quickly frustrated when the child showed no signs of understanding. The child complained that the teacher used new vocabulary that she found unfamiliar. Of course, the confusion here was based in the fact that the child did not speak French, but referred to her language as French.

NECESSARY KNOWLEDGE #3:
Misinformation in the Classroom

The consequences of misunderstandings such as have been outlined earlier (Myths 1 and 2) become clear at this point. First, many North Americans live under the misconception that there is one language called "Creole," when in fact, "creole" is a general designation for a type of language arising out of language contact. Second, as the "Language Barriers to Learning" article demonstrates, creole speakers do not necessarily come into North American classrooms with training in the linguistic structure or social history of their languages. The classroom becomes a place of confusion, and learning is impeded. Their non-creole-speaking classmates are at an even greater loss as to how to understand the complex social and linguistic issues surrounding their language. This should make evident to linguists and those interested in linguistic issues the intense importance of imparting the results of linguistic research to students as part of efforts to inform the general public. One important negative consequence for the classroom is the marginalization of the creole-speaking student, which may take various forms:

- When differences between a creole and the language of education are ignored, and the language of education is one of the creole's parent languages, there is no improvement in the student's ability to navigate effectively in the school setting. The creole-speaking student's variety is romanticized as a quaint "island" trait and her learning of significant linguistic differences between her first and second linguistic varieties is not encouraged.

- Normally developing students are enrolled in special education programs. Because their situation is not clinical, speech therapy is ineffective, and a waste of resources. "Barriers to Learning" tells of one such student, Felix. (Also see Ann & Peng, chap. 6, this volume.)
- Students are left back to repeat a grade and, without specific support in language learning, it is somehow hoped that they will figure out how to catch up on their own.

These examples of the disenfranchisement of creole-speaking students may arise not only from linguistic misinformation, but also from ideological stances related to a particular understanding of the sociocultural history of the student's home country. The following section explores three such ideological issues (Necessary Knowledge #4–6).

NECESSARY KNOWLEDGE #4: Attitudes Toward Anglophone Creoles Are Multivalued

Although it is important for the North American teacher to be aware that a number of new faces in their classrooms may come from countries where creoles are spoken, and that the grammars of these creoles are rule-governed, it is perhaps even more important for the teacher to be aware of the nature of the sociolinguistic experience these speakers bring. The body of research has been growing that clarifies ideological issues surrounding creole languages that coexist locally with one or more of their parent languages, including the impact of teachers' and students' attitudes toward language on the success of language arts instruction. (Some of these are provided under "Attitudinal Studies" in the Suggested Reading section of this chapter.) In this section, several basic findings of this research are characterized, and key consequences for the classroom are highlighted. The research exploring attitudes toward anglophone creoles may be summarized into the following three findings: language attitudes are multivalued, related to the social history of settlement of the region, and change as the society changes.

Researchers in the late 1980s and 1990s studied the attitudes of both laypeople and teachers to English-related creoles. At the center of the research has been a paradox: that, on the one hand, creoles such as the one spoken in Jamaica have been widely viewed by laypeople as nonstandard linguistic varieties whose demise is sure as English takes its rightful place in social, educational, or political life. However, decades after such predictions were made, these apparently low-prestige varieties continue to thrive in the same communities from which predictions of demise emerged. The continuity of these, and other language varieties the world over has been linked to the *multivalued* nature of language attitudes, a term used in scholarship into language ideology. Speakers' understandings of what their creole *is* are closely related to their attitudes regarding its *value*.

Several surveys found that lay attitudes toward creoles are often ambivalent and differ with age and educational background of the respondent. Wassink (1999) found that older Jamaican speakers did not appear to perceive Jamaican Creole as an independent variety, but rather as one that only exists relative to English (frequently calling it "Broken English"). Younger respondents, however, tended to say that Jamaican Creole was *mixed* with English, and to distinguish it from "slang," reserving "Broken English" for cases where English is used *inconsistently* (e.g., by foreign non-native speakers but not Jamaicans). Teachers were divided on the issue: Kindergarten and elementary teachers in the sample equated Jamaican Creole with slang and Broken English, while college and vocational teachers distinguished Jamaican Creole from these varieties. Only half of the sample felt that a Jamaican Creole monolingual could learn to speak English if not taught it in school.

Quite often, *audience* (type of listener) and *domain* (social setting) severely restrict use of a creole. Inappropriate audiences include one's supervisor, teacher, and non-familiars. While answering the telephone and professional settings constitute inappropriate domains of use, cultural events (theater, concerts), home, marketplace, and rural settings are typically appropriate. One 14-year old Jamaican boy said that he wants his children to know "when it's time for English, and when it's time for Patois." Thus, creole speakers often have a guarded pride in their Creole. They feel it is an asset but reflects negatively on the person who uses it in inappropriate domains—domains where everyone should use English. However, English is not welcomed in certain places, because it does not convey trustworthiness or cultural affinity. These findings echo those of research conducted in Guyana, the English-speaking Cameroon, and South Africa. Notably, such attitudes are not predicted if speakers are viewed as desiring the demise of a creole, as discussed earlier.

This balance of negative and positive attitudes toward the same language demonstrates that language attitudes are *multivalued*. Speakers simultaneously rate their language according to separate subjective criteria. On the one hand they value, and speak openly and positively about the language variety that is the most likely means of attaining socioeconomic advancement (this variety, then, receives *overt prestige*). At the same time, speakers value another linguistic variety as the one that communicates common culture, trustworthiness, political solidarity, and friendship. Because its worth is typically held silently or even denied in the presence of outsiders, it is said to receive *covert prestige*.

NECESSARY KNOWLEDGE #5: Attitudes to Language Are Rooted in Social History

The key to the apparent disparity between covert and overt language attitudes lies in part in the fact that the attitudes people hold toward language in the Caribbean are related to the social history of the settlement of the region. For example, the history of Jamaica, as an island that was home to Arawak peoples, then colonized by Spain (1494–1655) and Britain (1655–1838), is reflected in its words. Much of the island's industry and social structure developed under the enforced labor of slaves brought primarily from Western and West-Central Africa. We may consider, for example, ways in which contact with British culture, arguably the strongest colonial influence on the island, impacted attitudes and language use:

- Jamaica's systems of education and government were patterned on the British model (e.g., Jamaicans elect a Prime Minister and Ministers of Parliament)
- Migration of British settlers to Jamaica set British culture and values as prestige norms, reflecting the status of English speakers
- The English of the upper classes became the standard language in Jamaica for use in government and international affairs, although the emergent creole was the first language of the majority of the population

These facts enable us to understand how, in this postcolonial nation, English came to be viewed as the standard language and Jamaican Creole as the nonstandard. Students who emigrate from anglophone creole speaking countries carry their homeland's social history with them. (This elucidates why a Jamaican would refer to her language as "English," or why the Haitian child in the "Barriers to Learning" example referred to her language as "French.") It has only been since the 1940s that researchers have investigated Jamaican Creole and other anglophone creoles for retentions from their non-lexifier parent languages. Despite the high ratio of Africans to Europeans on the island through the 17th and 18th centuries, it was widely assumed that one need look no further than English to find the source for Jamaican linguistic forms. As has already been shown, the linguistic origin of creoles is considerably more complex than this. The resemblance between many creole and lexifier vocabulary items reinforces the view that non-lexifier linguistic structures prove a creole to be a "corrupt" variety of the lexifier. The use of creole features has long been perceptually associated with life on the former plantations, uneducated people, moral waywardness, and general backward living.

NECESSARY KNOWLEDGE #6: Attitudes to Language
Change as Society Changes

But despite the traditional ambivalence to some creoles, research suggests that as societies change, attitudes toward creoles also change. One study, exploring attitudes voiced in the Jamaican press, indicates that, "some are quietly sowing the seeds for change by using Creole in a wider range of areas than ever before" (Christie, 1995). Worldwide acclaim for Jamaican music and bolstered nationalistic fervor have been linked to increased pride in "things Jamaican." The domains of use appropriate for the creole are increasing, including, for example, the teaching of cultural history. In 1990, the National Association of Teachers of English in Jamaica (NATE) declared Jamaican Creole the "heart language" of the Jamaican people, and encouraged teachers to use as a resource the competence that students bring in Jamaican Creole to aid them on the road to mastery of English. Teachers were encouraged, not to teach Jamaican Creole in the classroom, but to use students' knowledge of this creole to enable them to understand the differences between its grammatical structures and those of English. Research conducted into the relationship between the attitudes of secondary school principals and students' test outcomes indicates that Jamaican students' scores on the verbal sections of the Common Entrance examinations are higher on average for those schools that are actively employing such "bridge methods." Crucially, the greatest advancements in mastery of English have not come when Jamaican Creole use was suppressed, but rather when student's verbal ability and knowledge of creole structure have been used to support the comparative learning of English grammatical categories. Thus, attitudinal change often advances alongside societal change, and these changes have clear outcomes for language arts education. It may be instructive to briefly present some of the "bridge methods" teachers employ.

RESOURCES FOR TEACHING

Creating a Bridge From Competence
in Creole to Competence in English

The final section of this chapter provides resources for building linguistic knowledge in the creole-speaking student and in their non-creole speaking classmates. Students from anglophone creole-speaking backgrounds are frequently developing competence simultaneously in multiple linguistic varieties and bring this linguistic experience with them to the classroom. However, unlike some populations in North America, these students are rarely regarded as developing two linguistic varieties, because they are considered to come from "English-speaking" countries, which is only partly true. Assuming that students from anglophone Caribbean countries come into the classroom with the same competence in English as American students is a mistake with at least two significant consequences: First, lessons designed for monolingual English-speaking children are often unsuitable for teaching basic concepts to the creole-speaking child. They may fail, for example, to recognize differences between Jamaican Creole and English of the types described earlier. Second, rather than being viewed as a resource to aid learning, the linguistic competence of the student is underused, or not tapped at all, and he or she becomes psychologically distanced from the material taught in class. Certainly, some of these issues have clear corollaries in wider discussions regarding bilingual education. For this reason, the teacher working in a traditional bilingual classroom may also find the discussion of language attitudes and suggested strategies for teaching quite relevant. (Also see MacGregor-Mendoza, chap. 9, this volume.)

This section presents methods currently in use to build a bridge between the creole-speaking student's knowledge of one creole (Jamaican) and North American English. We focus on the two types of linguistic difference introduced earlier:

1. Grammatical constructions different than those of English.
2. Different intonation/syntax relations.

Grammatical Constructions

Mary *drink* di wata.	Jamaican Creole
Mary *drinks* the water.	American English

Observation. Student has difficulty with use of English present tense agreement rules that relate a subject form to a verb of the same number and person. Teachers try to correct students' uninflected forms by teaching them that they incorrectly "leave off" forms. The result is hypercorrection because English marks only *third person* forms. The student overapplies the plural '-s' rule, adding it to all forms that she produces with no ending. Hypercorrection goes unaddressed.

Suggestions. Use oral exercises as one means of accessing the students' knowledge of parallel Creole ~ English forms. Record both sets of forms. Use this record as basis for further written exercises, reinforced by reading (speak-write-read).

Different Intonation/Syntax Relations

Mary will clean the blackboard (rising intonation)?   Jamaican Creole
Will Mary clean the blackboard (rising intonation)?   American English

Observation. Student uses rising intonation as the primary cue to the identity of an interrogative construction. Because this cue is present in her own constructions, she does not notice that subject/auxiliary inversion is required, and does not learn to marry syntax with intonation.

Suggestion. Draw student's attention to the idea that there are *two* steps to creating yes/no question sentences in English—changes in the melody of the voice, and changes in the order of the words in the sentence.

Resources for the Non-creole Speaking Student

Providing native speakers of North American English with accurate linguistic information about creoles also has several important benefits. Wolfram (1999) pointed out, in a discussion of dialect awareness education, that solutions that improve the educational environment for the regional dialect-speaking student and his or her classmates are ones that address both linguistic and attitudinal issues. The former is ineffectual without the latter. The same is true for creole and non-creole-speaking students. While the important linguistic axiom that grammars are *rule-governed* must be stressed, the systematicity and complexity of creoles will not be grasped unless the non-creole speaking student understands that the language has a speech community (just as their language does) with a history distinct from other cultures in the region. That is, it may be helpful to stress in history curricula that in the Caribbean, citizens of the English-speaking Caribbean do not view themselves as "Caribbean," but rather as citizens of different countries with unique histories. This will help to ameliorate the misconceptions that all creoles are based on French and that there is just one language called "Creole."

Principles of language acquisition are also important for the non-creole-speaking student. Particularly important is the understanding that *normally developing children all acquire language according to similar milestones.* Memorization of linguistic differences between a creole and American English will not take the weight they should if it is not understood that creole forms are natively learned in a manner identical to classmate's own acquisition process, and that creoles are sufficient for expressing every idea a speaker might want to express. Understanding this principle helps to address the misunderstanding that creole forms are minimally different from the language that is the medium of education.

DISCUSSION

This chapter has attempted to link language structure and language attitudes, that is, to demonstrate that *how* speakers think about a language influences *what* they believe about the language. When it is assumed that a creole-speaking child enters the classroom with a native competence in North American English, the very real problem emerges that the differences between their creole and English will go untaught and unrecognized. The importance of mastering English as a language of international communication is indisputable. However, there is a clear need for teaching around the linguistic characteristics of creole languages in North American settings where creole-speaking students are present. Approaches to teaching English that attempt to give English prominence in the mind of the student by claiming a nonlinguistic status for the Creole have proved over and over to be unsuccessful. A more realistic goal seems to be one which strengthens fluency in both varieties, recognizing the roles both languages play in social life. The teacher is best-prepared who can demonstrate to her bilingual or bidialectal students how they may become linguistic sleuths; detectives who actively seek to uncover the linguistic similarities and differences of their languages.

REFERENCES

Christie, P. (1995, January). *Attitudes to Creole: Some Jamaican evidence.* Paper presented at the Society for Pidgin and Creole Languages, New Orleans.

Pollard, V. (1992). *From Jamaican Creole to standard English: A handbook for teachers.* Kingston: University of the West Indies.

Wassink, A. B. (1999). Historic low prestige and seeds of change: Language attitudes toward Jamaican Creole. *Language in Society, 28*(1), 57–92.

Wolfram, W. (1999). Dialect awareness programs in the school and community. In R. S. Wheeler (Ed.), *Language alive in the classroom* (pp. 47–66). Westport, CT: Praeger.

SUGGESTED READING

Comparative Creole Studies and Studies of African Retentions in Anglophone Creole Languages

Holm, J. (1988). *Pidgins and creoles: Reference survey* (2 vols.). Cambridge, England: Cambridge University Press.

Holm, J., & Patrick, P. (Eds.). (2002). *Comparative creole syntax. Parallel outlines of 17 creole grammars.* London, England: Battlebridge.

Roberts, P. (1988). *West Indians and their language.* Cambridge, England: Cambridge University Press.

Turner, L. D. (1994). *Africanisms in the Gullah dialect.* Ann Arbor: University of Michigan.

Attitudinal Studies

Craig, D. (1971). Education and Creole English in the West Indies. In D. Hymes (Ed.), *Pidginization and creolization of languages*. Cambridge, England: Cambridge University Press.

Craig, D. (1976). Bidialectal education: Creole and standards in the West Indies. *Linguistics, 175,* 93–134.

Morgan, H. W. (1983). *An analysis of the attitudes of Jamaican principals toward Creole usage in secondary schools*. Unpublished doctoral dissertation, Texas Southern University.

Mühleisen, S. (1995, January). *Attitude change towards language varieties in Trinidad*. Paper presented at the Society of Pidgin and Creole Languages, New Orleans.

Rickford, J. R. (1986). Standard and non-standard language attitudes in a Creole continuum. In N. Wolfson & J. Manes (Eds.), *Language of inequality* (pp. 145–160). The Hague: Mouton.

Ryan, E. B. (1979). Why do low-prestige language varieties persist? In H. Giles & R. N. St. Clair (Eds.), *Language and social psychology* (pp. 145–157). Oxford, England: Blackwell.

Winford, D. (1976). Teacher attitudes toward language varieties in a Creole community. *Linguistics, 175,* 45–75.

Jamaican Creole Grammar, Phonology, and Vocabulary

Bailey, B. L. (1966). *Jamaican Creole syntax: A transformational approach*. Cambridge, England: Cambridge University Press.

Cassidy, F. G., & LePage, R. (1967). *Dictionary of Jamaican English*. Cambridge, England: Cambridge University Press.

Meade, R. (1999). *Acquisition of Jamaican phonology*. London: John Benjamins.

6

The Relevance of Linguistic Analysis to the Role of Teachers as Decision Makers

Jean Ann
Long Peng

This chapter is, in a broad sense, an attempt to address the twin questions of (a) what teachers do with language and (b) what implications this has for linguistics instruction in teacher education. Pre-service and in-service teachers clearly have many responsibilities and are involved directly or indirectly in making many kinds of pedagogical decisions. One main type of decision concerns the curriculum, determining what to teach and how to present it to students. This type of decision making is not new, forming most teachers' core responsibilities. However, largely as a result of social and political changes in the last 50 years, the society has placed upon teachers many other responsibilities, one of them being to identify students with special needs and to refer them for specialized services such as special education, ESL, or bilingual services. This chapter is concerned with the role of teachers in this type of decision making and its implications for linguistics instruction.

It was always clear to us that preschool and school teachers (both in-service and pre-service teachers) could use knowledge of some basic linguistic and sociolinguistic findings. These findings include, for example, the fact that (a) varieties of English such as African-American English, even though socially stigmatized, are systematic and have their own rules that are distinct from those of "standard" American English (Baugh, 1999; Hazen, 2001; Labov, 1972; Rickford & Rickford, 2000); (b) sign languages are real languages, with grammatical systems like those of spoken languages (Klima & Bellugi, 1979; Mancini, chap. 7, this volume; Messing, 1999; Stokoe, Casterline, & Croneberg, 1976); (c) language use and linguistic behaviors differ in communities of varied class backgrounds (Anyon, 1997; Delpit, 1995; Heath, 1983; Lopez, 1999). We knew that if teachers had some basic linguistic knowledge, they would have a better understanding and appreciation of their students' linguistic backgrounds. For example, students who don't speak English natively or who speak a different variety of English such as African-American English are sometimes considered linguistically and (sometimes) intellectually deficient, a position that would be impossible for anyone who is informed about linguistics to take. As Labov (1970, 1972), Jordan (1985), Smitherman (1973), hooks (1994), Lippi-Green (1997) and many others pointed out, even though African-American English and other varieties are socially stigmatized, speakers of these varieties are not linguistically or intellectually inferior; their abilities to think, reason, or communicate are not impaired. Instead of seeing the diverse linguistic backgrounds students bring to school as an obstacle to learning and academic success, teachers with an understanding of these sociolinguistic findings can view the linguistic diversity in their classrooms as an asset and use it to enrich instruction for everyone (Ann, 2002; Ann & Peng, 2002; Cummins, 2000; Wheeler, chap. 14, this volume). Research in educational psychology has consistently shown that those students whose linguistic and cultural backgrounds are respected by their peers and teachers have higher self-esteem and motivation to succeed academically.

A second much needed aspect of linguistic knowledge concerns knowledge of the grammar of English and grammar in general. Here we refer not so much to prescriptive norms (although some of these cannot be ignored in the context of schools) but to the knowledge of the phonological, morphological, syntactic, semantic, and discourse patterns in a language. There are good reasons for all teachers to have some knowledge of grammar, especially considering the fact that the student population that schools serve is becoming increasingly diverse linguistically. For instance, knowledge of grammar can be a way of beginning to talk about student writing and speaking. And even teachers who are not directly involved in language arts instruction are repeatedly confronted with linguistic and grammatical issues raised by their students.

Although we are constantly amazed at how much our own knowledge in these areas is tested and expanded in trying to answer our own and our students' questions, we have become aware that even an understanding of a large amount of linguistic and sociolinguistic knowledge is *not sufficient* for preschool and school teachers if they do not know how to apply such knowledge. We have come to believe that what teachers need to know is linguistic analysis, namely, the ability to apply their linguistic knowledge to real-life situations in which language is an issue. To do so, teachers must be able to look at language data, analyze it, and draw conclusions *on the basis of the data.* Increasingly, the pedagogical decisions that teachers make rely on both spoken and written language data. We argue that the ability to conduct basic linguistic analyses would greatly enhance teachers' abilities to identify the difficulties facing their students. The act of looking at language evidence, forming, testing and re-testing hypotheses, and drawing conclusions is not a luxury that teachers can do without. There is clear evidence that the pedagogical decisions that today's teachers make about their students depend increasingly on language data and that these decisions have serious (sometimes long-term) implications for the intellectual and psychological development of these students. The importance of these decisions for the students concerned provides a compelling case for teachers to develop the ability to conduct basic linguistic analyses so that they can accurately assess their students' needs and determine the type and amount of instruction needed.

To lay out our thinking, we first discuss the social and political changes that increasingly place teachers in the role of decision makers for the students they serve. We then consider two cases that highlight the need for learning how to do linguistic analysis. We conclude by drawing some lessons from the growing awareness of linguistics in the legal profession that shows the need for training in linguistic analysis.

THE CHANGING EDUCATIONAL LANDSCAPE AND TEACHERS AS DECISION MAKERS

The role of "teacher" has never been restricted solely to classroom instruction. Throughout the history of schooling in the United States, teachers have functioned in addition to offering classroom instruction as religious and moral guides, career counselors, and mentors for students (Spring, 1997; Tozer, Violas, & Senese, 1998). At any given time in history, the social and political conditions of the day drastically affect and determine the society's expectations of what teachers should do. For instance, the recent spate of high-profile school shootings has forced schools and teachers to address safety issues. One relatively new yet important responsibility brought about by social and political changes is the role of teachers in identifying their students' needs and referring them for appropriate services such as speech therapy, ESL services, or bilingual education. It is our belief that neither the scope nor the importance of this responsibility is fully understood or appreciated by the system that places teachers in that role.

The key structural forces that place teachers in this type of decision making emerge from changes taking place in our society. One such change is the growing recognition of issues facing specific groups of students and the need for specialized services to address these needs in fields such as special education, ESL, bilingual education, deaf education, and so forth. Until recently, schools were not required to provide specialized services for students with physical, mental and/or learning disabilities, for children from particular socioeconomic backgrounds, or for students whose native language is not English. Students with physical or mental disabilities rarely attended the same schools as students without such disabilities. Students with learning disabilities often went unnoticed, placed with other students, to fend for themselves. The students who spoke English as a second language were either placed directly in classes with native English-speaking students with little or no ESL support. Or they were placed with students with disabilities, with their lack of English language speaking abilities misconstrued as a sign of disability.

The advances in our understanding brought about by extensive research in fields such as education, sociology, anthropology, psychology, speech communication, and linguistics have resulted in a greater appreciation of the challenges facing these students. Today, public schools are required by various laws and regulations to provide services for these students. The availability of specialized services leads to an increase in the decisions that must be made about who should be provided such services. Teachers, as the personnel having the most frequent and direct contact with students, are often the first to identify the problems facing particular students and to make referrals. Depending on the procedures implemented in particular school districts, these referrals are often submitted to a team made up of specialists and classroom teachers, who have to determine whether specialized services are needed, what form of specialized services (such as push-in and pull-out services[1]) is appropriate, and for how long these services should be provided.

The push for educational accountability in the form of high-stakes testing has increased the scope and frequency of referrals that teachers make as well. Though we can debate the merits of these tests, they are here to stay for the time being. When standards are enforced by high-stakes assessments and the prospects of funding withdrawal or even school closure, the consequences extend well beyond holding schools accountable (Delandshere & Arens, 2001; Ford, Davern, & Schnorr, 2001). One such consequence is a dramatic increase in the number of recommendations or decisions that

---

[1]In American school settings, the expressions "push-in" and "pull-out" refer to the way in which specialized support services such as ESL or special education are provided to students with special needs. For instance, students with special needs may be placed with students without special needs. Those with special needs can be provided with instruction or support services directly in the classroom in which they are placed. Or students with special needs may be separated from or pulled out of the regular class and provided support services and instruction designed specifically for them. "Push in" refers to the first form of instruction while "pull-out" describes the second form of services.

teachers make so that their students are provided with appropriate academic support services. To prepare for these high-stakes tests, K–12 schools throughout the country have adopted a variety of measures such as summer classes, after-school programs, accelerated classes for advanced students and remedial courses for those who do not meet the benchmarks. These solutions increase the need for screening and referrals to determine who needs such services.

In addition, the standards-based reform has spurred the rapid rise and adoption of packaged educational programs. One widely adopted education program is Success for All (SFA), a reading program developed by Robert Slavin and his colleagues at Johns Hopkins University (Slavin, Karweit, & Wasik, 1994; Slavin & Madden, 2001). SFA is a reading program designed particularly for students from low social and economic backgrounds in urban high-needs schools. SFA bases its success partially on grouping students according to their abilities rather than their age. A SFA classroom is made up routinely of students from several grades. The assignment of students to classes depends on assessments and recommendations of classroom teachers, thus increasing the frequency of decisions that teachers make.

The need for language-based decisions is clearly highlighted by a situation in the school we visited. This school offers two separate curricular tracks. One is what the school calls the bilingual track and the other is the ESL track. The students placed in the bilingual track receive instruction mainly in Spanish with limited ESL services in the earlier grades. The students are gradually transitioned into English as they move up in grades. The students in the English track receive instruction only in English. To determine which track students belong in, the school currently follows a three-step process. First, a district-wide questionnaire is administered to the parents, asking questions such as whether their child is Spanish-dominant or English-dominant. On the basis of the responses, the teachers make a recommendation to the parents as to where their child should be placed. The final decision is left to the parents.[2] Here we see that language-based decisions start the moment a child enters the school. As we show through the stories recounted in the next section, the decisions that teachers make quite often rely on their ability to make sense of language data. Unless teachers are trained to conduct basic analyses, mistakes are inevitable, leading to short-term frustrations and worries for all parties concerned and sometimes lasting damages to the students' self-perceptions as learners and their academic achievements.

---

[2]After implementing this procedure for some time, the school administrators and teachers have realized a number of problems with the decision making process. One problem that has become obvious to the administrators and teachers is that parents do not fully understand the implications of the choices they make for their children. Fortunately for the children of this school, the problems are identified and active steps are being taken to address these problems.

REAL STORIES AND THEIR RELEVANCE
TO CURRICULAR PLANNING

We report two real stories that highlight the importance of developing teachers' ability to conduct basic linguistic analyses. We believe that teachers' decision-making abilities in these and other situations could be significantly improved with education in how to do linguistics. We have altered names and some nonessential details to conceal the identities of the parties concerned.

Darla

Darla's mother has a professional job with flexible and unconventional hours. Her father works at home. Darla sees both of her parents quite a bit, and gets a great deal of attention and care.

Darla has extremely expressive body language and facial expressions. Both are atypical of a girl her age (now 5), so much so that sometimes people feel like Darla is talking to them, when in reality, she isn't uttering any words. She loves to play and interact especially with adults. These interactions include cuddling, role-playing, storytelling, listening to stories, and the like. She displays the range of human emotions: Laughter, tears, rage, and joy are normal parts of her life. No professional who has evaluated Darla sees her as in any way abnormal emotionally, though they notice that she likes to be around adults and children who are, linguistically speaking, more like her. Her parents describe her as "sensitive," since she understands the things people say, and takes them to heart.

Darla began to speak independently at age 3½, though she could repeat and speak if prompted since age 2. She talked a great deal with family and friends and constructed multiword sentences. But Darla's speech was always hard to understand and gradually her parents became concerned. As Darla started to speak more and more, the intelligibility of her speech did not seem to improve with her age and increasing exposure to and use of English. All the adults around Darla realized that her speech was different, but they were not quite sure of how to describe it. Some of Darla's playmates began to realize that her speech was different and shunned her in social interactions.

Darla's worried parents brought her to a speech teacher supplied by a county-funded early intervention agency. The speech teacher was clearly startled upon hearing Darla's speech and, like other adults, had difficulty understanding what Darla said. She explained to the parents, within earshot of Darla, that she had never heard this unusual speech before. After some sessions, she told the parents she could no longer work with Darla because Darla couldn't get the hang of speaking the way she wanted her to.

Darla didn't enjoy working with this speech teacher and was somewhat relieved not to have to, but she still realized that something about her speech made her teacher reject her, and she told her parents tearfully that "nobody understands me."

What was it about Darla's speech that set her apart and caused her first speech teacher to stop working with her? We listened closely and transcribed the child's speech. As we examined the transcribed data and compared it with the same words in adult speech, a pattern started to emerge. Some of the data are presented next.

Darla	Adult	Darla	Adult
alk	talk	me	me
ad	dad	way	way
izuz	scissors		
ean	Jean		
astle	castle		
ink	drink		
ing	string		

Darla's speech pattern is clearly rare. While Darla was dropping most consonants that occur in the beginning or onset of a syllable, most children of her age drop coda (or ending) consonants. For example, instead of saying [dæd] a child of a language-learning age might say [dæ]. When children drop onset consonants, they do so to simplify the onset by eliminating not all but some onset consonants such as [bus] or [mus] for [brus] "Bruce." Our search through the psycholinguistic research has not uncovered one article that describes this kind of speech pattern. According to the psycholinguistics colleagues we consulted, Darla's speech pattern is rare with estimates ranging between 1% and 5% of children with speech issues exhibiting this pattern.

Darla's speech might throw anybody off initially because of its unusual pattern of onset dropping instead of the expected coda dropping. But is her speech so unusual that a teacher cannot figure it out? People who spend time with children first learning to speak know that early speech is highly contextual; children tend to talk about things in the immediate environment. With some exposure and perseverance, most adults can figure out what the kids are trying to say. We believe that with some knowledge of linguistic analysis, Darla's first teacher might not have panicked when she heard her unusual speech, even though it was something she had not heard before. She might have been able to make use of the truism that language (including children's speech) is rule-governed and systematic (taught in most introductory linguistics courses). It might have occurred to her that Darla's speech, however bizarre it might have seemed at first, is likely to follow a pattern and that the only logical step was to go through the process of trying to discover exactly what Darla's speech pattern might be. This process involves:

Analytic Steps to Determine Darla's Speech Pattern

a. listening closely to what Darla is saying;
b. writing down or transcribing what she is saying using phonetic transcription;
c. comparing it with what she intends to say, that is, with the adult forms;
d. identifying the systematic differences between Darla's speech and the adult forms, namely, the speech pattern.

The preceding four steps are parts of conducting a basic phonological analysis of human speech. It is not difficult to see that knowledge of the system in Darla's speech, which comes as a result of a linguistic analysis, is crucial for all parties involved in Darla's life. Speech teachers need to know it to address Darla's needs. Parents and other adults and children around her need to know it so they can make sense of what she tries to communicate, and perhaps lessen the frustration she feels.

When we talked about Darla's speech pattern with her parents, we showed why their daughter was not "deleting all initial consonants," or "not having certain sounds," as the speech teacher originally suggested. Even though Darla did delete initial consonants, there were a few simple onsets (such as [m] and [w]) that Darla always pronounced. Moreover, it was not the case that Darla did not have certain sounds. She did even though they appeared only in the coda in her speech. What set Darla's speech pattern apart from the speech patterns of most children is the deletion of beginning sounds. We explained that part of the evidence that suggested that Darla's pattern was so unusual is that onsets are not typically deleted or restricted in the world's languages, but codas often are. The information that we were able to share with the parents about language seemed to help them contextualize the linguistic behaviors of their daughter. Eventually Darla was assigned to a different speech teacher, who, according to the parents, has formed a much stronger bond with her and is not afraid of or upset by her linguistic characteristics. Today, at age 5, Darla is speaking well; her speech problems are almost gone.

Kenneth. We met Kenneth when he was in college. He grew up in Jamaica, West Indies speaking a language he calls "patois." With his family, he immigrated to the United States at around age 9 for the hope of a better life in New York City. Young Kenneth befriended other Black children in his neighborhood and, to his family's dismay, soon became a speaker of African-American English. In school, he learned that he had to read and write in standard American English. For some time, he maintained patois, African-American English, and standard American English. By the time he got to college, he could understand and speak patois if necessary (e.g., when visiting Jamaica) and he could readily switch between the other two. To a linguist, Kenneth is quite competent. Unfortunately, he was not seen this way in school. He writes:

> We have a tendency within the United States of America towards stereotyping, ridiculing and discriminating against things that are different . . . it is this belief that there is a "correct" form [of English] . . . that has plagued my lifetime . . .
>
> As I immigrated from Jamaica to the United States, Patois was my spoken language. However, Patois' similarity to English gave me enough knowledge to communicate with as well as understand any American citizen. The only difference between my English, and the English of any average American speaker, was that it was expressed with a Caribbean accent. Therefore, as I entered elementary school I was very optimistic about the many things I would learn. To my dismay I would learn that there was something very wrong with my language . . .
>
> Upon entering . . . school . . . , I was placed in a speech class . . . every day for an hour and a half. As my friends headed for the playgrounds and parks after school, I was learning how to speak. Students . . . would call me "retard" and "stupid."
>
> I graduated from elementary school as the valedictorian; ironically my self-esteem was very low. I could speak socially proper English. However I began to hide the existence of my heritage because of the ridicule that the foreign accent took . . .

Kenneth spoke freely with us about his belief that he was tracked into special education and provided speech lessons because he spoke a different variety of English from that spoken by his teachers. Instead of celebrating Kenneth's bi-dialectal capabilities (Jamaican and African-American English) and using them to enrich the linguistic experience of all children, professionals in his school diagnosed him as linguistically deficient (and intellectually deficient as well) and in need of remedial speech services. Despite his early school experiences in the United States, Kenneth graduated college with a 3.7 GPA. His intellectual ability was obviously not impaired or delayed.

In Kenneth's and many other similar cases (see e.g., Michie [1999] and Rodriguez [1982]), it is not hard to see that knowledge of sociolinguistics and linguistics is relevant here (also see Wassink, chap. 5, this volume). Knowledge of the unequal status of standard vs. non-standard varieties can benefit teachers who work with children like Kenneth (Fasold, 1998a, 1998b; Wardhaugh, 1998). Taken together, the works of Crawford (1992), Jordon

(1985), Kachru (1985, 1986), Labov (1970, 1972), Lippi-Green (1997), McCrum, Cran, and MacNeil (1995), Smitherman (1986) and many others yield a number of highly relevant conclusions for teachers:

Some Relevant Sociolinguistic Findings

a. There is more than one variety of English (clear as this may seem, many, including educators, remain convinced that there is only one in the United States);
b. each variety of English has its own system and rules;
c. each variety is equally capable of serving all of the linguistic or nonlinguistic functions of their respective speech communities;
d. the perceived deficiency of the non-standard varieties of any language is not based on any linguistic deficiency;
e. rather, it is the result of societal attitudes resulting mostly from the power relations among people who speak these different varieties.

It might be argued that many of these conclusions were not available until rather recently, perhaps not until the 1950s. Given the short history and the length of time it takes to disseminate research findings in any field, teachers cannot be expected to keep up with all recent developments in linguistics that are relevant to teaching. Perhaps the failure of Kenneth's teachers to accurately diagnose his linguistic capabilities is the direct result of the fact that such knowledge was not available.

We believe, however, that even if teachers do not know the latest linguistic research, teachers with training in linguistic analysis would be able to evaluate for themselves whether Kenneth and students like him have a language deficiency. There is plenty of linguistic information that can be collected about Kenneth if the teachers who work with him are willing to ask questions. For instance, an inquisitive teacher might want to ask Kenneth's parents whether he spoke with them and with his peers, whether they or Kenneth's playmates had trouble understanding Kenneth, whether he was ostracized from other children because of his speech, what he was capable of communicating when he spoke, and the like. Teachers themselves might want to observe young Kenneth in social settings (such as classroom or school playground) to see whether he talked with other students and whether he had trouble communicating. Such questions should provide sufficient information to determine whether Kenneth is linguistically deficient or just exhibiting some linguistic differences.

Kenneth's written passage addresses the emotional and psychological costs of the misdiagnosis to him as an individual. But there are other costs as well. By placing Kenneth in a speech class and segregating him from his standard American English-speaking peers, the school removed him from the natural and language-rich environment he needed to acquire standard American English. Unfortunately we will never know whether his acquisition of standard American English speech was actually delayed by the segregation imposed by the very speech lessons designed to help him. There is a social cost to misdiagnosis as well. The provision of special education services to students who do not need them drains the limited resources available to our cash-strapped public schools. This may result in the denial of these services to those students who desperately need them.

In our discussions with in-service and pre-service teachers, we have found other ways in which the lack of knowledge of linguistic analysis results in inaccurate conclusions. The inability to gather and process all the available information leads to errors in judgment. For example, we hear teachers claim that a student is "language delayed" or "linguistically deprived," meaning that their verbal abilities in the area of school language fall significantly behind the student's peers. But the same teachers might report that the student "talks up a storm" when given the right topic and the right environment. When the discrepancy between the diagnosis of "language deprived" vs. "talking up a storm" is pointed out, the talking-up-a-storm evidence is dismissed as insignificant either because the topic is not academic or because it is about something that the student has experience with. The talk-up-a-storm evidence is suppressed, while the attention is focused solely on the student's inability to speak on what teachers would consider to be relevant topics.

Apart from this, it is not infrequent that we see teachers equate the absence of evidence with evidence itself. Poor and working-class parents and parents from certain ethnic backgrounds such as Hispanic are often blamed for the deficiencies and poor academic performance of their children. The parents are said to be irresponsible, uncaring, too busy, too young, or morally incapable of being responsible for children (Delpit, 1995, p. 30). Teachers' evidence for these claims is that parents never call or contact the teachers to check up on their children's academic progress. So the absence of evidence that parents care is taken as evidence that they do not care.

The central point here is not that teachers are incompetent or should be blamed. Rather, our point is that while knowledge of linguistics is important and useful to classroom teachers, an understanding of linguistic findings alone is not sufficient. There is too much to know about linguistics even if we only consider those parts directly relevant to teachers. No teacher (no linguist, for that matter) can be expected to know everything there is to know about language. Precisely for these reasons, we must ask ourselves what is most relevant about linguistics that teachers should know to carry out their various responsibilities. The abilities to conduct basic linguistic analysis, to interpret linguistic (or nonlinguistic) data, and to distinguish the absence of data from evidence are some of the skills crucial to classroom teachers. These abilities are not inborn. The development of these abilities requires instruction about analysis, something that cannot be accomplished if linguistics instruction narrowly focus on imparting research findings to teachers.

Underlying the focus on knowledge transfer is an assumption that knowledge is equivalent to application. That is, that once teachers know something, they are necessarily able to apply this knowledge in their interactions with their students. (See Cochran-Smith and Lytle [1999] for an excellent discussion on the relation between knowledge and practice in education.) We believe that it is one thing to inform teachers that Jamaican English and African-American English are legitimate varieties of English with their own systems, while it is an entirely different matter to expect teachers to apply this knowledge when they are confronted by the tremendous pressures to teach their students to speak standard American English and pass high-stakes assessments all written in standard American English. The emphasis on linguistics in teacher education programs should be on applying linguistic knowledge to real situations that teachers confront in their schools. Critical thinking and problem solving cannot be divorced from the field in which students are expected to critically think or solve problems. In other words, critical thinking must be integrated with the real life situations that teachers are confronted with. Because of the linguistic nature of much of the evidence that teachers must evaluate to make decisions or recommendations about their students, the specifics of *linguistic* analysis should be learned. We believe that in order to develop this ability in teachers, linguistics education must involve the development of essential ingredients.

Essential Ingredients of Linguistics Instruction

    a. the ability to look at each child as an individual and not as a textbook example;

    b. the ability to collect linguistic and nonlinguistic information, and most importantly;

    c. the ability to analyze and interpret the collected linguistic information in an objective manner (that is, not suppressing some information or overemphasizing some data at the expense of other information).

With these skills, teachers can learn on their own or from their interactions with students what they need to know when the need arises.

CONCLUSION

The social and political changes in American society have drastically increased the availability of specialized services. The provision of these services has resulted in an increased demand on schools to determine who should be provided these services. The ability to determine who qualifies for such services and who does not often depends on analyses of language-based data. Unless teachers are trained to conduct basic analyses of language data, mistakes are inevitable.

To summarize, linguistics instruction for teachers cannot be reduced to memorization of linguistic facts, even if those facts are helpful to teachers. It must include training in conducting basic linguistic analysis such as data collection, pattern discovery, and data analysis. This training must link directly with the real life issues or problems that teachers face. That is, teachers must be shown how to apply their linguistic knowledge in school settings. They must be taught to look at each child and identify his or her needs and to refrain from trying to fit the child into what they know. Darla's story of an unusual speech pattern and Kenneth's story of being misdiagnosed as a child with a disability both highlight the peril of trying to fit every child into our existing knowledge frame and underscores the urgency for education in conducting basic linguistic analyses.

We conclude by drawing a brief comparison of linguistics in education with the emerging field of forensic linguistics. Language has always been linked to crimes, and in fact, in some crimes (perjury, offering bribes, or making threats), the crucial (sometimes the only) evidence is in the form of language. But it is not until very recently (perhaps since the 1980s) that linguists have been used as expert witnesses in legal proceedings. Even today, the use of a linguistic expert witness in a court case faces enormous resistance from judges and lawyers. According to Shuy (1993), the resistance stems from the widely held but mistaken belief that judges, lawyers, and the jury, because they themselves are speakers of a language, do not need assistance in interpreting language evidence, resulting in some cases in the mishandling of language evidence. (See Shuy [1993] and Lippi-Green [1997] for some discussion on this point.) The extensive research in areas such as phonetics and phonology, discourse analysis, and linguistic pragmatics has shown that human communication is extremely complex. What people mean and what they say are often different. For example, most people find it hard to imagine that a "yes" response to a question can be interpreted in any way other than confirmation. But "yes" can mean "no" given the right context, or it can simply be an acknowledgment that the listener has heard the speaker without necessarily confirming the information sought by the question. In order to correctly interpret what people mean on the basis of what they say, we must take into account many factors including the intonation, the discourse context, and the relationship between the speaker and hearer. With the growing use of expert witnesses in court cases, it is becoming increasingly clear that the skill, for instance, to consider factors such as intonation, discourse context, and speaker–hearer relationships in determining the communicative intention of a speaker is not a skill that everyone possesses just because he or she happens to be a native speaker. Because the American jury system uses average citizens as jurors, the jurors, in particular, need the expertise of linguists in interpreting language evidence. Today, some law schools have recognized the importance of linguistics training and have started to introduce courses in forensic linguistics.

The story of forensic linguistics offers a clear lesson to the teaching profession. Just because teachers are speakers of a language, it cannot be presumed that they possess the skill to analyze and interpret language-related data. Just as lawyers need awareness and training in linguistics, teachers need training in linguistic analysis so that they can make the right recommendations or decisions about the students they serve. The legal profession may be able to afford linguistics expert witnesses. But the frequency and extent of recommendations or decisions that today's teachers are called upon to make render it impractical and impossible to introduce linguistics experts into the school setting. Consequently, we have no choice but to rely on teachers and no choice but to offer them necessary training in linguistic analysis.

ACKNOWLEDGMENTS

The work reported here is based mostly on discussions with pre-service and in-service teachers in our classes, with ESL and bilingual teachers in a local K–6 elementary school and with Darla's parents. We would like to thank all of them for sharing their time and thoughts with us. Our work with this K–6 school is supported partially by a grant from Dwight D. Eisenhower Higher Education Professional Development Program to Pat Russo and Barbara Beyerbach through Project SMART, an Urban Education Initiative at SUNY Oswego. Our thanks also go to them for making our work with this local school possible. In the preparation of this article, we received comments and suggestions from Kristin Denham and Anne Lobeck (editors of this volume) and our education colleagues: Bonita Hampton, Mary Harrell, Sharon Kane, Faith Maina, Pamela Michel, Dennis Parsons, Pat Russo, Bobbi Schnorr, and Chris Walsh. We would like to thank all of them for their detailed and insightful comments and questions and for making us think about the relationships among language, linguistics, and schools. We are of course solely responsible for all of the errors that remain.

REFERENCES

Ann, J. (2002, February). *Your ESL students: Experts in your class.* Paper presented at meeting of the Education Club, SUNY Oswego.

Ann, J., & Peng, L. (2002). *Language inquiry leading to love of language.* Paper presented at the Passion for Learning and the Challenge of Teacher Education Session at the National Council of Teachers of English Conference, Atlanta, Georgia.

Anyon, J. (1997). *Ghetto schooling: A political economy of urban education reform.* New York: Teachers College Press.

Baugh, J. (1999). *Out of the mouths of slaves: African American language and educational malpractice.* Austin: University of Texas Press.

Cochran-Smith, M., & Lytle, S. L. (1999). Relationships of knowledge and practice: Teacher learning in communities. *Review of Research in Education, 24,* 249–305.

Crawford, J. (Ed.). (1992). *Language loyalties.* Chicago: University of Chicago Press.

Cummins, J. (2000). *Language, power and pedagogy: Bilingual children in the crossfire,* Buffalo, NY: Multilingual Matters.

Delandshere, G., & Arens, S. A. (2001). Representations of teaching and standards-based reform: Are we closing the debate about teacher education? *Teaching and Teacher Education, 17,* 547–566.

Delpit, L. (1995). *Other people's children: Cultural conflict in the classroom.* New York: The New Press.

Fasold, R. (1998a). *The sociolinguistics of language: Introduction to sociolinguistics.* Cambridge, MA: Blackwell.

Fasold, R. (1998b). *The sociolinguistics of society: Introduction to sociolinguistics.* Cambridge, MA: Blackwell.

Ford, A., Davern, L., & Schnorr, R. (2001). Learners with significant disabilities: Curricular relevance in an era of standards-based reform. *Remedial and Special Education, 22*(4), 214–222.

Hazen, K. (2001). *Teaching about dialects.* Washington DC: Center for Applied Linguistics.

Heath, S. B. (1983). *Ways with words: Language, life and work in communities and classrooms.* New York: Cambridge University Press.

hooks, b. (1994). *Teaching to transgress.* New York: Routledge.

Jordan, J. (1985). *On call: Political essays.* Boston, MA: South End Press.

Kachru, B. (1985). Standards, codification and sociolinguistic realism: The English language in the outer circle. In R. Quirk & H. G. Widdowson (Eds.), *English in the world: Teaching and learning the language and literatures* (pp. 11–33). Cambridge, England: Cambridge University Press.

Kachru, B. (1986). *The alchemy of English.* Oxford, England: Pergamon Press.

Klima, E. S., & Bellugi, U. (1979). *The signs of language.* Cambridge, MA: Harvard University Press.

Labov, W. (1970). The logic of nonstandard English. In J. Alatis (Ed.), *Linguistics and the teaching of standard English to speakers of other languages and dialects.* Georgetown University Round Table on Language and Linguistics 1969. Washington, DC: Georgetown University Press.

Labov, W. (1972). *Language in the inner city: Studies in the Black English vernacular.* Philadelphia: University of Pennsylvania Press.

Lippi-Green, R. (1997). *English with an accent: Language, ideology and discrimination in the United States.* New York: Routledge.

Lopez, M. E. (1999). *When discourses collide: An ethnography of migrant children at home and in school.* New York: Peter Lang.

McCrum, R., Cran, W., & MacNeil, R. (1995). *The story of English.* London: BBC Publications.

Messing, L. (1999). On the other hand. In R. Wheeler (Ed.), *The workings of language* (pp. 81–90). Westport, CT: Praeger.

Michie, G. (1999). *Holler if you hear me: The education of a teacher and his students.* New York: Teachers College Press.

O'Grady, W., Dobrovolsky, M., & Aronoff, M. (1997). *Contemporary linguistics.* Boston: Bedford/St. Martin's.

Rickford, J. R., & Rickford, R. J. (2000). *Spoken soul: The story of Black English.* New York: Wiley.

Rodriguez, R. (1982). *Hunger of memory: The education of Richard Rodriguez.* Boston: David R. Godine.

Shuy, R. W. (1993). *Language crimes: The use and abuse of language evidence in the courtroom.* Cambridge, MA: Blackwell.

Slavin, R. E., Karweit, N. L., & Wasik, B. A. (Eds.). (1994). *Preventing early school failure.* Boston: Allyn & Bacon.

Slavin, R. E., & Madden, N. A. (Eds.). (2001). *Success for all: Research and reform in elementary education.* Mahwah, NJ: Lawrence Erlbaum Associates.

Smitherman, G. (1973). White English in Blackface, or Who Do I BE? *The Black Scholar, 4*(8–9), May–June, p. 39.

Spring, J. (1997). *Political agendas for education: From the Christian coalition to the Green Party.* Mahwah, NJ: Lawrence Erlbaum Associates.

Stokoe, W., Casterline, D., & Croneberg, C. (1976). *A dictionary of American Sign Language on linguistic principles (new edition).* Silver Spring, MD: Linstock Press.

Tozer, S., Violas, P. C., & Senese, G. B. (1998). *Schools and society: Historical and contemporary perspectives.* Boston: McGraw-Hill.

Wardhaugh, R. (1998). *An introduction to sociolinguistics.* Cambridge, MA: Blackwell.

A Positive Sign: An Overview of the Benefits of Signing in the Classroom

Lynn S. Mancini

This chapter is very much a product of the times. Had this book been written a half century ago, no one would have thought to have included such a chapter in it. It was believed at the time that signing was at best a "broken" form of English on the hands, and at worst, mere hand-waving gestures. Signing therefore would not have been included in a book discussing linguistics. With the publication of Stokoe's (1960) groundbreaking book *Sign Language Structures*, linguists gradually began to recognize American Sign Language, or ASL, as a language in its own right. It has taken decades for this view of ASL to become widespread. Indeed, had the book you are holding been published as late as the 1990s, at least half of this chapter would have been devoted to providing evidence that ASL is a real language, and that it is distinct from English. The rest of the chapter would have been used in a justification of the use of ASL[1] with Deaf[2] students. However, the current climate is such that we can finally assume as background knowledge that ASL is indeed a language. The space thereby freed up can now be devoted to topics that are currently less widely known; specifically, how the use of sign in the classroom can benefit other populations of students.

---

[1] This chapter discusses education in the contexts of the United States, and so ASL will be the signed language under discussion; the contents of this chapter can easily be generalized to sign languages in other countries, as well.

[2] The word "deaf" with a lowercase "d" refers to an audiological condition. When "Deaf" begins with a capital "D," it refers to aspects of a culture; the most relevant aspect for this discussion being the use of a sign language such as ASL as the primary language of communication.

VARIETIES OF SIGN IN THE UNITED STATES

Before any discussion of the benefits of signing in the classroom is presented, it is important that the reader be aware of the sign varieties used in the United States. As mentioned earlier, ASL is a language completely distinct from English. It has its own phonology, morphology, and syntax. It also has dialects, age lects, and other variations, just as spoken languages do.

At one time, educators used the signs of ASL, along with several specially invented signs, in an attempt to make English visible on the hands, so that deaf students could better learn English. These Manually Coded English (MCE) systems included Seeing Essential English, Signing Exact English, and the Linguistics of Visual English. They attempted to capture the morphosyntax of English via signs. Each meaningful part of an English word (i.e., each morpheme) was given its own sign. If there was a readily available ASL sign to act as a counterpart to the English morpheme, it was used; otherwise, signs were invented to serve the purpose. For example, the English word *cats* would be signed using the ASL sign for "cat," and a sign made up to indicate the plural marker "s." (ASL does not use a single sign to indicate the concept of "plural"; however, it can indicate it in a variety of other ways.)

In between ASL and the MCEs is Pidgin Signed English (PSE). PSE is not one particular variety of sign; rather, it is a term used to describe signing that is neither ASL nor an MCE, but rather something in between. PSEs are most frequently used when hearing and Deaf individuals communicate with one another, and are generally used during simultaneous communication. Simultaneous communication is used when people try to sign everything they say when they say it. PSEs typically incorporate some of the morphosyntax of both ASL and English, and frequently leave out altogether many morphemes from the signing stream.

One should keep in mind the variety of signing that was used when evaluating research on the use of signing with students.

BENEFITS OF SIGN TO D/dEAF STUDENTS

Imagine you were given a choice of two possible learning environments. In which one do you think you would feel more comfortable, and in which one do you think you would learn more? In both situations, you are to learn an unfamiliar subject (the history of a particular foreign country, perhaps) by watching your teacher through a two-way video intercom. In both instances, there is no audio available. In the first scenario, everything the teacher says is captioned in English on the screen. In the second instance, there is no captioning, and the teacher is speaking in a language which you know minimally, if at all. Although neither learning situation is ideal, the former is clearly better than the latter. It should be obvious how this analogy, even faulty as it may be, applies to Deaf students. Now that ASL is recognized as a real language, the question of whether signing should be used in the classroom with Deaf students[3] is no longer relevant; the more appropriate question is which type of signing should be used.

The Rochester method involves fingerspelling everything that is said. In theory, students could learn not only English words and sentence structure, but also English spelling via this method. In practice, however, this method falls short of its promise. Fingerspelling for extended periods of time can be wearying on both the speller and the viewer. Fingerspelling demands that the arm remain relatively stationary with the hand approximately at shoulder level and the fingers and the hand making extensive fine motor movements. Because the movements are relatively small and fast, one must pay more attention to understand a fingerspelled communication than a regularly signed one. Furthermore, Bornstein (1979) has shown that fluent signers can only fingerspell approximately 40% as fast as they can speak. In a study by Reich and Bick (1977), 13 teachers conducting classes in the Rochester method legibly produced only 56% of the letters they were supposed to fingerspell; nearly one third of the letters were omitted entirely, and the remaining letters were indicated but not legible. Furthermore, nearly 15% of the English words were not fingerspelled at all. Caccamise, Hatfield, and Brewer (1978) review several other studies that support these findings. It is obvious that the Rochester method does not, in practice, provide Deaf students optimal communication.

Simultaneous communication using a variety of MCE also promised to provide Deaf students a visual representation of the morphology and syntax of the English language. Unfortunately, it has many of the same failings as the Rochester method. Grosjean (1979) found that speakers can utter 2.77 words (some of which might have multiple morphemes) in the time it takes a signer to make a single sign. Bellugi and Fischer (1972) similarly found that words can be produced approximately twice as fast as signs.

Despite the fact that individual signs in ASL take longer to articulate than do individual words in English, it takes approximately the same amount of time to express ideas, or propositions, in either one (Bellugi & Fischer, 1972). This seeming paradox can be explained by the fact that the basic forms of ASL signs can be modified to present multiple morphemes simultaneously. For example, a single sign with a single movement can be made to present the idea *He gave me a cup-shaped object*. The beginning and ending

---

[3]The mainstreaming of Deaf students is quite controversial. There is much debate about whether a classroom full of hearing students is truly the Least Restrictive Environment for Deaf pupils. Although the present author believes that such a class is not, in fact, the LRE for most Deaf students, she acknowledges that Deaf students are sometimes mainstreamed. The present discussion is intended to show how best to serve such students in a mainstream classroom; it is NOT intended as an endorsement for mainstreaming Deaf students.

locations of the sign indicate the giver and the recipient. The handshape is used to indicate the shape of the object being given.

Lieberman (1975) stated that if propositions are conveyed too slowly, the message becomes hard to process. Lieberman's research would suggest, therefore, that if people try to speak and sign an MCE at the same time, they might employ a strategy to avoid slowing down their communication too much. In fact, two such strategies have been documented: (a) Not signing everything that is said (e.g., Marmor & Petitto, 1979; Strong & Charlson, 1987), and (b) Employing the simultaneity of morphemes found in ASL, but not in MCEs (e.g., Kluwin, 1981; Crandall, 1974). Kluwin pointed out that Deaf signers and experienced hearing signers tend toward the latter strategy, and beginning hearing signers tend toward the former one. Marmor and Petitto's (1979) description of their research findings nicely summarizes what happens during simultaneous communication, "[S]igned utterances were predominantly ungrammatical with respect both to rules of English and to rules of ASL" (p. 99). Whatever the theoretical benefits of MCEs may be, they simply do not work in practice.

Moreover, Schick and Gale (1995) found that children not only attended more carefully to a storyteller when the story was related in ASL than when it was told via an MCE, but they also referred to the book more. Partly because of studies such as these, partly because of the poor results of the previous methods of educating Deaf children, and partly out of respect for the Deaf culture, classrooms for the Deaf are increasingly likely to use ASL rather than simultaneous communication as the primary form of classroom instruction. Written and/or spoken English is then taught as a second language.[4] Drasgow (1993) provided a more detailed description of the motivations for a bilingual/bicultural approach to Deaf education than there is room for here.[5]

BENEFITS OF SIGN TO HEARING SPECIAL NEEDS STUDENTS

Although the benefits of using sign with Deaf students are obvious, the benefits of signing with hearing special needs students might not be; nevertheless, a diverse population of special needs students do indeed benefit from

---

[4]It has long been known that inappropriate transfers from one's first language can result in errors made in one's second or foreign language. Researchers (Suri, 1991; Suri & McCoy, 1991) have shown that this phenomenon occurs between ASL and English as well. A knowledge of some of the basic syntax of ASL could help teachers understand the writing of native ASL signers.

[5]It is important to remember that different students may have different needs, based upon factors such as the etiology and severity of their hearing impairment, their current language abilities, their families' knowledge of and willingness to use sign, etc.

its use. For example, English and Prutting (1975) showed that hearing children who cannot produce intelligible speech (e.g., because they have tracheotomies) can learn to communicate using a natural signed language.

A more common use of signing is with nonspeaking or minimally speaking autistic or mentally retarded children.[6] Bonvillian, Nelson, and Rhyne (1981) reviewed 20 studies of more than 100 hitherto nonspeaking autistic children and found that most of the subjects learned to produce between 5 and 350 signs, and about 40% went on to make combinations of at least two signs. Although these numbers are small in comparison to the number of words that nonautistic hearing children learn to use, they represent significant progress in the children's ability to communicate. Carr (1979) suggested that not only will the ability to use some signs improve some children's ability to communicate, it may also be a factor in improvements in their behavior.

Carr, Pridal, and Dores (1984) studied autistic children who had had no functional use of speech, and found that those who were successful with verbal imitations could gain an understanding of six spoken words, but that many who could not imitate were unable to do so. Both the imitators and the nonimitators, however, could learn to comprehend six signs. Similarly, Kahn (1981) found that nonverbal hearing mentally retarded children who had sign language training outperformed those who had a similar amount of verbal training with respect to the number of signs or words they learned and to the number of subjects demonstrating the ability to produce sign or word combinations.

Why can children who cannot understand speech learn to understand and produce some signs, and why do some of these hitherto nonspeaking children proceed to utter some words after training in simultaneous communication? Several answers to these questions have been proposed by Bonvillian and Nelson (1978), Bonvillian et al. (1981), Bryen and Joyce (1986):

1. Teachers are able to mold their students' hands to make the signs, but they are unable to manipulate the students' mouths in a similar fashion to help them form words. This molding provides kinesthetic feedback which may be useful to the students. Furthermore, teachers can articulate signs slowly and "freeze" their own hands at the start or end of a sign for as long as

---

[6]Many, but by no means all, autistic children are mentally retarded. On the other hand, mental retardation may arise from other causes than autism. Unfortunately, some studies do not make this differentiation; some researchers have grouped together mentally-retarded and non-mentally-retarded autistic children in the same study; others have combined children with varying etiologies of mental retardation into a single study. For the purposes of the present chapter, such co-mingling of subject pools is not disastrous; but such a confusion might prove detrimental to individual students in the classroom with a teacher who is uninformed of these differences.

necessary for the students to perceive the shape and location of the signer's hands.

2. Many of the signs taught to the children can be perceived as iconic.[7] Konstantareas, Oxman, and Webster (1978) showed that autistic subjects who were taught sign via simultaneous communication learned iconic signs better than noniconic ones.

3. The visual modality is processed better than the aural one by many autistic individuals. Grandin (1995) noted that some autistic individuals have hypersensitive hearing; for others, the volume heard varies over time. Many autistic individuals find it impossible to tune out background noises or conversations and to focus in on a single voice.

4. The cross-modal redundancy of information present in simultaneous communication may help individuals with minor or no auditory processing problems comprehend what is said. Poizner, Bellugi, and Klima (1987) noted that both signed and spoken languages stimulate the same area of the brain. Bonvillian et al. (1981) pointed out that signs can be used to differentiate acoustically similar words.

Signing has also been shown to improve the literacy of trainable mentally retarded students (Sensenig, Mazeika, & Topf, 1989, and Daniels, 2001), and to help improve the behavior of emotionally disturbed individuals (Daniels, 2001).

How does the foregoing information help the educator in a typical classroom? First, some special needs students might well be mainstreamed into their classes, and the more they know about such students, the better they will be able to teach them. Next, some information gained on how best to teach special needs students can transfer to other students. For example, it is known that even non-special-needs individuals may learn best in different modalities, and may benefit from the presentation of information in a multimodal manner. Finally, the previous information serves as a good background for the next two sections of this chapter.

BENEFITS OF SIGN TO ENGLISH AS A SECOND LANGUAGE STUDENTS

As surprising as it may seem, students who are studying English as a Second Language (ESL) learn English better when they also learn ASL at the

---

[7]Native signers pay no more heed to the iconicity of signs than native speakers of English pay, for example, to the onomatopoeic nature of the first syllable of the word "popcorn" when they are discussing what they will bring to a party. This does not, however, negate the fact that nonnative learners of ASL often employ the iconicity of some signs to help them remember them.

same time. Hafer and Wilson (1986) reported on a 7-year-old Nigerian student who didn't know much English and was acting up in the classroom. When he was taught to sign, he not only learned sign, but he calmed down enough to be receptive to English tutoring. There seemed to be two reasons for this, both related to self-esteem: He was able to succeed in learning to sign, whereas he may have been feeling frustrated with his attempts to learn English; and he found that he knew something his classmates didn't. His teacher built upon this second benefit by having him teach his classmates to sign.

Daniels (2001) discussed a school's two third-grade classes which contained Hmong students learning English. The first class scored poorly on the standardized start-of-the-year pretest for English. The other scored much better on the pretest. The second class was taught English by traditional means, including one hour a day of specialized ESL training. The first class was taught ASL along with English. On the end-of-the-year posttest, the traditionally taught class made far fewer gains than the class taught with sign. The teacher of the first class believed that her students did so well because she was able to use sign to explain English words, and also because the ability to picture the ASL signs in their minds helps the students to retrieve their English counterparts.

Admittedly, the reports just mentioned are anecdotal in nature, and should not be taken as proof that learning ASL at the same time as English will help improve one's English abilities; nevertheless, they indicate that further research in this area is warranted.

BENEFITS OF SIGN TO HEARING STUDENTS WITHOUT SPECIAL NEEDS

Even teachers who never have Deaf, special needs, or ESL students can help their students by using signs in their classrooms. Hafer and Wilson (1986) and Daniels (2001) both suggested the use of signs for classroom management. The teacher needs to know only a handful of signs (no pun intended) to be able to do this. Some sample signs that could be used are TOILET, DRINK, PLEASE, YES, NO, SIT-DOWN, and LINE-UP. With these signs, a student can request to go to the bathroom, and the teacher can respond to the request, without interrupting the concentration of the other students. If the class needs to be told to sit down or to line up, the teacher can flick the lights on and off and then sign the instruction to the students. Students quickly learn that they need to look at the teacher to be able to understand what is going to happen next. This makes the use of sign in the classroom an effective classroom management technique.

Hafer and Wilson (1986), Daniels (2001), and Lawrence (2001) have all indicated that students who learn to fingerspell and to sign outperform their nonsigning peers in learning to read. Daniels (2001) reviewed a series of increasingly more strictly controlled experiments that she conducted which revealed that students learning to sign show larger increases in performance on English vocabulary tests than do peers who do not have training in sign.

Several hypotheses have been proposed for these findings; among them:

- Signing and fingerspelling provide kinesthetic and visual reinforcements, thereby permitting the benefits of multimodal learning. (Hafer & Wilson, 1986; Daniels, 2001)
- Learning individual fingerspelling letters and signs, and learning to combine them into larger wholes, gives the students the conceptual "hook" needed to understand that the spoken stream of English can be broken into words whose parts can be represented by written letters. (Daniels, 2001)
- Students inherently find signing fun and it motivates them to learn. (Hafer & Wilson, 1986; Daniels, 2001; Lawrence, 2001)
- Fingerspelling lets children practice spelling in a modality that is inherently easier and faster to produce than writing. (Daniels, 2001)
- The iconicity of some signs may make their English counterparts more meaningful to the students. (Hafer & Wilson, 1986; Daniels, 2001)
- Having two languages with which to store and retrieve concepts permits a dual pathway in the brain to access information. (Daniels, 2001)
- Learning a second language stimulates brain development. (Daniels, 2001)
- Both sides of the brain are stimulated with signing: The right hemisphere is used to process the visual input, and the left hemisphere is used for a linguistic processing of the signs. (Daniels, 2001)
- The ability to sign may increase the students' self-esteem, since they have learned something which their families and friends might not know. (Hafer & Wilson, 1986; Daniels, 2001; Lawrence, 2001)

CONCLUSION AND FURTHER READINGS

This chapter showed how the use of sign can provide a number of benefits to a wide variety of students; however, it was merely intended to serve as an introductory overview to the topic. Readers interested in learning more about the linguistics of sign are encouraged to read the excellent, if slightly outdated, book by Klima and Bellugi (1979). Valli and Lucas (2000) provided a much more recent, but somewhat more technical, overview of the linguistics of ASL. Hafer and Wilson (1986) and Daniels (2001) are good references for more information on using sign in a mainstream classroom. And of course readers are encouraged to take a course in sign language.

REFERENCES

Bellugi, U., & Fischer, S. (1972). A comparison of sign language and spoken language: Rate and grammatical mechanisms. *Cognition, 1*, 173–200.

Bonvillian, J., & Nelson, K. (1978). Development of sign language in language-handicapped individuals. In P. Siple (Ed.), *Understanding language through sign language research* (pp. 147–212). Orlando, FL: Academic Press.

Bonvillian, J., Nelson, K., & Rhyne, J. (1981). Sign language and autism. *Journal of Autism and Developmental Disorders, 11*(1), 125–137.

Bornstein, H. (1979). Systems of sign. In L. Bradford & W. Hardy (Eds.), *Hearing and hearing impairment.* New York: Grune & Stratton.

Bryen, D., & Joyce, D. (1986). Sign language and the severely handicapped. *The Journal of Special Education, 20*(2), 183–194.

Caccamise, F., Hatfield, N., & Brewer, L. (1978). Manual/simultaneous communication (M/SC) research: Results and implications. *American Annals of the Deaf, 123*(7), 803–823.

Carr, E. (1979). Teaching autistic children to use sign language: Some research issues. *Journal of Autism and Developmental Disorders, 9*(4), 345–359.

Carr, E., Pridal, C., & Dores, P. (1984). Speech versus sign comprehension in autistic children: Analysis and prediction. *Journal of Experimental Child Psychology, 37*, 587–597.

Crandall, K. (1974). *A study of the production of chers and related sign language aspects by deaf children between the ages of three and seven years.* Unpublished doctoral dissertation, Northwest University.

Daniels, M. (2001). *Dancing with words: Signing for hearing children's literacy.* Westport, CT: Bergin & Garvey.

Drasgow, E. (1993). Bilingual/bicultural Deaf education: An overview. *Sign Language Studies, 80*, 243–266.

English, S., & Prutting, C. (1975). Teaching American Sign Language to a normally hearing infant with tracheostenosis: A case study. *Clinical Pediatrics, 14*(12), 1141–1145.

Grandin, T. (1995). *Thinking in pictures and other reports from my life with autism.* New York: Doubleday.

Grosjean, F. (1979). A study of timing in a manual and a spoken language: American Sign Language and English. *Journal of Psycholinguistic Research, 8*, 379–405.

Hafer, J., & Wilson, R. (1986). *Signing for reading success.* Washington, DC: Kendall Green.

Kahn, J. (1981). A comparison of sign and verbal language training with nonverbal retarded children. *Journal of Speech and Hearing Research, 46*, 113–119.

Klima, E., & Bellugi, U. (1979). *The signs of language.* Cambridge, MA: Harvard University Press.

Kluwin, T. (1981). The grammaticality of manual representations of English in classroom settings. *American Annals of the Deaf, 126*(4), 417–421.

Konstantareas, M. M., Oxman, J., & Webster, C. D. (1978). Iconicity: Effects on the acquisition of sign language by autistic and other severely dysfunctional children. In P. Siple (Ed.), *Understanding language through sign language research* (pp. 213–237). New York: Academic Press.

Lawrence, C. (2001). *Using sign language in your classroom.* Paper presented at the Annual Convention and Expo of the Council for Exceptional Children. ERIC Document 459 557.

Lieberman, P. (1975). *On the origins of language: An introduction to the evolution of human speech.* New York: Macmillan.

Marmor, G., & Petitto, L. (1979). Simultaneous communication in the classroom: How well is English grammar represented? *Sign Language Studies, 23,* 99–136.

Poizner, H., Bellugi, U., & Klima, E. (1987). *What the hand reveals about the brain.* Cambridge, MA: MIT Press.

Reich, P., & Bick, M. (1977). How visible is Visible English? *Sign Language Studies, 14,* 59–72.

Schick, B., & Gale, E. (1995). Preschool deaf and hard of hearing students' interactions during ASL and English storytelling. *American Annals of the Deaf, 140*(4), 363–370.

Sensenig, L., Mazeika, E., & Topf, B. (1989). Sign language facilitation of reading with students classified as trainable mentally-handicapped. *Education and Training in Mental Retardation and Developmental Disorders, 24*(2), 121–125.

Stokoe, W. (1960). *Sign language structures.* Silver Springs, MD: Linstok Press.

Strong, M., & Charlson, E. (1987). Simultaneous communication: Are teachers attempting an impossible task? *American Annals of the Deaf, 132*(6), 376–382.

Suri, L. Z. (1991). *Language transfer: A foundation for correcting the written English of ASL signers* (Tech. Rep. 91-19). Department of Computer and Information Sciences, University of Delaware.

Suri, L. Z., & McCoy, K. (1991). *Language transfer in deaf writing: A correction methodology for an instructional system* (Tech. Rep. 91-20). Department of Computer and Information Sciences, University of Delaware.

Valli, C., & Lucas, C. (2000). *Linguistics of American Sign Language* (3rd ed.). Washington, DC: Gallaudet University Press.

8

A Critical Approach to Standard English

Anne Lobeck

When I ask my students what they think about grammar, their responses are typical. They tell me that grammar is boring and hard and they hated studying it. When I ask them about Standard English, they tell me, unequivocally, that knowing Standard English is necessary to get a good job and to be taken seriously. For them, Standard English is the oral and written language deemed to be "correct" by teachers, parents, grandparents, English majors, or "anyone with more education than you." They assume that the rules of Standard English can be found in grammar books and usage guides, and they describe "non-standard" or "bad" grammar with examples: *I seen it*, using *good* rather than *well*, using double negatives as in *I don't know nobody*, and failing to use apostrophes and commas in the right places. My students often simply admit that "they know bad grammar when they hear it," and sometimes, that it "makes them cringe."

My students' attitudes about Standard English are familiar: Standard English is defined in terms of social prestige connected with sounding educated, and is often described in terms of arbitrary rules of oral and written language that reflect an awareness of stigmatized versus non-stigmatized forms. Language authorities are defined in terms of their perceived expertise correlated with social prestige and power (which in turn often correlates with being perceived as educated). Writing and usage handbooks are viewed as authoritative repositories of the rules of Standard English, but perhaps most importantly, what is "standard," and for that matter "non-standard," is often identified based on one's perceptions: Something can just not *sound right*. These attitudes illustrate traditional ideas about grammar are alive and well in the public schools, despite the alternative approaches to understanding grammatical structure and usage that modern linguistics offers.

In this chapter, I discuss some of the weaknesses of teaching traditional grammar (the grammar of "Standard" English found in usage and writing handbooks commonly used in the public schools), in particular, evidence that teaching grammar from this perspective does little to raise awareness of the actual structure and use of language. I provide some insights into why this method of teaching grammar nevertheless remains so entrenched in the public schools and in the public consciousness.

I offer an alternative approach, in which teachers and students approach Standard English critically, using tools of descriptive linguistic analysis. In this approach, students and teachers investigate different aspects of Standard English by studying dialect differences, differences in register and "formal" versus "informal" English, differences between oral and written speech, and the sources of language "errors." Students also study the history and ideological foundations of Standard English and notions of language authority. This model of grammar teaching allows teachers to teach forms and usage that they see as important for student success, but at the same time it allows teachers to raise students' awareness not only of grammatical structure, but of the idealized nature of Standard English, and how our attitudes about it form the roots of language discrimination and stereotypes.

EVIDENCE FOR THE PERSISTENCE OF TRADITIONAL GRAMMAR

The foundations of the social perceptions of Standard English and "good" grammar have their origins in 16th and 17th century England, with the rise of prescriptive rules of oral and written English to which social prestige was attached. (See Milroy and Milroy, 1999 for in depth study of the origins of "Standard" English; see also Millward, 1996.) This traditional, prescriptive perspective is reflected in grammar handbooks and usage guides today, where what I refer to as "traditional" grammar is taken to include rules of both oral and written sentence structure, writing and style conventions such as punctuation and paragraphing, cohesion, organization, etc. Such handbooks also typically include various prescriptive grammatical rules, including rules on how to "correctly" use *who/whom* and *lie/lay*, etc. These handbooks generally support the idea that grammar is either "good" or "bad," and perhaps most importantly, that grammatical rules are uniform and consistent, promoting the idea that grammar questions have simple, accessible answers.

However, Battistella (1999) pointed out a number of ways in which traditional grammatical rules fail as a theory of sentence structure. For example, he observes that traditional definitions of *subject* (either as a *who* or a *what*, or as *doer of the action*) fail when applied to non-referential subjects such as *it* and *there* in sentences such as *It was snowing* and *There were three cows in the field*. In these sentences, *it* and *there* are merely placeholders in the subject position, and have no semantic content at all. Traditional approaches to parts of speech are also typically flawed; in many handbooks, quantifiers such as *each, all* and *every* are defined as "adjectives," as is, quite often, the definite article *the*. There are obvious distinctions between quantifiers, articles, and adjectives that are missed in this simple generalization, one of which is that adjectives can be modified by degree words such as *very/so/ too*, but quantifiers such as *all/each/every* cannot (*The very red barn* versus * *very all barns*), and only adjectives can occur in predicate position, after a linking verb (*The barn is red* versus *The barn is all*).

Perhaps a more immediate problem with traditional grammar, which Battistella observes is of direct relevance in the classroom, is that traditional grammar fails as a description of educated usage, in spite of the expectation that grammar and usage handbooks provide a list of invariable "dos" and "don'ts" of Standard written English. For example, the traditional rule "Never begin a sentence with a conjunction" is consistently violated in highbrow essays in the *The New Yorker*, and the prohibition against sentence fragments is routinely ignored in both academic writing and contemporary literature by highly respected writers.

Because of its limitations and oversimplifications, traditional grammar, which is intended to reflect the rules of Standard English, does little to support an interest in the real workings of language, and limits our exploration of it. Grammar becomes irrelevant, arbitrary, and no fun, particularly when teachers cannot provide satisfactory explanations to students' questions. Rather, traditional grammar requires one to accept (and typically, memorize) arbitrary distinctions and rules that do not correspond to our intuitions about linguistic structure. It is not surprising then that in many classrooms the approach to grammar is one of "correction," with the teacher as authority on what constitutes "good" and "bad" or "standard" or "nonstandard" English, and students' intuitions about language structure and use have little value. To further complicate this picture, students often relate to me that they become aware of the fact that what is considered "standard" or "correct" varies from teacher to teacher, and that what they are taught about grammar in school is inconsistent with what they find in their own reading. Traditional grammar teaching is therefore also at odds with the school emphasis on reading to learn to write.

Yet, the reliance on traditional grammar persists for a variety of reasons, which I briefly outline next.

WHY TRADITIONAL GRAMMAR PERSISTS

- Teachers are provided no alternative approach. Teacher preparation programs may lack courses in descriptive grammar,[1] and/or courses in the applications of linguistics to teaching Standard English. This is often because linguistics and descriptive grammar are viewed as academic and irrelevant to classroom practice.
- Well known studies suggest that teaching grammar is irrelevant anyway, even though ironically, these studies are based mostly on the efficacy of teaching traditional grammar (Braddock, Lloyd-Jones, & Schoer, 1963).
- Grammar is seen only as relevant to writing, without any connection to other subjects. The popular idea of teaching grammar only "in context" perpetuates a narrow view of the applications of grammatical knowledge to other areas of study in the K–12 curriculum, including literature, history, social studies, etc. (in ways addressed in this volume).
- Understanding descriptive grammar takes time and study. Traditional grammar is immediately accessible (in writing handbooks, for example).
- Many teachers share the public attitude that no expertise is required to teach grammar because they speak English and know "what sounds right."
- Public attitudes support traditional approaches. It is assumed that in the public schools teachers will teach "good grammar," for student success. Traditional grammar is accessible, available, and widely accepted. (For further discussion, see Battistella, 1999, and *What Teachers Need to Know About Language* [Wong Fillmore & Snow, 2000]).

All of this suggests that although we want our students to succeed, and thus to learn to speak and write in ways that do not invoke prejudice and

---

[1]Descriptive grammar includes rules of sentence structure (syntax), word structure (morphology), sound patterns (phonology) and word and sentence meaning (semantics) of a language. Descriptive grammar "describes" a speaker's unconscious knowledge of language—what a speaker must know in order to speak English or some other language, and descriptive grammatical analysis is therefore based on speaker intuitions about what is a possible utterance in the language. *Girl the dogs six bought* is therefore descriptively ungrammatical, while *The girl bought six dogs* is grammatical. Prescriptive grammatical rules, on the other hand, are those rules to which social values are attached. Typically, we learn these rules consciously—for example, the rule "never end a sentence with a preposition" is a prescriptive grammatical rule, deemed by some authority (in this case 18th century grammarians) to be "correct." Speakers of English routinely violate this prescription, producing sentences such as *Who did you talk to*, which ends in a preposition. This sentence is thus descriptively grammatical, but prescriptively unacceptable, and "incorrect."

discrimination, we also need to raise students' awareness of linguistic diversity so that they will in turn not discriminate against others. Traditional grammar and its reliance on correction and memorization does not allow us to do this, and in fact increases what I call *grammar anxiety* in both students and teachers, namely, the lack of confidence in ones' understanding and command of language and standard usage.

A CRITICAL APPROACH TO STANDARD ENGLISH

We can reduce the reliance on traditional grammar in the schools, however, by preparing teachers to approach Standard English critically in the classroom, using tools of linguistic analysis to investigate language structure and use. This approach allows teachers (and their students) to explore language in ways that move us from grammar anxiety to grammar confidence. I discuss each of these in turn from the perspective of teacher preparation— what aspects of linguistic knowledge can help teachers teach Standard English, but raise language awareness at the same time?

DESCRIPTIVE GRAMMAR

First and foremost, central to a critical approach to language is a foundation in the descriptive grammar of English. Teachers must have the linguistic tools to be able to analyze sentences based on linguistic intuitions, as it is such tools that will allow them to work with students to formulate adequate answers to questions about syntactic categories and structure. In terms of teaching Standard English, tools of descriptive grammatical analysis are particularly valuable because they allow us to compare and contrast (and thus *understand*) differences between descriptive and prescriptive grammatical rules (in ways I make clear shortly).

To take a simple example, teachers often teach the prescriptive rule *Never begin a sentence with because*. This rule is designed to help students avoid sentence fragments, such as *I got my coat. Because I wanted to leave.* This prohibition does little to enlighten students about the larger class of modifiers introduced by other subordinating conjunctions (*because* falls into a class of subordinating conjunctions including *when, since, while, although, even though*, etc.), nor does it help students understand the difference between a modifier (which alone is a fragment) and a clause (which alone is not). A foundation in descriptive grammar allows teachers to identify grammatical patterns and concepts, and to explain these patterns and concepts in a way consistent with students' intuitive knowledge of grammatical structure. This moves teachers away from the role of language authority to one of language investigator. Students are empowered as well by relying on what they *do* know about grammar intuitively, rather than emphasizing what they *don't* know, and must be *taught*.

DIALECT AWARENESS AND STANDARD ENGLISH

Second, it is crucial for teachers to understand why Standard English is not an actual dialect, if we are truly going to raise their awareness of what dialects are and what they are not. Definitions of *dialect* and of *Standard English*, from a widely used introductory linguistics textbook, are given next.

What Is a Dialect?

A dialect is any variety of a language spoken by a group of people that is characterized by systematic differences from other varieties of the same language in terms of structural or lexical features.
(*The Language Files*, 8th Edition, 2001, OSU Linguistics Department p. 301)

What Is Standard (American) English?

As with any standard dialect, SAE is not a well-defined variety but rather an idealization, which even now defies definition because agreement on what exactly constitutes this variety is lacking. SAE is not a singe, unitary, homogenous dialect but instead comprises a number of varieties.
(*The Language Files*, 8th Edition, 2001, OSU Linguistics Department p. 308)

Descriptively, a dialect is a language variety spoken by a community, which has systematic morphological, syntactic, phonological, and semantic rules that distinguish it from other varieties of the same language. Dialects are identified based on shared oral, rather than written patterns. Standard English, on the other hand, is an idealized collection of rules of oral and written language that we can think of as spoken and written by an idealized speech community to which we attach social prestige. The idealized nature of Standard English is reflected by evidence that what is considered "standard" varies from speech community to speech community. Standard English is therefore perhaps more appropriately defined as "language that one perceives as having the fewest number of prejudicial forms." Also, Standard English, particularly in school, is not restricted to oral language, but rather is considered the language appropriate for writing. It therefore also includes rules of written language, unlike naturally occurring dialects, which are defined solely in terms of their oral descriptive grammar.[2]

---

[2]This is not to say that there are not some "supra-regional" forms that are widely viewed as "standard," and, for that matter, as "non-standard." For example, most educated speakers avoid

To take an example of how knowledge of dialect can be applied to teaching Standard English, suppose that a teacher encounters a student who speaks a dialect in which past participles are often used as past tense verbs (producing utterances such as *I seen it, I done my homework, I run the race,* etc.) and the teacher wants the student to avoid such usage in their writing because it will prejudice readers. The typical approach to such stigmatized forms is simply to correct them, and often, to view them as "sloppy" English, and to consider speakers of such forms as less intelligent and as members of a less socially acceptable group. Descriptively, however, such constructions are completely rule governed and systematic for speakers of that dialect, and from a linguistic point of view just as "grammatical" and rule governed for speakers who use them as *I saw it, I did my homework,* and *I ran the race* are for speakers of another dialect. Asking students to use the less stigmatized *I saw it* instead thus involves not correction of "bad grammar," but rather showing students how to move to from one valid linguistic code to another one (see Wheeler, chap. 14, this volume, for in depth study of such dialect "codeswitching"). In such an approach, students become aware not only of dialect differences, but also how terms such as *standard* and *non-standard* English, and *good* and *bad* grammar are social labels that are not based on linguistic fact.[3]

LANGUAGE IDEOLOGY

Teachers can also benefit from exploring the sources of the social attitudes about Standard English. We can do this by studying the origins of language prescription in 16th and 17th century England. London dialect comes to be considered standard, largely because London was the locus of the printing

---

double negatives and using *ain't*, and most would recognize *I seen it* as non-standard. Though there is some agreement over these forms, it is still impossible to come to complete agreement over what does or does not comprise Standard English, just as it is impossible to come to complete agreement over who does or does not speak it. This is not to say, either, that we don't consider certain dialects "standard." We certainly do, but as Preston has shown in his studies of students in Michigan (Preston, 1997), what is considered a standard dialect varies from region to region, and oftentimes speakers designate their own speech as the norm (often to support group identity and prestige).

[3]It is impossible, in my view, to teach Standard English without somehow also teaching students that certain linguistic forms are more highly socially valued than others. Teaching students that their "home" language is as linguistically valid as their "school" language is a step in the right direction, but students nevertheless understand that one variety is more highly valued in certain situations than another variety. Were we able to eliminate social norms about language altogether, we would move toward a more egalitarian approach to linguistic difference, but this is unrealistic, given how entrenched these social norms about language are. What I propose here is to provide students and teachers with the tools to challenge and perhaps reshape those norms by critically analyzing them.

press, and the standard language of print media became London dialect. With the rise of sentiment for an English Academy to "purify" the language in the 17th century, Standard English comes to incorporate prescriptive rules of both oral and written language, including grammatical constructions unnatural to English based on Latin grammar. By examining early grammar and usage handbooks we observe firsthand not only the arbitrariness of these rules (using generic *he* is an example, as is a prohibition on double negatives and split infinitives) but also how what is considered *standard* varies from authority to authority (e.g., Joseph Priestley's *The Rudiments of English Grammar*, published in 1761, contrasts rather remarkably with Bishop Lowth's more prescriptive *A Short Introduction to English Grammar*, published in 1762). The foundations of this language ideology are still with us today. It is very useful to examine the ideological approach to grammar in modern usage handbooks, such as *English Grammar for Dummies* by Geraldine Woods (2001), and in "grammar rants" discussed, for example, by Dunn and Lindblom (chap. 16, this volume). Students can see how decisions about usage and *good* and *bad* grammar are often arbitrary and based on social (often moral) considerations. Students can examine their own grammar rants and the ideologies they reflect about notions of language authority, correctness, and discrimination.

REGISTER

Many of the rules and forms associated with Standard English are rooted in differences in *register*. For example, the Standard English prohibition on contractions in written language involves avoiding patterns of casual speech in one's writing, and using, instead of *gonna* or *wanna, going to* and *want to*, saying *yes* instead of *yeah*, and ellipses evident in such exchanges as *Staying here long? Nope. Leaving tomorrow.* An understanding of register provides teachers with an excellent opportunity to explore with students their intuitive command of register and their awareness of audience. Discussion of register can also lead to discussions of word choice and vocabulary, and a critical analysis of distinctions among slang, jargon, euphemism, synonyms, etc.

Crucially, an understanding of register allows us to tease out differences between "formal" and "informal" language. That is, often students are taught that *standard* is a synonym for "formal" language. This suggests, however, that language varieties that are considered *non-standard*, such as African-American Vernacular English, or AAVE, are simply "informal," and that what speakers of this dialect need to learn is a "formal" language variety to use in school. All dialects have different registers, however; speakers of AAVE use formal AAVE in certain situations, and informal AAVE in others. (For an excellent study of grammatical and stylistic aspects of AAVE see Mufwene, Rickford, Bailey, & Baugh, 1998, and references cited there.) Similarly, speakers of dialects that are considered *standard* use different registers as well. An understanding of register therefore allows us to recognize the linguistic choices available to speakers of any dialect, and to avoid perpetuating the stereotype that *standard* is "formal."

WRITTEN VERSUS ORAL LANGUAGE

Because Standard English includes rules of written English, understanding differences between oral and written language, and how to make the transition from one to the other, is central to a critical approach. Two central aspects of this topic that teachers and their students must understand are listed next.

- understanding that oral and written discourse follow different rules
- analyzing prejudicial writing errors and how these have different sources in dialect, register, mechanics, etc.

To take an obvious example of the transition from oral to written discourse, consider punctuation. In order to master rules of period and comma placement, for example, students must learn to make oral intonational pauses graphic, a transition that is not always easy for student writers, but which does not indicate a lack of mastery of English, nor does it indicate "sloppiness" or "carelessness." Rather, this transition requires making unconscious knowledge of grammatical structure (and the pauses that mark phrase and clause boundaries) conscious.

Noguchi (1991) observed that sentence fragments, to take another example, are completely appropriate in oral discourse where given information in a conversational exchange can be omitted, and only new information expressed, as illustrated in the following exchange.

Speaker A: What city do the Mariners play in?
Speaker B: Seattle.

In order to teach students to avoid fragments in written English, however, teachers can benefit from understanding the differences between oral and written discourse, and the role that given and new information play in the transition between the two. For example, an amended response to Speaker A is given below. Here, the response includes given as well as new information, and is, as a result, an independent clause, rather than a fragment.

Speaker B: The Mariners play in Seattle.

Teachers often approach sentence fragments as "incomplete thoughts," but observe that in oral speech, a sentence fragment is, for the speaker, certainly a logical response, and thus a complete thought. A more explanatory approach, Noguchi suggests, is to highlight distinctions between oral and written discourse, particularly how given information is crucial in writing, but not in speech. This approach to teaching about sentence fragments provides an opportunity to exploit students' intuitions about clause structure and boundaries, using tools of descriptive grammatical analysis. For example, instead of relying on the traditional notion of a clause as a "complete thought," (and its immediate confusion with fragments, which to students also constitute "complete thoughts") a more reliable, syntactic test for a clause is to embed it as the complement of a verb such as *say* or *think*, both of which require clausal complements. Notice that a sentence fragment cannot occur in this position, but that a clause can.

a.   *I think (that) *Seattle.*
b.   I think (that) *the Mariners play in Seattle.*

Finally, perhaps the most important reason for providing teachers with linguistic tools to approach Standard English critically is that these tools help them identify and understand the sources of prejudicial error (or, forms that occur in writing, and that are not only seen as errors, but as errors that actually prejudice a reader against the writer), and to in turn approach such error from an informed perspective.

In their studies of prejudicial error, both Hairston (1981) and Beason (2001) surveyed professionals in areas other than English teaching. Hairston's list of "status marking errors" includes a number of stigmatized dialect features. Her list of "very serious errors" includes examples of transitions from oral to written discourse such as fragments and run on sentences, punctuation and spelling errors, and also the mildly stigmatized dialect feature *set* versus *sit*. Purely stylistic errors are judged as moderately serious. (The following lists include only a selection of Hairston's examples.)

Status marking errors: (Hairston, 1981)

- Nonstandard verb form: *I brung it.*
- Lack of subject-verb agreement: We *was/were*
- Double negatives (*He don't know nothing.*)

- Objective pronoun as subject (*Him and Richard were the last ones hired.*)

Very serious errors

- Fragments
- Run on (or fused) sentences
- Non capitalization of proper nouns
- *Would of* instead of *would have*
- Lack of subject verb agreement (non-status marking)
- Insertion of comma between verb and its complement
- Non-parallelism
- Adverb forms (*He treats his men bad*)
- *Set* versus *sit*

Moderately serious

- Use of *whoever* instead of *whomever*
- Lack of commas to set off an appositive (*My dog Skip jumped the fence.*)
- Inappropriate use of quotation marks
- Comma splices

Hairston's study shows that the errors perceived as most serious are those associated with social status and viewed as nonstandard usage, a point also made in Beason's (2001) study of attitudes of business professionals toward writing error. Stylistic errors, on the other hand, are much less prejudicial, and less noticed. These studies seem to support the widely held belief that perceptions of social status reflected in writing can crucially affect one's credibility in the workplace.

Though it is unrealistic to think that with more knowledge of linguistics people will cease to negatively evaluate one another's language, nevertheless, a linguistically informed approach to such errors at least keeps us, in Beason's words from making "erroneous generalizations about students' linguistic aptitude based on dialect-based error, that in truth reflect valid grammatical systems . . . and that errors in formal writing do not necessarily reflect a person's overall personality, demeanor, or competence" (Beason, 2001, p. 60). A linguistically informed approach to teaching Standard English also allows teachers to explore and critique conceptions of prejudicial error with their students, to understand the linguistic patterns involved, and the social stigmas that might be attached to them.

CONCLUSION

In conclusion, we can't eliminate the normative approach to language, nor can we totally eliminate linguistic discrimination and stigmatization. We can, however, by integrating more and more linguistic analysis into the schools, and by offering alternatives to traditional grammar, shift language norms away from being purely socially based, to being informed by linguistic science. Teaching Standard English critically provides just this opportunity.

REFERENCES

Battistella, E. (1999). *The persistence of traditional grammar*. In R. Wheeler (Ed.), *The workings of language*. Westport, CT: Praeger.

Beason, L. (2001). Ethos and error: How business people react to errors. *College Composition and Communication, 53*, 33–63.

Braddock, R., Lloyd-Jones, R., & Schoer, L. (1963). *Research in written composition*. Urbana, IL: NCTE.

Hairston, M. (1981). Not all errors are created equal: Nonacademic readers in the professions respond to lapses in usage. *College English, 43*, 794–806.

Millward, C. L. (1996). *A biography of the English language*. Fort Worth, TX: Harcourt Brace.

Milroy, J., & Milroy, L. (1999). *Authority in language: Investigating standard English* (3rd ed.). London and New York: Routledge.

Mufwene, S., Rickford, J., Bailey, G., & Baugh, J. (Eds.). (1998). *African American English: Structure, history and use*. London and New York: Routledge.

Noguchi, R. (1991). *Grammar and the teaching of writing*. Urbana, IL: NCTE.

The Language Files. (2001). (8th Ed.). Ohio State University Linguistics Department. Columbus, OH: Ohio State University Press.

Preston, D. (1997). *A handbook of perceptual dialectology*. Beverly Hills, CA: Sage.

Wong-Fillmore, L., & Snow, C. E. (2000). *What teachers need to know about language*. Center for Applied Linguistics. Available online at: http://www.cal.org/ericcll/teachers/teachers.pdf

Woods, G. (2001). *English grammar for dummies*. New York: Wiley.

9

Bilingualism:
Myths and Realities

Patricia MacGregor-Mendoza

Of the more than 53 million school-aged children in the United States today, nearly one in five comes from a home where English is not the primary or sole language spoken (U.S. Bureau of Census, 2002). With the increase in immigration and the global ties the United States has with other nations, this linguistic trend is likely to increase in the future. Moreover, given the migration of speakers of languages other than English within the United States, it is conceivable that teachers in every school district, no matter how distant from popular immigration points, will serve students who come from homes where languages representing a family's ethnic heritage are spoken.

The notion of language and the schools is often hotly debated. Recall the controversy a few years ago regarding Ebonics or the ongoing arguments questioning the virtues of bilingual education. These deliberations stress the value placed on language, particularly Standard English, as not only a vehicle for providing education, but also as a measure of individual and curricular success toward that end. When students enter the school system with skills in a language other than English, they represent a challenge to the educational status quo and are often pushed to perform academic tasks without a full understanding by teachers of what the students' linguistic skills, needs, or potential are. Today's K–12 teachers, therefore, need to have a solid understanding of what being bilingual entails in order to recognize and promote the linguistic abilities of the potential bilingual students in their classes.

Defining bilingualism has challenged even the scholars who study language. Definitions have ranged from Bloomfield's (1933, p. 56) notion that a bilingual is someone who has "native-like control of two languages" to a recently compiled list of more than 35 terms (Wei, 2000, table 0.1). Although Bloomfield's definition is a popular representation of bilingualism, it is far from the reality for most bilingual individuals, who vary in their skills based on the time at which they acquired use of their two languages, the context in which they were learned, the level of proficiency in one language as compared to another, the opportunity they have had to use both languages, the stage of development of their two languages, as well as a host of other characteristics (see Bahtia & Ritchie, 1999; Grosjean, 1982).

Because so little is truly understood about bilingualism, several popular myths have developed. I examine each myth, present the realities, and offer suggestions to help K–12 teachers meet the needs of bilingual students.

Myth #1: Exposing a heritage language child to two languages will only confuse her; it's best that her parents only speak to her in English.

The diverse nature of bilingualism makes addressing the needs of bilinguals a daunting task in a school context. As such, many teachers assume that the easiest or most beneficial strategy is to adopt a uniform policy for all students and concentrate on developing the skills in the majority language (e.g., English in the United States). This "all or nothing" approach is sometimes even adopted by parents who are eager for their child to learn English and fear that their home language will hinder her progress. These fears are unwarranted. Most children who speak a non-English (i.e., heritage) language at home quickly develop conversational abilities in English within a few years although academic skills in English may lag behind (Collier, 1987; Cummins, 1979, 1981).

The assumption of a negative effect associated with bilingualism arose from faulty research over a century ago. Although throughout the 19th century and continuing up until the 1960s bilingualism was considered potentially damaging to an individual's intellectual acuity, those assertions have been successfully refuted by the meticulous research of linguists, psychologists, and educational scholars over the last four decades. To wit, there is *no* evidence that a child will be permanently hindered, either cognitively or academically, by their knowledge of two languages. Much to the contrary, studies have demonstrated that bilingual children possess a number of cognitive advantages over monolingual children. By virtue of their exposure to more than one language, bilinguals understand and exploit the arbitrary connection between the sound of a word and the object it identifies, as well as make the most of the flexibility and creativity of human language at an earlier stage than do their monolingual peers. As a result, bilinguals are graced with enhanced creative thinking abilities and superior communicative sensitivity as well as the acquisition of early cognitive skills at a faster pace than monolinguals (Baker & Prys Jones, 1998; Cummins, 2000).

Although the assumption of disadvantages to being bilingual can be soundly discounted, there is evidence, however, of the detrimental effects of a forced decline of the home language in favor of the school languages. When heritage language parents exclusively promote the development of English skills, either by their own desire or on the advice of school officials, they unwittingly foster a gap between their home and school environments; one that increases as the years go by (Wong-Fillmore, 1991). This breach in the ties of the family does more harm to the student's self-esteem and academic progress than could any purported language deficit.

Similarly, MacGregor-Mendoza (2000) noted the damaging long-term effects for students who were pushed to speak only English in school and who were physically, verbally, or emotionally punished for speaking Spanish. Her informants reported that the negative experiences they had as young children shaped their overall academic achievement, their self-esteem as adults, and their beliefs regarding the language they should speak to their own children. Moreover, several informants reported being trained to think they were "stupid" because their teachers viewed their Spanish speaking background as a hindrance to their education. (Also see Ann and Peng, chap. 6, this volume; Wassink, chap. 5, this volume.)

Reality #1: Although a heritage language background is not detrimental to a child's academic achievement, the negative perceptions of bilingualism can hinder her scholastically.

The most forceful challenge bilingual children routinely face is not related to the acquisition of linguistic or academic skills, but rather their teachers' underestimation of their academic potential. As a case in point, Bloom (1991) found that teachers less frequently recommended students whose home language was not English for participation in gifted programs, even though these students displayed no differences on independent academic measures from their native English speaking peers. In sum, because of a lack of understanding of bilingualism, many K–12 teachers lower their expectations of a bilingual child, or assign blame for whatever academic or social difficulty that arises in that child's school career on their non-English background.

What Teachers Can Do

Teachers can provide an environment that supports and promotes the development of both a bilingual's languages. This task means engaging both community members and school personnel in an effort to provide abundant, well-rounded linguistic and cultural experiences.

One key area in which teachers can help is to encourage the development of literacy skills in both languages among both students and parents. Tse (2001) found that heritage language students who are part of a peer group that reads will retain the use of and develop a broader range of abilities in their home language and carry those abilities through adulthood. Mulhern, Rodriguez-Brown, and Shanahan (1994) discovered that adult literacy aided in restoring ties across generations in families that speak a language other than English at home.

To build a bilingual's language and literacy skills in her heritage language K–12 teachers should encourage parents to use their home language freely and encourage their child to do the same. Teachers should also keep parents informed of upcoming themes of units and lessons so that parents can supplement schoolbooks and homework with materials and discussions in the home language. Teachers could also send home assignments that highlight the use of the home language. Another idea is to start a family journal in which family members establish an informal dialogue with teachers.

Myth #2: English is the key to success in school; other languages can be "picked up" at home if needed.

Although only a small staunch group of people would stubbornly oppose bilingualism, most individuals would agree that developing skills in more than one language is both laudable and beneficial. Nonetheless, there is often controversy as to what role U.S. schools should play in developing non-English language abilities. Given the overwhelming social pressure in the United States for heritage language children to develop English language skills, the acquisition of English is often favored over the expansion of heritage language abilities during school hours. Consequently, the process of acquiring skills in the children's heritage languages is frequently placed in the hands of parents. Although this arrangement may appear to be a reasonable compromise and division of linguistic duties, such an informal agreement risks failing to aid students in realizing both their full academic potential and linguistic competence.

Although English is the dominant language spoken in the United States, proficiency in English, on its own, does not guarantee academic success for bilingual students. MacGregor-Mendoza (1999) found that Spanish–English bilinguals who had dropped out of school demonstrated no differences in their English abilities when compared to bilingual high school students and college students. Even more noteworthy, the dropout informants reported feeling that their English skills were better developed than their Spanish skills. By contrast, the bilinguals who were attending college reported feeling nearly equally as confident in both their Spanish and English abilities. Thus, while the English abilities of all three groups of students were relatively equivalent, they differed in the development of their heritage language.

Hence, the more academically successful students, by virtue of their superior command of both languages, possessed the linguistic tools that aided them in effectively navigating both their home and school environments.

Acquiring advanced skills in language is not realized by accident; rather, these abilities are honed by repeated exposure to a wide range of people, media, contexts, and topics. Whereas most parents can provide their children with the necessary foundations to develop basic communicative skills in their home language, they often do not have access to additional resources (print materials, speakers) that would expose their children to a greater breadth of linguistic styles.

Reality #2: When bilingual students are encouraged to acquire skills in both of their languages they benefit culturally, linguistically, cognitively, and academically.

Making greater links between the home and school environment and increasing opportunities for bilinguals to exercise their skills in both languages will minimize the cultural and linguistic gaps warned of previously, as well as promote the acquisition of a broader range of vocabulary and communicative styles in both languages. From a scholastic standpoint, studies have demonstrated that more highly developed bilingual skills correspond to higher outcomes on verbal and nonverbal intelligence measures (Hakuta, 1986; Thomas, Collier, & Abbot, 1993). Thus, K–12 teachers should be actively involved in encouraging the development of a bilingual's heritage language as part of the school curriculum.

What Teachers Can Do

Finding ways to promote a bilingual's heritage language should not be viewed as "taking time away from the regular curriculum," rather should be incorporated as a meaningful part of each lesson. Teachers can supplement class materials by inviting a range of members from the heritage language community to the classroom to give presentations on various educational and cultural topics.

Teachers should also keep apprised of the resources for learning materials in the bilingual's heritage language. In addition to bookstores specializing in foreign language texts or internet sites, educational materials are sometimes available through foreign embassies and consulates.

Myth #3: Someone who is bilingual is aware of the languages she speaks and, at any given moment, can consciously choose to speak one language or the other.

Truth be told, even monolinguals switch among codes within their language. A teacher may refer to a student as "Billy," but on occasion he may be called "Mr. Foster" if she is displeased by his behavior in some way. Likewise, a judge might be addressed on a fishing trip as "you ornery s.o.b." by his buddies, but as "your honor" if they ever meet up in a courtroom. Thus, by shifting between these different styles of speaking, monolinguals can linguistically demonstrate a range of formality, sensibility to other speakers and listeners, as well as communicate approval, disdain, or an abundance of other intentions. Bilinguals, by virtue of their knowledge of more than one language, have at their disposal a variety of devices in both of their languages to signal a change in rapport, communicate a desire, signal solidarity or status, or accomplish a whole host of other linguistic functions.

Despite the wide range of communicative goals one can achieve by adjusting one's form of speech, code choice is not always conscious, particularly for bilinguals. Hamers and Blanc (1982) noted that for bilinguals,

> the code that is optimal at one point may cease to be so later as a result of changes in the situation, the topic, role relations, etc. One should add that speakers are not necessarily conscious of using these strategies. (p. 145)

Thus, while bilinguals (just as monolinguals), *may* consciously adjust their speech under particular circumstances, a bilingual's modifications in speech are not made any more consciously than are those of a monolingual speaker. To test the degree to which bilinguals were consciously aware of their use of either of their two languages, Brown, Sharma, and Kirsner (1984) presented Hindi-Urdu bilinguals with task focusing on the attention to written and oral forms. Although the two languages are similar in their spoken forms, their scripts are radically different and are read from opposite directions. Informants were asked to read aloud cards that contained objects written randomly in one script or the other. When later asked to identify the language in which each word had appeared, informants could only correctly name the language 42% of the time; an outcome less accurate than if they had simply guessed. Thus, even when bilinguals perform a simple task highly focused on the separation of their two languages, they do not necessarily place a high degree of attention on the language they are speaking. It follows then, that when bilinguals interact in daily conversations with persons who share their linguistic repertoire, they are going to be even less likely to be *consciously* aware of which language they are using at any given point in the conversation.

Reality #3: A bilingual's instinctive sensitivity to her conversational partner, the topic, cultural norms, as well as a host of other factors dictate a shift from one language to another more often than deliberate or conscious effort.

In the classroom, all students exercise various linguistic shifts, from chatting with peers, to answering a teacher's question, to reading aloud.

These shifts are often so routine; they become automated and go largely unnoticed. When a bilingual shifts from one language to another she may draw the attention of individuals who do not share her same linguistic repertoire. Teachers need to understand that when bilinguals shift between languages with each other, they often do so out of habit; not as a result of a conscious attempt to offend, exclude or breach the courtesy of others. Teachers, therefore, should recognize that code switching is a natural element of a bilingual's social interaction.

What Teachers Can Do

To gain a better insight on bilingualism, teachers can interview someone who has more than one language in their background. They might inquire about the context in which they learned their languages and to what degree their abilities in each language are developed now. Can they accomplish all activities in one language or another to a similar degree of success? Which language(s) do they have the opportunity to use now in their daily lives? Are there particular contexts in which they use one language or another? Do they feel more comfortable discussing formal topics like science and politics in one language or another? Do they feel more comfortable discussing family, religious, and cultural matters in one language or another? Do they feel more comfortable expressing emotions like anger or love in one language or another? Do they associate one language or another with a particular group of people? After the interview, the teacher should reflect on the interviewee's experiences in acquiring his or her languages and how those experiences have shaped his or her abilities today.

Myth #4: If someone who is bilingual switches between two languages, it shows that she doesn't know either one well.

Code switching is a linguistic feature that is virtually universal among bilingual communities (Romaine, 1989, p. 2). Although in some instances code switching can indicate a lack of vocabulary (either momentary or more permanent), this reason is neither the sole nor the most common motivation for a bilingual's alteration between her two languages. Much to the contrary, code switching from one language to another requires bilinguals to activate a host of largely unconscious knowledge they retain about their two languages. Thus, rather than suggest a linguistic debility, bilinguals who are able to switch between their languages fluently bring to bear highly specialized lexical, grammatical, and conversational knowledge about their two languages.

Regarding vocabulary, a bilingual's expanded lexical resources allow her to draw upon terms in one language that are not readily translatable in another, or which contain additional shades of meaning. Even when both languages have comparable terms, a bilingual may switch languages because the switched term comes to mind first or is less awkward.

From a syntactic standpoint, switches involve integrating two possibly very distinct grammars at points where they don't conflict. That is to say, when bilinguals do employ switches, they do so without breaking the grammatical rules of either language (see Clyne, 1987/2000; Pfaff, 1982; Poplack, 1982/2000 for details). The following example demonstrates this principle:

SI TU ERES PUERTORRIQUEÑO (if you're Puerto Rican), your father's a Puerto Rican, you should at least DE VEZ EN CUANDO (sometimes), you know, HABLAR ESPAÑOL (speak Spanish). (Poplack, 2000, p. 235)

In addition to having a command of the vocabulary and grammatical structures of their two languages, bilinguals employ switches to achieve various social and communicative functions. For example, each of a bilingual's languages may have particular social attributes. Consequently, the employment of one code or another or switching between them has a social implication. Thus, speaker's interjection of stock phrases in a more familiar code (e.g., Spanish "*Andale pues*" meaning "Ok, then" to signal you're beginning to take leave of someone) may assist in communicating friendship and solidarity. On the other hand, interspersing terms from a more prestigious language in some bilingual communities may signal educational level and an elevated social status.

Similarly, the emotional and cultural values associated with a bilingual's two languages may promote a shift. Because of the emotional attachment associated with a heritage language, a bilingual may chose to express personal feelings through her heritage tongue. Alternately, a bilingual may switch to her second language to distance herself psychologically and emotionally from a sensitive topic. Moreover, Bonvillain (1997, p. 325) noted that some words are more culturally charged in one's heritage language and that "in order to avoid [the cultural] expectations associated with native norms," a bilingual speaker may switch to her other language to signal a lesser degree of obligation.

When recounting stories or engaging in conversations, Bonvillain (1997, pp. 322–323), noted bilinguals can employ code switches to mark the boundaries of internal quotes (e.g., "*El me dijo* (he told me) 'Call the police.' ") as well as to qualify, explain or elaborate on a topic (e.g., "*Va chercher Marc* (go fetch Marc) and bribe him *avec un chocolat chaud* (with a hot chocolate) with cream on the top"). Moreover, she explains switches that consecutively repeat information may be used to provide an elaboration or clarification of a point being made (e.g., "*Baju-me jao beta, andar mat* (Go to the side son, not inside). Keep to the side"), or may provide added force to a command (e.g., "Go sit down, go. SIEN-TA-TE (SIT DOWN!)"). Lastly, because the languages in a bilingual's repertoire are frequently associated with particular groups of people and specific topics, a switch may also occur when addressing a new person or when changing topic of conversation.

Reality #4: Code switching does not promote linguistic decline; rather it is a linguistic tool whose use requires a command of a broad range of lexical, grammatical, and pragmatic skills.

Because of the complexity involved in code switching, it has been demonstrated that young children, whose linguistic skills are less developed, shy away from this practice more than older children, whose linguistic competence is greater (McClure, 1977). Bilinguals who are skilled in shifting between their two languages are better aware of grammatical gateways that allow switches to occur and moreover, are able to draw upon not only the lexical stores of both languages but also the subtle rhetorical cues that the use of a given word in one language or another might convey.

What Teachers Can Do

Because the skills involved in code switching are largely unconscious, yet signal linguistic progress, teachers can aid their students in developing an awareness of their growing language abilities. Teachers should encourage students to explore their own bilingual abilities by having them log their interactions with different people for 2 to 3 days. Their log should include who they were talking to, where they were, what they were talking about, and what their general mood was at the time. Afterward, students should examine their notes and try to see if they can identify any patterns in the ways in which they use their languages. Such a task will not only signal a teacher's validation of the bilingual's heritage language, but will help make the bilingual student more aware of his or her language skills and language use.

Myth #5: If someone can speak two languages, she can readily and accurately translate or interpret anything between the two.

Often, heritage language students or any available school personnel are pressed into service as interpreters for their parents for school registration or orientation sessions, conferences with school officials, or requested to provide a written translation of information regarding school events and policies communicated in school memos in the same caliber register in which the original message is being communicated. However, an established informal conversational ability in two languages does not presume a highly developed command of more formal or academic registers (Valdés & Geoffrion-Vinci, 1998).

Both translation and interpretation skills are highly complex and require that the bilingual not only have an extensive range of grammar and vocabulary knowledge at her avail, but also require her attention to discourse features such as intent, message, tone, and sometimes even the artistic qualities of language, such as the use of metaphors. Thus, since we've already acknowledged that the term *bilingualism* spans a wide range of abilities, we must also assume that competency in translation and interpretation is equally as variable.

Individuals that are recognized as good interpreters are highly competent in terms of their grammatical and pragmatic knowledge of both languages. Investigating the reliability of this practice, Valdés et al. (2000) placed student interpreters in situations that required them to mediate a conflict between a parent and a school administrator. The researchers found that the students often "softened the blow" of potentially insulting remarks and/or eliminated parenthetical information that was not relevant to resolving the conflict. In doing so, the interpreters demonstrated their awareness of discourse features by maintaining focus on the message as well as their pragmatic skills in retaining the lines of communication open. Moreover, the cultural knowledge the student interpreters possessed allowed them to effectively negotiate the different backgrounds and expectations of the individuals for whom they were interpreting. Effective interpreters and translators, therefore, possess a wide range of vocabulary and are sensitive to shifts in register and cognizant of differing cultural norms.

Reality #5: Translation and interpretation skills develop with practice.

Translation and interpretation skills involve understanding the intended meaning of the original message and being able to render that message in another code. The skill that a bilingual individual demonstrates as a translator and/or interpreter will be a direct reflection of the breadth of linguistic experiences in her two languages, her practice at performing these tasks in the past, as well as her intuitions about her two languages. If teachers require the assistance of a bilingual student to bridge a communication gap between the bilingual's home and the school, they need to actively promote the translation and interpretation skills they seek in their students.

What Teachers Can Do

To promote translation skills in bilingual students, teachers can design activities that focus a bilingual student's attention on shades of meaning, formal styles of expression, and poetic uses of language. For example, the notion of *walk* changes dramatically when realized as *strut, amble, saunter, sashay,* or *creep*. Similarly, we can recognize that the utterance, "please use caution upon exiting the building," is more formal and impersonal than "be careful as you leave," although both communicate the same type of warning. Likewise, the statement, "the sun singed even the clouds" is more fanciful than simply saying, "it was hot." By drawing the student's attention to the broad spectrum of linguistic expression and encouraging her to seek equivalent terms in both languages, teachers can expand not only the bilingual's vocabulary knowledge, but also his or her sensitivity to different linguistic registers.

REFERENCES

Bahtia, T. K., & Ritchie, W. C. (1999). The bilingual child: Some issues and perspectives. In W. C. Ritchie & T. K. Bhatia (Eds.), *Handbook of child language acquisition* (pp. 569–643). San Diego: Academic Press.

Baker, C., & Prys Jones, S. (1998). *Encyclopedia of bilingualism and bilingual education.* Clevedon, UK: Multilingual Matters.

Bloom, G. M. (1991). *The effects of speech style and skin color on bilingual teaching candidates' and bilingual teachers' attitudes towards Mexican American pupils: A dissertation.* Unpublished doctoral dissertation, Stanford University.

Bloomfield, L. (1933). *Language.* New York: Holt, Rinehart and Winston.

Bonvillain, N. (1997). *Language, culture and communication: The meaning of messages* (2nd ed.). Upper Saddle River, NJ: Prentice-Hall.

Brown, H. L., Sharma, N. K., & Kirsner, K. (1984). The role of script and phonology in lexical representation. *Quarterly Journal of Experimental Psychology, 36A*, 491–505.

Clyne, M. (2000). Constraints on code-switching: How universal are they? In L. Wei (Ed.), *The bilingualism reader* (pp. 257–280). London: Routledge. (Reprinted from *Linguistics* (1987), *25*, 739–764)

Collier, V. P. (1987). Age and rate of acquisition of second language for academic purposes. *TESOL Quarterly, 21*, 617–641.

Cummins, J. (1979). Cognitive/academic language proficiency, linguistic interdependence, the optimum age question and some other matters. *Working Papers on Bilingualism, 19*, 121–129.

Cummins, J. (1981). Age on arrival and immigrant second language learning in Canada. A reassessment. *Applied Linguistics, 2*, 132–149.

Cummins, J. (2000). *Language, power, and pedagogy. Bilingual children in the crossfire.* Clevedon, UK: Multilingual Matters.

Grosjean, F. (1982). *Life with two languages.* Cambridge, MA: Harvard University Press.

Hakuta, K. (1986). *Mirror of language.* New York: Basic Books.

Hamers, J. F., & Blanc, M. H. A. (1982). *Bilinguality and bilingualism.* Cambridge, England: Cambridge University Press.

MacGregor-Mendoza, P. (1999). *Spanish and academic achievement among Midwest Mexican youth: The myth of the barrier.* New York: Garland.

MacGregor-Mendoza, P. (2000). Aquí no se habla español: Stories of linguistic repression in Southwest schools. *Bilingual Research Journal, 24*(4), 333–345.

McClure, E. (1977). Aspects of code-switching in the discourse of Mexican-American children. In M. Saville-Troike (Ed.), *Linguistics and anthropology* (pp. 93–116). Georgetown University Round Table on Languages and Linguistics. Washington, DC: Georgetown University Press.

Mulhern, M., Rodriguez-Brown, F., & Shanahan, T. (1994). Family literacy programs lead to academic success. *Forum, 17*(4), Washington, DC: National Clearinghouse for Bilingual Education.

Pfaff, C. (1982). Constraints on language mixing: Intrasentential code-switching and borrowing in Spanish/English. In J. Amastae & L. Elías-Olivares (Eds.), *Spanish in the United States: Sociolinguistic aspects* (pp. 264–297). Cambridge, England: Cambridge University Press.

Poplack, S. (2000). Sometimes I'll start a sentence in Spanish y termino en español": Toward a typology of code-switching. In L. Wei (Ed.), *The bilingualism reader* (pp. 221–256). London: Routledge. (Reprinted from J. Amastae & L. Elías-Olivares (Eds.), (2000), *Spanish in the United States: Sociolinguistic aspects* (pp. 230–263). Cambridge, England: Cambridge University Press.

Romaine, S. (1989). *Bilingualism*. Oxford, England: Blackwell.

Thomas, W. P., Collier, V. P., & Abbott, M. (1993). Academic achievement through Japanese, Spanish, or French: The first two years of partial immersion. *Modern Language Journal, 77*, 170–180.

Tse, L. (2001). Resisting and reversing language shift: Heritage-language resilience among U.S. native biliterates. *Harvard Educational Review, 71*(4), 676–708.

U.S. Bureau of Census; P035. Age by language spoken at home by ability to speak English for the population 5 years and over—Universe: Population 5 years and over, Data Set: Census 2000 Supplementary Survey Summary Tables; (n.d.), accessed February 28, 2002, <http://factfinder.census.gov/servlet/DTTable?ds_name=D&geo_id=D&mt_name=ACS_C2SS_EST_G2000_P035&_lang=en>

Valdés, G., Chávez, C., Angelelli, C., Enright, K., González, M., García, D., & Wyman, L. (2000). Bilingualism from another perspective: The case of young interpreters from immigrant communities. In A. Roca (Ed.), *Research on Spanish in the United States: Linguistic issues and challenges* (pp. 42–81). Somerville, MA: Cascadilla Press.

Valdés, G., & Geoffrion-Vinci, M. (1998). Chicano Spanish: The problem of the "underdeveloped" code in bilingual repertoires, *Modern Language Journal, 82*, 472–501.

Wei, L. (Ed.). (2000). *The bilingualism reader*. London: Routledge.

Wong-Fillmore, L. (1991). When learning a second language means losing the first. *Early Childhood Research Quarterly, 6*(3), 323–347.

10

Spanish Maintenance and English Literacy: Mexican-Descent Children's Spanish and English Narratives

Robert Bayley
Sandra R. Schecter

In 2000, approximately one out of every six school-age children in the United States came from a home where a language other than English was spoken, up from one in seven children reported in the 1990 Census (Bayley, 2004). Not only did the number of language minority children increase during the past decade, but the 1990s witnessed the spread of language minority populations to areas of the country where they had not previously settled in great numbers. To give just one example, the Latino population of Siler City, North Carolina, a small town located in the middle of the state, increased from 3% to 40% during the 1990s (Moriello & Wolfram, 2003).

These changes in population structure present challenges to all teachers. The best available evidence indicates that a child who enters kindergarten without a knowledge of English will take from 5 to 7 years to become fully proficient in English, although most children acquire conversational proficiency much more rapidly (August & Hakuta, 1997). Children are seldom enrolled in bilingual education or English as a second language programs for more than 3 or 4 years. It is evident, then, that almost all teachers will work with English language learners (ELLs) during their careers.

In this chapter, we deal with one of the main issues facing teachers of ELLs—the relationship between minority language maintenance and children's developing proficiency in English. Specifically, we address the question of whether children who use a minority language at home—and thus develop oral proficiency and sometimes literacy in that language—do as well on English writing tasks as children who have become English-dominant.

Our inquiry is motivated by numerous comments we heard from parents during the course of our own research on language use in Mexican-background families (Schecter & Bayley, 2002). On a number of occasions, parents reported that their children's teachers had urged them to refrain from teaching their children to read in Spanish or to avoid speaking Spanish at home. For example, one California mother, a university-educated member of the middle class from Guadalajara, was strongly advised by her daughter's kindergarten teacher not to teach the child to read in Spanish so as not to "create a conflict" (Schecter & Bayley, 1997). Another mother, a monolingual Spanish speaker who lived on a ranch in south Texas, recounted how the teachers at her children's school blamed the difficulties her middle child was having on the fact that the family only spoke Spanish at home. The oldest child in the family, however, was an honor student. No one at the school attributed his academic success to the exclusive presence of Spanish in his home environment (Bayley, Schecter, & Torres-Ayala, 1996). The teachers in both examples were well-intentioned. Here, however, we are concerned not with intentions, but with the accuracy of the information that motivated the teachers' advice to parents of these language minority children. Does teaching a child to read in Spanish cause the child problems later in school? Does maintaining Spanish (or another minority language) as the language of the home negatively impact on a child's academic progress? (see MacGregor-Mendoza, chap. 9, this volume).

We address these questions on the basis of a larger study of language use in Mexican-background families in south Texas and northern California (Bayley, Alvarez-Calderón, & Schecter, 1998; Bayley et al., 1996; Schecter & Bayley, 1997, 1998, 2002, 2004). Specifically, we focus on narrative production across the Spanish–English bilingual continuum. Although the participants in our study represent only a single nationality and single language-background, the 40 families with whom we worked (20 in Texas and 20 in California) represent a broad social and geographical spectrum. Parents traced their origins to many different areas in Mexico and came from widely differing socioeconomic backgrounds, ranging from economically marginalized single parents to upper middle-class professionals (see Schecter & Bayley, 2002 for a full description of family characteristics). On the basis of narratives from children in Grades 4, 5, and 6, we examine writing across the bilingual continuum in order to understand children's developing literacy in both English and Spanish, including the relationship between Spanish maintenance and English writing.[1] Although school success requires command of many genres in addition to narratives, we chose to focus on narratives because narratives are the

---

[1]We selected children in grades 4–6 because the focus of the larger study was on home language use and its effect on minority language maintenance. By the time language minority children reach fourth or fifth grade, they are usually transitioned out of bilingual education. Hence, the role of the home in supporting minority language maintenance becomes even more important.

earliest written form that children are expected to master at school. Moreover, narratives are a primary means by which human beings make sense of their experience (Hymes, 1982).

For the purposes of investigating children's developing literacy, we describe two different measures of writing proficiency and examine the relationships between them. First, at the *discourse* level, we look at children's command of narrative structure as evidenced in both their Spanish and English written production. Second, we look at an array of features associated with the children's writing in both languages, features that practicing bilingual teachers have found important. The use of the "Teachers' Assessment Rubric," developed in cooperation with practicing bilingual teachers, enables us to view in more detail the dimensions of children's literacy development that are of concern to educators. Finally, recognizing that language proficiency is a multidimensional construct (Bachman, 1990; Valdés & Figueroa, 1994), we examine the ways in which children's performances with regard to these different assessments relate to one another and we explore the implications of these relationships for children's language and literacy development. In particular, we examine the relationship between Spanish writing ability and children's development of English writing skills.

Our focus is on the written narratives obtained from children by means of the following essay prompts:

English: Could you tell us about something that happened *in school* that you will always remember? An event or an incident that happened in school that you will never forget. It could be something really exciting, or happy, or scary. Remember . . . something that happened in school.

Spanish: *¿Puedes escribir sobre un evento muy memorable que tu tuviste "afuera" de la escuela? Algo que nunca se te olvidará: Puede ser algo muy emocionante, o felíz, o miedoso. Recuerda . . . algo que pasó afuera de la escuela.* (Can you write about a very memorable event that happened *outside of school*? Something that you will never forget. It can be something exciting, or happy, or scary. Remember . . . something that happened outside of school.)

The elicitation resulted in 71 compositions, 41 in English (in one family two brothers participated) and 30 in Spanish. Essays ranged from fully developed and elaborated narratives in English and Spanish to minimal lists of the few words that a child was able to recall in Spanish.

NARRATIVE STRUCTURE ANALYSIS

Our analysis of narrative structure is based on the framework developed by Labov (Labov, 1972; Labov & Waletsky, 1967). Although a number of more fine-grained analytic schemes have been proposed in the years since Labov and Waletsky's seminal essay (see, e.g., Gee, 1986; McCabe & Peterson, 1991; Peterson & McCabe, 1983), Labov's general scheme proved best suited to our purpose. Within this scheme, a minimal narrative is defined as two temporally ordered clauses in the past tense (Labov, 1972, p. 360). The main sections into which narratives may be divided are: an Abstract (one or two clauses that summarize the story), an Orientation (setting the stage for the narrative, providing background information), at least one Complicating Action (what happens that makes it a narrative), a Resolution (how the issue, question, or problem got resolved or what the outcome was), an Evaluation (the narrator's reflections on the meaning of the event, providing the purpose of the story), and a Coda (a final clause or series of clauses closing off the series of complicating actions and often bridging the gap between the time of the story and the present). In addition, the flow of the narrative may be interrupted on one or more occasions by a Suspension—additional information about participants in the action, for example, that is not part of the story line.

Using this general framework, the research team devised a scale to measure the degree to which children's written narratives made use of the sections outlined by Labov.[2] Because the ordering of sections, as well as the amount of emphasis given to each, may well be affected by cultural differences (McCabe, 1995), essays were rated only on whether they used the elements outlined earlier, not whether the elements were used in a particular order or in the amount of emphasis given to each.[3] The Narrative Assessment Scale is shown in Table 10.1.

Although the majority of scores clustered about 3 or 4, the narratives illustrated the full range of scores. The following English example, one of the most elaborate narratives in our data, received a top rating of 6. (In the interests of space, the line divisions used in the coding have not been retained here. The spelling has not been normalized.)

Abstract: Boy, I will never forget the time someone at school when we were playing on the structor at lunch time and one of my

---

[2]The Narrative Assessment Scale was developed by Ann Robinson in cooperation with Adriana Boogerman.

[3]Prior to rating, essays were entered into a computer in order to minimize distractions arising from extraneous matters such as handwriting. The original orthography and punctuation, however, were maintained. The essays were then divided into clauses. Line divisions were made at every discourse marker (e.g., *and, then, because, so, also, but, while, suddenly, boy!, well, you know, y, y luego, entonces*) and at every sentence ending whether or not it had a period. The narratives were then divided into sections and rated by two project assistants. Ratings were reviewed by Bayley. In the very rare cases where ratings diverged by more than a point, the two closest scores were used.

TABLE 10.1
Narrative Assessment Scale

Organization

a. abstract = summary
b. orientation = who, when, what, where (often characterized by past progressive clauses; often placed at strategic points, not just at the beginning)
c. complicating action (= then what happened)
d. suspension (= additional information, not part of the story line)
e. evaluation (= the point of the narrative; why it is told; answers question "so what?")
f. result/resolution (= what finally happened)
g. coda (= signal that the narrative is finished)

Rating Scale

6 has 6 of the above; must have action; action is detailed and clear; must have evaluation or resolution
5 has 5 of the above; must have action; action is somewhat detailed and clear; some evaluation or resolution
4 has 4 of the above; must have action; action has minimal detail and clarity; minimal evaluation or resolution
3 has 3 of the above; must have action; action borders on minimal
2 has 2 of the above; must have minimal action
1 no action = not a narrative

	friends fell off and an ambulanc came to the school to take him to the hospital.
Orientation:	It was about a month ago when this happened. Joel, Jetta, James, Vincent and me were standing on a concreat tube while the other kids tride to pull us down. We played this fore a long time. But we grew tired and stopped playing that game and left, except for James and the kids at the bottom of the tube. We went to the upstares part of the yard And played tag there.
Action:	Suddenly kids started running down to the lower yard. We followed them. At the bottom we saw a crowd of people around some police who were knelt down over someone. When we got down there, we saw James on his back crying.
Suspension:	Someone had pulled him off and he wasn't expecting it when he fell.
Action:	Then they took him away.
Evaluation:	I felt real bad because I could have saved him from herling him self. And if I had stayed there, it could have bin me moneing and growning on my way to the hospital.
Resolution:	Later on that day, people said Mardin, another 6th grader who was down on the lower year playing the game with James, was

responsibal for James, and they wouldn't beleav him that he
didn't. Then I felt sorry for Mardin because he was crying.

Evaluation: That was a realy skary experience. My stomach felt sick. I hope
never to have a expereance like that again.

Fin: P.S. James was fine.

The following narrative, also in English, represents a more typical example. It was rated a 3 on the narrative assessment scale:

Orientation: Wen I met my frinds at shool one is leslei she was the first And
esmeralda was the second Mary is the thir and Katy the forth I
didn't feel loenly anymoer in that shool it hapend in 1992 and
1993.

Action: they shode my arunde the shool and we wen't to the same
clasrom and we yousto play novels Katy alwas yous to be Plar
and I ider was Fernanda or Maria Mersedes Sometimes leslei
was Fernanda we played that we wantes to be atris and we new
how to sing good but they said we waer to yung and we yousto
say Pastas de sanaoria y Care de bruja to the Lady.

Evaluation: I mis leslei she was the won that alwas made me lafe and I remember me and my friends yousto bring maykup to shool and
we yous to get in trubel. Katy was the last so I hade to show her
arunde.

Finally, we show a mid-range narrative in Spanish. The following account
of a visit to Mexico to attend a cousin's wedding was rated a 3.

Orientation: *a mi me justo cuando fui a la boda de mi primo se caso en Culiacan
Sinaloa toda mi familia de mexico y todas nosotras estavamos vien
feliz.*

Action: *I me diverti vien mucho porque fuimos muchas a la misa I era muy
vonita porque no mas vi a toda my familia. Y me sentí muy feliz I
me dio muchas ganas de yorar y todas fuimos a la fiesta estabamas
vailando y comienda todas feliz y mi familia ayudando a todas y
uvo muchas personas vailanda me divertí porque mi ermana se
dio al casada un viveron de vino en su boca.*

Evaluation: *Y era en navidad y conosi a muchas de mis primas trana (=?) mas
omtes (=?) I me divertimos mucho.*

Orientation: I liked it when I went to my cousin's wedding. He got married in
Sinaloa. My whole family went.

Action: And I enjoyed myself a lot because went to the Mass a lot And it
was very beautiful because I had never seen my whole family.
And I felt very happy And I really felt like crying and we all went
to the party and were were all happily dancing and eating and

	my family was helping everyone and there were a lot of people dancing.
Evaluation:	It amused me because my sister gave the bride (?) a bottle of wine in her mouth And it was Christmas and I met many of my cousins ??? And we had a lot of fun.)

THE TEACHERS' ASSESSMENT RUBRIC

Beyond our interest in children's development of narrative structure, we wished to know how teachers would react to the types of essays our participants produced. We therefore brought together four experienced bilingual teachers to develop the "Teachers' Assessment Rubric."[4] The teachers were recorded while they examined and rated a number of sample essays. They were asked to describe as fully as possible their reasons for rating the essays as they did. Subsequently, their discussion was summarized and the Teachers' Assessment Rubric was developed. The instrument went through a number of revisions as a result of the teachers' responses to the various iterations. In its final version, it consists of 10 separate categories ranging from organization and narrative content to breadth of vocabulary to handwriting and spelling. The full list of categories is as follows:

ORGANIZATION

Cohesion: has a "beginning, middle, end"

Maintains topic: "revisits" opening point/s at end of narrative

Paragraphing: sense of transition between subsections

Sentence transitions: appropriate and varied use of adverbs to mark next point (e.g., entonces, despues)

DESCRIPTION

Clarity: all points are clearly stated

Elaboration: develops point further, provides evidence, substantiates, provides details

Use of detail: "paints the evidence"

NARRATIVE CONTENT

Setting: specifies setting

Character development: includes descriptive information that will help reader understand the characters' motives

---

[4]The Teachers' Assessment Rubric was developed by Sandra Schecter in cooperation with Lucinda Pease-Alvarez of the University of California, Santa Cruz.

Plot: includes evidence of plot development (e.g., movement toward statement of problem and its resolution)

Message: includes moral or stance on issue

CHOICE OF LANGUAGE

Rich and varied vocabulary; "*vocabulario amplio*"

Non-redundance: does not over-rely on same words

Verb tenses: uses different verb tenses to develop narrative and to make sequence clear

PRESENTATION

Handwriting: includes legibility

Appearance on paper: (e.g., use of indentation, location of writing on page)

SPELLING

Spelling

Appropriate word segmentation (e.g., "no sé" vs. "nose")

MECHANICS

Punctuation

Appropriate use of accents for Spanish

Capitalization

SYNTAX

Complete sentences

Appropriate sentence segmentation (e.g., "no run-on sentences")

CREATIVITY

Sense of author: (e.g., personality, maturity)

Original content: (e.g., interesting "twists")

EMOTION/TONE

Creates a feeling or mood (e.g., sorrow, suspense, humor)

These categories were rated on a five-point scale that took into account the age of the writer: 1, not at all developed (for this age group); 2, somewhat developed; 3, average; 4, well developed; 5, very well developed. In accordance with the preferences expressed by the teachers with whom the Teachers' Assessment Rubric was developed, all categories were weighted equally.

The essays were read and assessed by two practicing bilingual teachers, one of whom had been involved in developing the rating instrument. In cases where ratings on any category diverged by more than a point, the essays were read by a third teacher and the two closest (usually identical) scores were used.

COMPARING DIFFERENT ASSESSMENT MEASURES AND PERFORMANCE IN TWO LANGUAGES

Performance on the Narrative Assessment Scale

Here we compare Spanish and English results on the narrative assessment scale for children who were able to produce at least a minimal essay in Spanish. We then examine the English narratives separately, including narratives from children who were not able to write in Spanish.

Overall, there was very little difference in the narrative structure ratings for the English and Spanish essays, although, as we might expect given the wide range of language proficiency represented in the Spanish essays, the scores on these essays varied greatly. The mean on the English essays was 3.65 out of a possible 6 points. On the Spanish essays, the mean was 3.40. Moreover, although the correlation between performance in English and Spanish as measured by the Narrative Assessment Scale was statistically significant, the correlation was not particularly strong ($r = .3111$, $p < .05$).[5] Finally, when the English essays written by participants who were unable to produce a Spanish essay were included along with the essays by children who produced essays in both languages, the mean changed only slightly, decreasing from 3.65 to 3.51. While the ability to write in two languages may not convey an advantage in English writing, this result suggests that maintaining Spanish did not interfere with participants' development of English literacy.

We turn now to the results from the Teachers' Assessment Rubric to see how well they agree with the results for narrative development.

Performance on the Teachers' Assessment Rubric

The results for the ratings with the Teachers' Assessment Rubric are highly correlated with the results of narrative structure analysis. Thus, the correlation between the English essay ratings according to the Teachers' Assessment Rubric and the Narrative Assessment Scale was .7685 ($p < .001$). The correlation between the ratings of the Spanish essays on the two measures

---

[5]A correlation coefficient (r) may range from 0, indicating that the two elements examined are not associated, to 1.00, indicating that the two elements examined are always associated. The significance of the association is indicated by the p value given in parentheses. Normally, a value of .05, meaning that the outcome reported could have come about by chance only one out of 20 times, is required in educational research.

was even higher, .8352 ($p < .001$). Like the Narrative Assessment Scale, the Teachers' Assessment Rubric shows a correlation between children's performance in the English and Spanish essays that, while significant at the .05 level, is comparatively weak, at only .3347. However, while the means for the Spanish and English essays did not differ significantly on the Narrative Assessment Scale, the mean rating for the Spanish essays according to the Teachers' Assessment Rubric was significantly lower than the mean rating for the English essays ($p < .005$). On the latter measure, the mean score for the Spanish essays was 1.97, or "somewhat developed for this age group." (Recall that 3 is defined as "average for this age group.") The mean rating of the English essays was 2.67, or only slightly below average for their age group. Finally, as with the ratings on the Narrative Assessment Scale, the inclusion of essays by English-dominant participants who were unable or unwilling to produce a Spanish essay had only a negligible effect on the mean rating for English essays according to the Teachers' Assessment Rubric. (See Appendices A and B for the details of the statistical analysis.)

The results summarized earlier lead to several conclusions. First, the magnitude of the correlations between our two measures for the English and Spanish essays respectively suggests that when rating the essays, teachers using the Teachers' Assessment Rubric attended more closely to questions of structure and organization than they did to details of punctuation and spelling. In fact, the instrument is structured to promote just such an outcome. Although each main heading was worth an equal number of points in determining the overall score, only three of the ten main categories deal with prescriptive grammar, mechanics, and presentation, areas that the Narrative Assessment Scale does not cover. Seven categories in the Teachers' Assessment Rubric are concerned with higher level questions of organization, description, and so forth. Second, participants who have acquired sufficient Spanish literacy to at least attempt to produce a Spanish essay did as well (or slightly better) on the English essays as children who lacked sufficient written Spanish to attempt an essay. On this measure, then, we can make the argument that the participants who have acquired at least some writing ability in Spanish have indeed outpaced their peers because, in addition to doing as well in English writing, they have acquired a second writing system (cf. Krashen, 1999; Krashen & Biber, 1988).

THE STORY THE STORIES TELL

Let us now review what we have learned from the stories the children produced. First, we found correlations, albeit not strong ones, between the measures of written production for Spanish and English. We have reason to believe that writing ability in fact does transfer across languages, although there are others who have made a more forceful case for this position than we have been able to provide (see, e.g., Cummins, 1985, 2001).

Second, we found a strong correlation between the results on the different writing assessment measures, suggesting that good linguists and good teachers are not only developmentally and cross-culturally sensitive, but also in agreement about the attributes that constitute good writing. The four teachers who participated in developing and applying the Teachers' Assessment Rubric organized their assessments to privilege content, overall structure, and coherence over more surface and mechanical features such as handwriting and punctuation.

Third, the difference in the results between the English and Spanish essays on the Teachers' Assessment Rubric (the Spanish writing was rated lower) may be attributed to patterns of language use in schools and to policies that encourage children to shift to all-English classes at the earliest opportunity. Considering that many of our participants had received no formal Spanish literacy instruction at school and that even those who did receive such instruction were usually transitioned to English by third grade, it is not surprising to see that the ratings for the Spanish essays on the Teachers' Assessment Rubric were lower than they were for the English essays, written in the language in which most of our participants had received the greater part of their formal literacy instruction. Further, many of the children were from homes where the parents had never had the opportunity to acquire literacy in Spanish. These children exhibited varying degrees of oral proficiency in Spanish. Some could decode Spanish texts. However, few were able to engage in operations that require readers to extract core meaning from text or engage critically with text.

Finally, children who felt sufficiently confident to write in Spanish did as well on their English essays as children who could not or would not write in Spanish. Results such as this should, we argue, allay the concerns of teachers—and of some immigrant parents as well—that maintaining a language other than English at home will result in problems for the child in English-medium schools. On the basis of results such as those we have presented here, we would argue otherwise. Bilingual children who do *as well* as their monolingual counterparts on measures of English language proficiency, especially on measures that assess reading and writing, have benefited considerably from minority language maintenance because, as citizens of an increasingly interconnected world, they have access to two languages rather than only one.

ACKNOWLEDGMENTS

The research on which this chapter was based was supported by grants from the Spencer Foundation and from the Field-Initiated Studies Program

of the U.S. Department of Education. Alicia Alvarez-Calderón and Adriana
Boogerman assisted with the analysis.

APPENDIX A

Comparison of Results of Measures of Writing: Descriptive Statistics

Instrument	Mean	Std Dev	Min	Max	N
TAR, Spanish	1.97	1.05	.00	3.80	30
Narrative, Spanish	3.40	1.89	.00	6.00	30
TAR, English	2.67	.86	1.00	4.30	30
Narrative, English	3.65	1.33	.00	6.00	30
TAR, English (all)	2.63	.83	1.00	4.30	41
Narrative, English (all)	3.51	1.32	.00	6.00	41

Note. TAR, Teachers' Assessment Rubric; Narrative, Narrative Assessment Scale. TAR, English and Narrative, English include essays from participants who attempted to produce essays in both Spanish and English. TAR, English (all) and TAR, English (all) also include the English essays from participants who were unable or unwilling to attempt a Spanish essay.

APPENDIX B

Correlations Among Measures of Language Proficiency

	Narr. Str. English	Narr. Str. Spanish	TAR English	TAR Spanish
Narr. Str. Eng	1.000			
Narr. Str. Sp.	.3111*	1.000		
TAR English	.7685***	.3104*	1.000	
TAR Spanish	.3106*	.8352***	.3347*	1.000

*p < .05. ***p < .001.

REFERENCES

August, D., & Hakuta, K. (Eds.). (1997). *Improving education for language minority children.* Washington, DC: National Academy Press.

Bachman, L. (1990). *Fundamental considerations in language testing.* Oxford, England: Oxford University Press.

Bayley, R. (2004). Linguistic diversity and English language acquisition. In E. Finegan & J. R. Rickford (Eds.), *Language in the USA: Themes for the 21st century* (pp. 268–286). Cambridge, England: Cambridge University Press.

Bayley, R., Alvarez-Calderón, A., & Schecter, S. R. (1998). Tense and aspect in Mexican-origin children's narratives. In E. V. Clark (Ed.), *The proceedings of the twenty-ninth annual Child Language Research Forum* (pp. 221–230). Stanford, CA: Center for the Study of Language and Information.

Bayley, R., Schecter, S. R., & Torres-Ayala, B. (1996). Strategies for bilingual maintenance: Case studies of Mexican-origin families in Texas. *Linguistics and Education, 8*, 389–408.

Cummins, J. (1985). The role of primary language development in promoting educational success for language minority students. In California State Department of Education, *Schooling and language minority students: A theoretical framework* (pp. 3–49). Los Angeles: Evaluation, Dissemination and Assessment Center, California State University, Los Angeles.

Cummins, J. (2001). *Negotiating identities: Education for empowerment in a diverse society* (2nd ed.). Ontario, CA: California Association for Bilingual Education.

Gee, J. (1986). Units in the production of narrative discourse. *Discourse Processes, 9,* 392–422.

Hymes, D. (1982). Narrative form as a "grammar" of experience: Native Americans and a glimpse of English. *Journal of Education, 2,* 121–142.

Krashen, S. D. (1999). *Condemned without trial: Bogus arguments against bilingual education.* Portsmouth, NH: Heinemann.

Krashen, S. D., & Biber, D. (1988). *On course: Bilingual education's success in California.* Sacramento: California Association for Bilingual Education.

Labov, W. (1972). The transformation of experience in narrative syntax. In *Language in the inner city: Studies in the Black English vernacular* (pp. 354–396). Philadelphia: University of Pennsylvania Press.

Labov, W., & Waletsky, J. (1967). Narrative analysis: Oral versions of personal experience. In J. Helm (Ed.), *Essays on the verbal and visual arts: Proceedings of the 1966 annual spring meeting of the American Ethnological Society* (pp. 12–44). Seattle: University of Washington Press.

McCabe, A. (1995). *Chameleon readers: Teaching children to appreciate all kinds of good stories.* New York: McGraw-Hill.

McCabe, A., & Peterson, C. (Eds.). (1991). *Developing narrative structure.* Hillsdale, NJ: Lawrence Erlbaum Associates.

Moriello, B., & Wolfram, W. (2003). New dialect formation in the rural South: Emerging Hispanic English varieties in the mid-Atlantic. *University of Pennsylvania Working Papers in Linguistics, 9*(3), 135–147.

Peterson, C., & McCabe, A. (1983). *Developmental psycholinguistics: Three ways of looking at a child's narrative.* New York: Plenum.

Schecter, S. R., & Bayley, R. (1997). Language socialization and cultural identity: Case studies of Mexican-descent families in California and Texas. *TESOL Quarterly, 31,* 513–541.

Schecter, S. R., & Bayley, R. (1998). Concurrence and complementarity: Mexican-background parents' decisions about language and schooling. *Journal for a Just and Caring Education, 4,* 47–64.

Schecter, S. R., & Bayley, R. (2002). *Language as cultural practice: Mexicanos en el norte.* Mahwah, NJ: Lawrence Erlbaum Associates.

Schecter, S. R., & Bayley, R. (2004). Language socialization in theory and practice. *International Journal of Qualitative Studies in Education, 17,* 605–625.

Valdés, G., & Figueroa, R. (1994). *Bilingualism and testing: A special case of bias.* Norwood, NJ: Ablex.

PART

II

INTEGRATING KNOWLEDGE
OF LANGUAGE INTO
K–12 TEACHING

This section offers a variety of practical ways for teachers to apply aspects of their knowledge of language in their classrooms. Chapters discuss how teachers can construct exercises and activities that raise knowledge and awareness about language change and the history of English, activities for writing instruction (both fiction and nonfiction) as well as other language arts lessons involving metaphor and the teaching of Standard English and its variants, and ways to expand students' linguistic and multicultural awareness through linguistic corpora investigation and internet exploration. Each chapter demonstrates how selected aspects of knowledge of language can be integrated into existing K–12 curricula in productive and useful ways. Though many of the activities described in this section seem targeted for secondary classrooms, they can be fairly easily modified for K–6 students as well.

Anne Curzan's chapter, "Spelling Stories: A Way to Teach the History of English," provides a brief history of English spelling, to explain the reasons behind the apparent "chaos" of the system. The chapter begins by describing the regularity masked by the chaotic exceptions, which is useful material for all teachers working with students on reading and writing. The rest of the chapter explains the exceptions. It works from the premise that spelling provides an interesting and accessible vehicle for students to learn about the history of English. The chapter ends with suggestions for practical ways in which teachers can integrate a discussion of spelling into their curricula. All of these activities ask students to think critically about the language around them—both written and spoken—and how it changes over time.

Kristin Denham's chapter, "Teaching Students About Language Change, Language Endangerment, and Language Death," reviews some of the important reasons that K–12 students should know about language change in general and the reasons that they should have some understanding of language death and what the loss of languages means for us. Denham includes suggestions for how to incorporate information about language change and language death into the classroom by providing a list of topics, discussion points, and further resources. Some of the questions posed include the following. Is language loss a scientific loss? Does language loss mean loss of a culture? Aren't new languages being born/created? What about creoles? Wouldn't it be better if we all spoke the same language so we could all understand each other and then get along? Can not multiple languages result in lack of communication and, therefore, lack of cultural understanding? Then, for each hypothetical student question, the author offers some possible responses for the teacher, suggested classroom activities, and a list of further resources.

Janet Higgins' chapter, "Language as a Reflection of our Social and Physical World: What Students Can Learn From Metaphor," shows how a series of classroom exercises based on how we socially construct linguistic metaphors can help students become more critically aware of how language reflects our social and physical world. The author provides a step-by-step guide to constructing different classroom activities that lead students to reevaluate how they view other people, the economic system, the environment, etc., and to also find alternative ways to conceiving our social and physical world. Students can then move on to analyze the metaphorical content of different texts, learning to read more critically.

Rebecca Wheeler's chapter, "Contrastive Analysis and Codeswitching: How and Why to Use the Vernacular to Teach Standard English," examines how training in linguistics can be put to use in a bidialectal classroom by using contrasts between African American Vernacular English (AAVE) and Standard English syntax and morphology as a teaching tool and positive motivator. In particular, the author shows how teachers can introduce language analysis that highlights and validates dialectal difference. Such an approach builds students' self-esteem and deepens their understanding of language variety, helping to break down linguistic discrimination and stigmatization.

Kirk Hazen's chapter, "English LIVEs: Language in Variation Exercises for Today's Classrooms," explains how the study of language variation can help students learn how language works, and how our social judgments of "difference" are often linguistically based. In analyzing both stigmatized and nonstigmatized dialects through a variety of basic, accessible exercises based on both their own speech and the speech of others, students themselves engage language to learn about regional and social phonological and grammatical variation. Teachers with basic training in linguistics can easily implement these exercises in their classrooms, raising awareness of language structure and language discrimination.

Patricia Dunn and Kenneth Lindblom's chapter, "Developing Savvy Writers by Analyzing Grammar Rants," focuses on the controversy in education involving the role of grammar in teaching writing at the high school level. The authors synthesize and analyze both major voices in the debate and those heard from less often, and argue for a more sophisticated and nuanced view of "grammar" in teaching writing. They suggest specific pedagogies that address the political and rhetorical implications of grammar issues as they affect the teaching of writing. The goal of the chapter is to inform teachers of the varied perspectives on teaching grammar, and to offer practical classroom strategies for addressing this controversial issue.

Donna Jo Napoli's chapter, "Linguistics as a Tool in Teaching Fiction Writing," focuses on the knowledge that the ordinary speaker's ear has of his or her own language in terms of what the way we speak tells us about characteristics of a given speaker—including age, sex, race, ethnicity, religion, social class, educational level, where the person grew up, what the native language of the person is, and other factors. Effective mappings from real to rendered (i.e., fictional) speech that aim to capture these characteristics are examined. The author also discusses how to handle dialogue that cannot be heard today—such as in works that take place far in the past or far in the future.

Tony Hung's chapter, "Applications of Corpus Linguistics in Language Teaching," is a practical guide for using corpus linguistics as a teaching tool, in particular for non-native speakers, but also as a means of raising awareness of native speakers about English syntax and morphology. The author shows how students, using the 300-million-word Bank of English, can study differences between prescriptive grammatical rules and descriptive rules of naturally occurring language firsthand. For example, when students investigate the use of *who* and *whom*, they find that this distinction has virtually disappeared from conversational English. The language corpus also provides a rich resource for constructing language-learning tasks, with readily available data on unusual or difficult constructions.

Anca Nemoianu's "English *Gairaigo*: Learning About Language Structure From the Margins of Japanese," shows how students learn inductively about semantic, syntactic, morphological, and phonological principles at work by using lexicons of loanwords adapted from English into Japanese and a web site of signs and ads in English used widely in Japan—that is, a

natural rather than an artificial language corpus. In the process, students increase their awareness of English and of descriptive techniques used in linguistics. The chapter details ways of performing inductive linguistic analyses on the corpus: how students can understand how sounds of one
language are handled within the sound system of another; how new words
are coined; how meaning changes, and so forth.

And finally, Anne Curzan's second chapter, "Opening Dictionaries to Investigation," shows how dictionaries have the potential to be a productive
resource far beyond their standard use as an authority on questions of
meaning and pronunciation. In fact, the status of "the dictionary" as a linguistic authority is where the investigation can begin. This chapter examines how dictionaries can be incorporated into the curriculum as a subject
of study, to enhance investigations of the lexicon, word meaning, and language change as well as to encourage discussions of language and power.

11

Spelling Stories: A Way to Teach the History of English

Anne Curzan

Since 1925, American high school students have been competing in the National Spelling Bee, a competition that is interesting only because of the idiosyncrasies of English spelling—such as the final *-asy* of the word *idiosyncrasy*. Many English speakers think of English spelling as an obstacle to be surmounted or as a hassle to be managed, with dictionaries, spellcheckers, and mnemonics (a spelling bee-worthy word). Writers are well aware that they may be judged by an unfortunately placed misspelling, and many of those who are not successful spelling-bee competitors view English spelling with trepidation if not contempt. The fundamental argument of this chapter is that English spelling, despite its reputation, can actually be a rich and exciting area for teaching students about language: in the regularities of English spelling, they can discover the many rules they intuitively grasp; and in the irregularities, they can learn much about the history of the English language.

The irregularities in English spelling abound, and they tend to get the most attention. Mark Twain once wrote, "I don't give a damn for a man that can spell a word only one way," and English spelling seems to provide us many ways to spell the sounds we utter. Is it *catalogue* or *catalog*, *centre* or *center*? How did the *b* in *doubt* get there? Where did the *u* in *forty* go? And what in the world happened with *colonel*? In brief, the answer to the first question depends on whether you live in Britain or in the United States. The second question: Renaissance scholars put it there. The third question: historians of English don't know (Chaucer could still write *fourty* but somewhere the *-u-* disappeared). The fourth question: It's a long story. And it's all about patterns of borrowing in the history of English.

This chapter provides a brief history of English spelling, to explain some of the reasons behind the apparent "chaos" of the system. In fact, English spelling is more regular than most English spellers realize. But the exceptions can be spectacular, as *colonel* demonstrates. The chapter begins by describing the regularity masked by the chaotic exceptions, which is useful material for all teachers working with students on reading and writing. The next section explains some of the common exceptions. It works from the premise that spelling provides an interesting and accessible vehicle for students to learn about the history of English. English spelling is, often, a museum that captures earlier pronunciations of words, so students can learn both about how, for example, Chaucer sounded and about how sounds can change over time. The final section provides suggestions for classroom activities focused on exploring English spelling rather than simply learning it by rote.

BACKGROUND ON ENGLISH SPELLING:
PATTERNS OF REGULARITY IN THE SYSTEM

The historian of English Mario Pei once wrote, "English spelling is the world's most awesome mess." And although it can sometimes feel that way, there is more "method behind the madness" than many speakers realize. While Bernard Shaw could spell *fish* as *ghoti*, he could only do so by violating basic rules of spelling-to-sound correspondence linked to position in the word (Johnston, 2000, 2001, p. 372): the spelling <gh> cannot represent /f/ word initially, and <ti> can represent /š/ only medially.

In *Why Our Children Can't Read*, a rich resource for reading and writing instructors at all levels, Diane McGuinness (1997) lays out an argument for the nonrandomness of English spelling patterns, and she explains how this understanding can reshape how we teach reading and spelling. McGuinness describes English spelling as a code, not from spelling to sound but from sound to spelling: "The alphabet is a letter code for phonemes in speech, not a 'sound code' for letters on the page" (p. 209). This perspective on the system, she argues, allows teachers to approach teaching English spelling with a logic explainable to children, about the main way or ways that a sound is spelled. Straightforward tables capture the possibilities and probabilities of the main sound-to-spelling correspondences, as the excerpts from her tables below demonstrate (the representation of phonemes has been changed to correspond to the IPA; rare spellings are excluded from her tables):

Single Consonant Spelling Alternatives
(excerpted from McGuinness, 1997, p. 103)

Sound	Key Word	Word Beginning	Word Ending
m	man	m	m mb mn
n	not	n kn gn	n gn
p	pig	p	p
r	red	r wr	r
s	sat	s c sc	ce se ss s
t	top	t	t bt

Vowel Spelling Alternatives (excerpted from McGuinness, 1997, p. 105)

Sound	Key Word	Spelling Alternatives in Order of Most to Least Likely						
		1	2	3	4	5	6	7
æ	had	a						
ɛ	bed	e	ea	ai				
e	made	a-e	ai	a	ay	ei	eigh	ey
i	see	ee	ea	y	ie	e	e-e	ey
ay	time	i-e	i	y	igh			

The less probable spellings in these charts, particularly of consonants, can seem less difficult in their irregularity if students are presented with lists of the common exceptions that take these spellings, which turn out to be manageable in length. For example, the exceptional spellings /s/ can be described as follows (excerpted from McGuinness, 1997, p. 259):

Sound /s/	Key word: see.	Spell s except:
ce	cease, cedar, cede, ceiling, celebrate, celery, celestial, cell, cement, cent, centennial, center, centi- (100), central, century, ceramic, cereal, ceremony, certain, certify	
ci	cider, cigar, cigarette, cinch, cinder, cinema, cinnamon, cipher, circle, circuit, circulate, circus, cite, citizen, citrus, city, civic, civil	
cy	cycle, cyclone, cylinder, cymbal, cynic, cypress, cyst	
sc	scene, scent, science, scepter	

Some well-known patterns in English spelling captured in these kinds of charts can be traced back to medieval conventions and sound change. Doubled consonants (as well as some clusters such as *ck* and *tch*) often indicate that the preceding vowel is "short" (or lax). Single consonants followed by a vowel often indicate that the preceding vowel is "long" (or tense): hence spellings in the chart such as <a-e> for /e/ and <e-e> for /i/.

Another set of minor but regular spelling patterns relies on knowledge of etymology. For example, as Stockwell and Minkova (2001, pp. 166–168) explain, the pronunciation of <ch>, <g>, and <x> varies depending on whether the word is borrowed from Latin or Greek. The spelling <ch>, which represents /č/ in native English words, works this way in words from Latin and Greek:

Latin		Greek	
/č/	channel	/k/	character

If the Latinate word was borrowed directly from French, rather than Latin, then <ch> typically represents /š/: *moustache, chagrin*. Spelling bee participants, groping for clues, ask about word origins to narrow the possibilities of how the sounds might be spelled.

BACKGROUND ON ENGLISH SPELLING: SOURCES OF IRREGULARITY IN THE SYSTEM

David Crystal (1995, p. 272) quotes estimates that 80% of the English lexicon is spelled according to regular patterns, and only 3% is so irregular that speakers must learn the spellings individually by heart. So although the problem is not as unwieldy as it may sometimes seem to English speakers, 3% to 20% of a large lexicon is still a reasonably large number. This section summarizes five major sources of irregularity or idiosyncrasy in the English spelling system. Two full-length book treatments of English spelling, while dated, can provide teachers with many more details: D. G. Scragg's *A History of English Spelling* (1974) and G. H. Vallins' *Spelling* (1954). Mario Pei's *The Story of the English Language* (1967) and David Crystal's *The Cambridge Encyclopedia of the English Language* (1995) also contain informative and entertaining sections on the history of English spelling, and Richard L. Venezky's *The American Way of Spelling* (1999) is the most comprehensive treatment of American spelling to date (for a shorter treatment, see Venezky, 2001). C. M. Millward's *A Biography of the English Language* (1996) provides extensive information about the history of English generally and the history of English spelling within particular historical periods specifically. Diane McGuinness' *Why Our Children Can't Read* (1997) contains highly readable sections on the development of alphabets and of the English spelling system specifically. The *Oxford English Dictionary* often provides information about the historical spellings of specific words.

The Alphabet Problem.   English was first written with the Latin alphabet after the introduction of Christianity to England, beginning in 597 A.D. with the mission of St. Augustine. One fundamental problem is that the Latin alphabet we use today has only 26 letters for more than 40 sounds in English. So we have letters doing "double time": for example, *c* for /s/ as well as /k/; and *h* not only for /h/ but as part of representing /θ/, /ð/, /š/, and /č/. When the Latin alphabet was first introduced, scribes kept a few runic characters for English sounds that did not occur in Latin: for example, thorn (þ) and eth (ð) for /θ/ and /ð/, wynn (shaped similarly to thorn without the extended vertical stroke at the top) for /w/, and ash (æ) for /æ/.

After the Norman Conquest, in 1066, when French scribes began writing down English, some French spellings were introduced into English: for example, <c> for the sound /s/ in words like *city* and *cellar*; <ou> for /u/ in a word like house; and <qu> for the sound /kw/ (which was spelled <kw> or <cw> in Old English). It is during this Middle English period that the Old English spelling <hw> is turned around to be <wh>, probably by analogy with the spellings <th> (which replaced the runes), <sh> (which replaced Old English <sc>), <ch> (which replaced Old English <c>). Scribes also tried to handle the fact that long and short vowels had the same letter form. Often they doubled the following consonant if the vowel was short and added an extra vowel if it was long. But they did not apply either practice entirely consistently and there was not universal agreement in the second case about what the extra vowel should be (e.g., *see, seas, seize*).

The Sound Change Problem. Many of the reasons why the spelling of English words does not correspond to their sound is that the spelling preserves an older pronunciation of the word. In some ways, spelling in English is a "museum" of older pronunciations. After the introduction of the printing press to England in 1476, the more widespread standardization of spelling began, but, of course, the sound of the language was still changing. For example, in the Early Modern English period, initial /k/ and /g/ in the clusters /kn/ and /gn/ were lost (both sounds really were pronounced before this time), but they are preserved in the spelling of words such as *knight* and *gnat*. The final −*e* in English words such as *name* represents a vowel that used to be pronounced, and this pronunciation is still preserved in the spelling.

In terms of English vowels, a vowel change called the "Great Vowel Shift" (GVS) happened roughly between the fifteenth and seventeenth centuries, as spelling was becoming standardized, so the spelling of words often reflects vowels before the GVS. The shift involved the historically long vowels (many of which we would now label as tense vowels), and they rose or "moved up" in their articulation. In other words, low vowels became mid vowels, mid vowels became high vowels, and high vowels (with "nowhere higher to go") became diphthongs. In a highly simplified schema, the GVS had these effects:

$$/\text{i:}/ \rightarrow /\text{ay}/ \qquad /\text{u:}/ \rightarrow /\text{aw}/$$
$$/\text{e:}/ \rightarrow /\text{i}/ \qquad /\text{o:}/ \rightarrow /\text{u}/$$
$$/\text{ɛ:}/ \rightarrow /\text{e}/, /\text{i}/ \qquad /\text{ɔ:}/ \rightarrow /\text{o}/$$
$$/\text{a:}/ \rightarrow /\text{e}/$$

Here are a few examples of the many English spellings that still reflect pre-GVS pronunciation: *mouse* (formerly /u:/ which became /aw/), *mice* (formerly /i:/ which became /ay/), *boot* and *goose* (formerly /o:/ which became /u/), *see* and *meet* (formerly /e:/ which became /i/), *mate* (formerly /a:/ which became /e/).

The "Return to Etymologies" Problem. The interest in classical Greece and Rome which characterizes the Renaissance period had effects on the written form of the language, as Renaissance scholars sometimes made efforts to change English spelling to conform to the Latin forms of the words. English spellings often reflect the French forms, from which English borrowed the words; but scholars could trace the forms back to Latin, and they would sometimes insert letters that had been lost in the French and, therefore, in the English. In many cases, the spelling had no effect on pronunciation: for example, the silent *b* in *debt* (Middle English *dette* but Latin *debitum*) and *doubt* (Middle English *doute*, but Latin *dubitare*), as well as the silent *c* in *indict* (Middle English *enditen*, but Latin *indictare*). In other cases, the new spelling eventually altered pronunciation so that the modern spelling and pronunciation correspond; for example, Modern English *falcon* (Middle English *faucon*, but Latin *falco*) and *adventure* (Middle English *aventure*, but Latin *aduentas*).

In some cases, we find "incorrect" Latin spellings, based on false etymologies. For example, the English word *island* is a native English word, which appeared as *ealand* in Old English (*ea* 'water' + *land*). Renaissance scholars seem to have assumed that the word was, however, related to the Latin word *insula*, and so they "unetymologically" inserted the *s* "back into" (although it was never there!) *island*.

The Foreign Borrowings Problem. English has a long history of borrowing words from the world's languages, which means English also borrows foreign spelling patterns. For example, the initial spelling clusters <psy> (for /s/) and <rh> (for /r/) are originally Greek; the initial <ll> (pronounced /l/ in English) is Spanish. The silent consonants at the end of words like *patois* or *corps* reflect French pronunciation patterns.

The British Versus American Spelling Problem. Many of the most noted spelling differences between American and British written English can be traced back to American spellings introduced by Noah Webster in his important 1828 *American Dictionary of the English Language*, which were then picked up by the Government Printing Office. Webster, an advocate of spelling reform in general, saw the reform of American spelling away from British spelling as symbolic of American independence and the establishment of a uniquely American form of English. He introduced the use of American *-or* for British *-our* (*honor* vs. *honour*), *-er* for *-re* (*theater* vs. *theatre*), *-ence* for *-ense* (*offense* vs. *offence*), and *-ize* for *-ise* (*industrialize* vs. *industrialise*). Webster also introduced the single *l* in inflected forms of verbs such as *travel* (so *traveled*, not *travelled*), dropped the final *-k* from words such as *public* and *music*, and introduced final *-or* for *-er* when it corresponded to the Latin (e.g., *instructor*).

The Odd and Sometimes Inexplicable Problems. Some odd spellings result from idiosyncratic word histories. One of the more mysterious spellings in English is the word *colonel*. The odd pronunciation of this word, given its spelling, seems to result from a "double borrowing" in this history of English. In the mid-16th century, English borrowed the form with "r" from the French form *coronelle*, ultimately derived from the Italian form *colonello*. During the period, the Italian form, with the "l," was also borrowed and the two forms seem to have coexisted for a period of time before the Italian spelling was standardized with the French pronunciation.

These examples are only the tip of the iceberg, but they describe several of the main categories of irregularities in English spelling—in other words, the reasons and regularity behind the irregularity.

SPELLING IN THE K–12 LANGUAGE ARTS CURRICULUM

Most classroom activities focused on spelling involve drills and memorization, asking students to learn the exceptions and the rules. These activities are clearly important, given the ways in which students' education will, in some circumstances, be judged by their ability to spell. But spelling can be much more interesting than memorization drills, and the following activities encourage teachers to use English spelling as an avenue for exploring the structure and history of English.

Spelling to Sound Correspondence. Teachers can pick a sound like /k/ and challenge students to come up with as many different spellings as possible. My own students have come up with as many as 13 spellings for /k/, including the obvious <k, ck, c>, the less obvious <kh, qu, q>, and the truly not obvious <gh> (*McLaughlin*). The activity can be made more specific, such that students first come up with spellings for initial /n/ (e.g., <n, gn, kn>) and then final /n/ (e.g., <n, mn>). The activity can also be reversed, so that instructors provide a spelling (e.g., <ea> or <gh>) and students try to come up with as many different pronunciations as possible. These activities ask students to scan their own lexicons for patterns and exceptions. Students can also pursue "scavenger hunts" in written text for particular spelling patterns, such as <gh>, <ea>, or <ou>. Once students have collected lists of words with a particular spelling sequence, they can describe patterns of pronunciation. In other words, students create charts of patterns and probabilities such as those described earlier in this chapter.

In such searches, students will, undoubtedly, find exceptions, but often the exceptions are much more limited than the general pattern. For example, <ough> is notoriously capricious in its pronunciation (e.g., *though, through, cough, enough, thought*), but a hunt for the spelling sequence shows students what a small subset of words use this sequence—that is, how few exceptions this troublesome sequence involves. If students search for *mn*, they will probably only find *autumn* and *column*, and suddenly this "odd spelling" does not feel so chaotic in the system because it is so limited in its distribution.[1]

Or students can scan texts for silent consonants. This exercise requires both sight and sound recognition, and once students have compiled lists, they can, once again, find patterns where these consonants appear. Instructors can use this as an opportunity to explain some of the historical reasons for silent consonants (e.g., sound change and Renaissance respellings) and reinforce for students a sense of the limited scope and of the patterns of these spellings.

Testing Intuitions About Spelling. The fact that we all know that *ghoti* cannot really spell *fish* exemplifies our intuitions, as readers, of which kinds of spellings are acceptable and which are not, even when we do not recognize the word. Teachers can create lists of nonsense words, including words spelled in ways that conform to English spelling patterns (e.g., *blag, murnot, priggle, yote*) and ones that do not (*ngors, ftung, oofpsy, yoaet*), and ask students to identify which are possible or acceptable English word spellings. For the latter set, students should try to articulate why the spelling seems unacceptable; for example, is it that English does not have a particular consonant cluster or is it that the cluster cannot appear in that particular place? For the nonsense words that conform to English spelling patterns, students can provide a probable pronunciation and explain why that pronunciation seems likely. For a word like *yote*, they can also try to provide alternate spellings for the same pronunciation (e.g., *yoat*). With all these exercises, students are identifying and playing with spelling patterns.

---

[1] I would like to thank Arthur Evenchik at the Maya Angelou Public Charter School in Washington, D.C., for this example.

Spelling Reform. Students can be presented with the opportunity to develop specific proposals for reforming English spelling. What would they reform, and how? Students can devise their own reformed alphabet (for example, do they want a letter for every sound?) and/or principles for spelling-to-sound correspondences. Instructors can ask them to rewrite a given passage in their new spelling system. If students then exchange passages, they can evaluate a peer's reformed system—and often they see that they are more attached to traditional spelling than they realize.

With this exercise, students are participating in a long tradition of spelling reform efforts in the history of English, dating back at least into the 16th century. Noah Webster is unusual in terms of the success of several of his proposed reforms of American spelling, but it must be noted that many more of the reforms he advocated failed: for example, dropping the final *−e* to create words such as *determin, definit, medicin,* and *infinit* (the only one of these that may be succeeding now is *ax* for *axe*). Other efforts at reform have been less successful. The American Philological Reform Association has published suggested new spellings with few results; the American Spelling Reform Association proposed a modified alphabet with 32 letters; and the Simplified Spelling Board, while not successful in most of its proposed reforms, is responsible for the shortening of words such as *catalog* and *program,* and the substitution of *f* for *ph* in *fantasy* (but not in other *ph* words).

Some spelling changes occur without the advocacy of specialized groups—and, in fact, they sometimes occur in the face of general resistance. Students can argue for or against spelling changes such as: *donut* for *doughnut, lite* in reference to low-calorie food product, *thru* for *through, gonna* for *going to, nite* for *night, womyn* for *women.* These examples raise a host of different issues, from creating spelling distinctions to correspond to semantic distinctions (e.g., *lite*), to combining two words to reflect both pronunciation and a new grammatical function (e.g., the modal *going to/gonna*), to searching for more "politically correct" spellings that could replace spellings considered potentially sexist (e.g., *womyn*). Students can also keep an eye out for new spellings in advertisements and on public signs, and bring these to class for discussion.

The questions involved in spelling reform touch on topics raised in many of the chapters of this book. Given that the language is always changing, how would spelling ever keep up if it is supposed to correspond to current pronunciation? And do students really want to destroy the "museum of English spelling" that preserves the visual connection between, for example, *south* and *southern,* even though they are now pronounced with different vowels? Given the richness of English dialect variation, whose pronunciation would become standardized in a reformed spelling system (e.g., would *cot* and *caught* be spelled the same way or differently? *Pin* and *pen*?)? If students find that they are more attached to traditional spellings than they realized, why? Do they feel comfortable judging other people's education based on their spelling? Until the introduction of printing, spelling was much more individualistic and less consistent, such that a word might appear with several different spellings within one document (even Shakespeare seems to have spelled his name several different ways).[2] Why do we put so much weight on having just one spelling for each word, and who gets to determine what that spelling is? Spelling opens up discussions not only about language change, but also about the nature of Standard English and language authority.

All of these activities ask students to think critically about the language around them—both written and spoken—and how it changes over time. They actively search out and describe patterns in the written language, to create a context for the exceptions. And discussion of the exceptions opens the door to conversations about language change and the history of English.

REFERENCES

Crystal, D. (1995). *The Cambridge encyclopedia of the English language*. Cambridge, England: Cambridge University Press.

Johnston, F. R. (2000/2001). Spelling exceptions: Problems or possibilities? *The Reading Teacher, 54*(4)(Dec/Jan), 372–378.

McGuinness, D. (1997). *Why our children can't read: And what we can do about it*. New York: The Free Press.

Millward, C. M. (1996). *A biography of the English language* (2nd ed.). Fort Worth, TX: Harcourt Brace.

Oxford English Dictionary. (1989). Second ed. Oxford: Clarendon.

Pei, M. (1967). *The story of the English language*. Philadelphia and New York: J. B. Lippincott.

Scragg, D. G. (1974). *A history of English spelling*. Manchester, England: Manchester University Press.

Stockwell, R., & Minkova, D. (2001). *English words: History and structure*. Cambridge, England: Cambridge University Press.

Vallins, G. H. (1954). *Spelling*. London: Andre Deutsch.

Venezky, R. L. (1999). *The American way of spelling: The structure and origins of American English orthography*. New York and London: Guilford Press.

Venezky, R. L. (2001). Spelling. In J. Algeo (Ed.), *The Cambridge history of the English language: English in North America* (Vol. VI, pp. 340–357). Cambridge, England: Cambridge University Press.

---

[2]Students often find it hard to believe that medieval readers could have tolerated, let alone not have noticed, this kind of spelling variation. One useful (although not perfect) analogy for students can be handwriting. Many of us have several variants of any given letter: for example, my handwriting mixes cursive and print versions of a letter like <f> within one paragraph, line, and even word. If, at some later point in time, handwriting were standardized to the point that there were only one version of each letter, users of this system might look at my handwritten documents with amazement: how could people not notice and/or be confused by my random variation in letter forms?

12

Teaching Students About Language Change, Language Endangerment, and Language Death

Kristin Denham

Every time I tell students in my classes about language death and language endangerment, they are surprised and shocked, not only at the information itself, but that they had never heard about it before. Here in Washington state, we are surrounded by scores of Native American tribes with endangered or dead languages, yet public knowledge of these languages and the languages' status is nearly nonexistent.

Students should have such basic knowledge about language change, language endangerment, and language death well before they happen upon that information in a college classroom. In this chapter I explain why the study of language change and language death is important for every child to know. Although ideally linguistics should be taught as its own subject in the public schools (see Denham, 2003), making that sort of change is a longer, more difficult process. We can effect change now, however, by working within the system and acknowledging the existing standards and benchmarks set by schools and administrators and then determining how linguistic knowledge can help meet those standards. For example, the Washington state standards—and likely those of most other states—require discussion of both national and global "native" cultures. Discussion of language death, language endangerment, and language revitalization can easily become part of those discussions, and the information can form the basis for issues related to cultural and linguistic diversity, colonization and imperialism, intellectual history, and other topics that I mention later. I first offer some background information on language change, which could be part of language arts or English classes in various forms. Some of the information discussed in the latter parts of this chapter might be of broader value when placed within a social studies curriculum. The background information and the discussion points introduced next provide teachers with some launching pads for general discussion of linguistic issues that are not only interesting and relevant for all students, but also help teachers and students meet the curriculum standards.

FIRST, EXAMPLES OF LANGUAGE CHANGE

What evidence do we have that English has changed? One need only look at an excerpt from *Beowulf* to see that it is not possible for a speaker of modern English to read it without prior study of Old English. And though Chaucer, written in the 1300s in what we now call Middle English is a bit more recognizable, we still need a hefty dose of footnotes and grammatical explanation. Shakespearean English is much easier to read and finally seems like our own language, although footnotes are necessary here too. We have quite a lot of evidence that English has changed in its phonology, morphology, and syntax, and that the meanings of many words have changed as well. We even have evidence of language change in progress. For example, it is now very rare to hear *whom* in spoken language—a morphological change. We also seem to be losing the phoneme /ʍ/ in American English. This change is not one that is restricted to a particular geographic region or class, but largely a generational distinction. That is, many (most?) people over, say, age 50 still have the /ʍ/; that is, they have a distinction between the words *which* and *witch*, whereas most speakers under age 50 no longer have this distinction and do not have the phoneme /ʍ/ at all in their consonant inventories.

It can sometimes be difficult to distinguish language variation from language change, but basically, the majority rules. When a substantial number of speakers have adopted the variation as their own accepted pronunciation or grammatical form, then we say that the language has changed. Some changes are incorporated into the written language (mainly, morphological and syntactic changes), some are not (pronunciation changes).[1]

AND WHY IS IT THAT LANGUAGES CHANGE?

It is useful to be reminded of why languages change in order to reduce our tendency to think of change as degradation. Because the acquisition of lan-

---

[1]Why are pronunciation changes not incorporated into the written form of the language? Largely because our spelling system is not a reflection of our pronunciation anyway. There is not a one-to-one correspondence between our spelling symbols (alphabet) and our pronunciation. Also, of course, there is much more dialectal variation for pronunciation than for other grammatical differences.

guage is an innately determined behavior, the same patterns of change will emerge in all languages. One of the primary motivations for sound change is ease of articulation; that is, phonetic and phonological changes come about as a result of making certain sequences of sounds easier to say. Some sound changes that took place before our spelling system was standardized are reflected in the spellings of the words. The prefix on words such as *impossible* and *illegal* used to be the regular prefix *in-* meaning "not." However, this *in-* changed in certain words in order to make the sound sequences easier to say. So in + possible → impossible or in + legal → illegal. This process of assimilation—making one sound more like a neighboring sound in some way—is one of the most common processes in language change and language variation. Another common reason for language change is *regularization* or *analogy*. For example, in Old English, there used to be many different ways to form the plurals of nouns. (See Curzan (on spelling), chap. 11, this volume.) Those words which we now think of as having irregular plurals (*oxen, geese, mice, women*), were members of larger groups of nouns that formed their plurals in the same way. Gradually, by analogy and because of the tendency to regularize, the *-s* plural became the dominant form and other kinds of plural endings dropped out (for the most part).

Another major reason for language change is language contact—one community of speakers comes into contact with speakers of another language. This can result not only in borrowing of words (as in the huge number of words English borrowed from French following the Norman Invasion of England in 1066), but in changes to the phonology, morphology, and syntax of a language. For example, English acquired a phonemic /v/ due primarily to the influence from French (which had a phonemic /v/) after the Norman Invasion. And American English acquired the names for many plants and animals (such as *squash, raccoon, hickory, persimmon, moose, skunk*) from various Native American languages, primarily languages of the Algonquin (or Algic) families of the East Coast.[2]

TODAY'S LANGUAGE IS JUST GOING DOWN THE TUBES

Despite the naturalness of language change and its pervasiveness throughout the history of any language, change is generally regarded by those living through it as a bad thing, as language degradation. (See also Dunn and

---

[2]The influence on English from Native American languages, however, was quite minimal—not surprisingly, since they were conquered peoples—and all of the borrowed words are nouns, indicating a lack of any true mingling of cultures. Place names, including the names of 28 states, are from Native American languages (including one from Inuit and one from Hawaiian).

Lindblom, chap. 16, this volume.) Some of the reasons for this attitude have to do with the standardization of English, with mass literacy, and simply with the notion of "otherness." (See Lobeck, chap. 8, this volume.) If we hear an unusual word or linguistic structure, we tend to think that it is "wrong" or "bad"; the way we have learned it and the way we see it in print must be the "better" and "right" way. However, looking again at the historical record can help put these attitudes in perspective, allowing us to see that our attitudes about language change are based on what is familiar, not what is "correct." For example, if someone today says *bringed* instead of *brought*, it might be viewed as quite "incorrect" according to some standard form of English. However, in older English, up through the 15th century, the accepted past tense of *work* was *wrought*; this form was viewed as the more "standard" form of the word. Now, of course, it is more accepted to use the regularized *worked*, although one can imagine the parents and teachers of the day cringing when their children said *worked*, as some may do now when they hear *bringed*. What started out as a quite patterned example of language variation, likely viewed as language degradation at the time, eventually became accepted by the people in positions of power and thus became the so-called "standard" form.

An additional example illustrates another kind of pattern regularization. Many dialects use the form *you was* rather than *you were*, and though this may not be the standard form anymore, *you was* used to be quite standard in speech and showed up frequently in literature until it was condemned by prescriptivists in the late 1700s. Table 12.1 summarizes how the use of *was* regularizes the pattern. Using *was* for the second person singular *you* regularizes the pattern, making all of the singular subjects take *was* and the plurals *were*. Though this is a logical pattern that serves to make the system more regular, it is now stigmatized and considered by most speakers to be nonstandard.

Another change that can help students see how their attitudes about language are not necessarily rational is the pronunciation of words that have an "al" or "ol" followed by another consonant. For most of these words, the /l/ is not pronounced by most speakers: *half, calf, walk, salmon.* According

TABLE 12.1
Past Tense Forms of "Be"

standard				nonstandard			
person (singular)	*to be*	person (plural)	*to be*	person (singular)	*to be*	person (plural)	*to be*
I	**was**	we	were	I	**was**	we	were
you	**were**	you	were	you	**was**	you	were
he/she	**was**	they	were	he/she	**was**	they	were

to Pyles and Algeo (1982), this /l/ before a consonant had disappeared across the board by Early Modern English (1500–1800). However, the /l/ has returned in some Modern English speakers' pronunciation because of what we call a "spelling pronunciation," an effect of seeing the /l/ in the word in print. (This has also happened with the /t/ of *often*, which used to not be pronounced, but now is for some speakers.) Some words with an *l* + consonant have two standard pronunciations, so you may hear *folk* or *psalm* with or without the /l/, though other /l/s are not pronounced, as in *yolk*. And though most speakers do not pronounce the /l/ in *half* or *calf*, those same speakers might pronounce the /l/ in *wolf* and criticize those who do not have an /l/ in *wolf*. It is a useful exercise to have students consider other words that contain an /l/ before a consonant and discuss their own pronunciations and attitudes: *salve, calm, talk, golf, Rudolph, elf, shelf, myself*, for example.

Perhaps it is just human nature to resist change and with language change that resistance is quite evident. However, acknowledging the naturalness and inevitability of language change, as well as its systematic and rule-governed nature, reminds us that the attitudes about language change (and variation) come not in response to the language itself, but in response to society's attitudes toward the *speakers* of that language variety.[3]

So it would indeed be an oddity, if not an impossibility, for a language not to change. At least when we view language change from a distance (of either space or time), we seem to understand and accept that languages do affect and influence each other—no one would argue that French or Spanish should become Latin again—and such influence is not necessarily regarded negatively. However, when we are talking about our own language in the present, there is widespread resistance to change and to influence. Consider, for example, the *Academie Francaise*, France's language academy which charges itself with "fixing" the language and resisting outside influences, or consider the negative attitudes toward different dialects of English. Our language becomes part of our identity and so we resist any sort of change or variation. We need to keep in mind how closely we guard our own language (or dialect) when we consider cases in which language contact has led to complete obliteration of a language.

Everyone is likely aware that languages die, but some of the languages mostly commonly thought of as "dead" languages didn't die, they simply morphed into other languages. Latin, for example, is often called a dead language, though it simply developed into Spanish, Portuguese, French, Italian,

---

[3]Perhaps it's also human nature to seek out differences to give definition to one's clan/tribe/ class and language certainly provides an effective platform for this kind of societal behavior. This desire to belong to a group is why speakers of particular language varieties maintain their own way of speaking even when they know it is nonstandard and stigmatized by the social elite.

and Romanian; much as Old English changed into Modern English. And Ancient Greek did not die, but changed into Modern Greek. When a language has no descendants, however, then it can more accurately be called a dead language. Ancient Hebrew is often brought up as an example of a dead language that has been successfully revived as Modern Hebrew. However, the language was not quite dead, having been used as a lingua franca among Jews in the Muslim world, and perhaps elsewhere, at least into the 1400s.[4] Also, the fact that the language remained alive in religious contexts as well as the fact that there was a wealth of written records enabled the language to again become—or perhaps remain—a language spoken by children as a first language.

WHAT'S REAL LANGUAGE DEATH?

If Latin, Greek, and Hebrew are not examples of dead languages, what are? Which languages have left no descendants and why? Michael Krauss (1992) proposed that, in this century, as many as 95% of the estimated 6,000 languages currently spoken in the world may become extinct and that they are dying out at the highest rate ever. Krauss also claims that the remaining 5% will belong to at most 20 language families, and more than half of the remaining languages will belong to just two families, Indo-European and Niger-Congo. What is causing this forecasted rapid decline? How do languages die? Speakers of a language have all died from disease or genocide, as happened with some Native American tribes upon contact with Europeans. Such scenarios have been uncommon, however; as James Crawford (1998) noted: "More often language death is the culmination of language shift, resulting from a complex of internal and external pressures that induce a speech community to adopt a language spoken by others. These may include changes in values, rituals, or economic and political life resulting from trade, migration, intermarriage, religious conversion, or military conquest" (p. 3).

Discussion Points

With some background information now in hand, the K–12 teacher and students can tackle the following set of discussion points that are organized as a series of questions and answers, the questions being those raised by hypothetical students, the answers being some suggestions for the kinds of topics that the questions could lead to. I have organized it this way so that

---

[4]Thanks to Ray Jackendoff for this point.

a teacher can pull out questions and answers for different kinds of classes, age groups, and focuses. They also can be read together as a unit on language change and language death.

WHAT'S SO BAD ABOUT LANGUAGE DEATH?

It is a common public belief that we would be better off if we all spoke the same language—such linguistic homogeneity would mean we could all understand each other and consequently all get along, right? Some would argue that having multiple languages results in lack of communication and, therefore, lack of cultural understanding. The teacher should lead the class in a discussion of the practical problems of getting everyone in any given community of speakers with more than one language to speak the same language. It simply won't happen. And if it is attempted by force, it is rarely effective, and rather than promoting mutual understanding and respect, can have the opposite effect. It may be useful to introduce the term *lingua franca* (a language adopted as a common language by speakers who do not share a common native language) and to discuss the role of English as a global language. Even if students agree that a lingua franca is useful, it should be pointed out that multiple languages are also useful and that most people in the world can speak more than one language. Also, discussion of imposing a language by force could naturally lead to a discussion of English Only laws (legislation which seeks to make English the official language) and can provide a platform to talk about the dangers and constitutional questions of outlawing public use of immigrants' languages and, in effect, legalizing discrimination against minority languages. Surely, such questions can lead to a discussion of how language and identity are so closely intertwined; people are not willing to simply give up their language for another, especially when that other language is one spoken by a more powerful (economic, social, racial) group. Having students investigate which states have English Only laws and what the (quite varying) effects of those laws are, is a useful and informative activity, especially since many students may assume that English already is the official language of the country.

Language loss is tragic because it is a scientific loss (for linguists and for others) and a loss of diversity, in a broad sense. Hale (1992) argued that linguistic diversity—having a wide variety of languages and language types—is very important to human intellectual life, not only for the amount and variety of data that such diversity provides for linguists, but "also in relation to the class of human activities belonging to the realms of culture and art" (p. 35). Hale adds that "some forms of verbal art—verse, song, or chant—depend crucially on morphological and phonological, even syntactic, properties of the language in which it is formed" (p. 36). In such cases, the art cannot exist in the same way without the language. There has therefore already been profound loss of culture due to the deaths of the hundreds of languages in North America alone.

ISN'T IT JUST THE "NATURAL" WAY FOR SOME LANGUAGES TO DIE AND OTHERS TO BE CREATED/BORN?

Although it is true that new languages are being born as creoles, they are not emerging at nearly the rate that other languages are dying out. (See Wassink, chap. 5, this volume, for more on pidgins and creoles.) It is important to discuss the idea of what is "natural" with respect to language change. Language change is *natural*—that is, languages change and to try to prevent it is nearly always futile—but the kinds of external influence that result in language change are quite varied. For example, if communities with different languages come together by choice (migration), that can result in those languages affecting, changing, each other. However, when there is colonization, forced assimilation, or some other prohibition against a community's language, there will be a *natural* reluctance—or even overt resistance—to let go of a language. Understanding the reasons behind language death, especially the language death in the United States, provides perspective on and an understanding of the effects of colonization and the resulting power of English worldwide.

WHAT'S STOPPING LANGUAGE MAINTENANCE?

Many may wonder why, if a group of people does not want their language to die, they don't just start speaking it more. In most cases, language loss results from assimilation of one culture to another more powerful or dominant culture. Along with that assimilation comes loss of a language. What we are seeing now in many Native American communities is a desire to bring back a language that no one speaks (at least fluently) anymore. The challenges these communities face in that task are enormous. In some communities, there are no speakers left. Some have only a few elderly speakers. The languages vary somewhat in how much material has been documented, but they often lack a dictionary or grammatical description of the language. And the ones that do have those materials may not have educational materials that have been developed to make the often quite technical linguistic description and explanation useful for the classroom. So although there may be a desire by the community to have their children speak the language, it is not as easy as that. In many discussions of imperialism and colonialism, language is not typically discussed, and, as a result, "folk knowledge" persists. For example, many people assume there is a single Native American tribal group and/or a single Native American language. Discussion of the current plight of Native languages, discussion about the residential schools and the punishment endured by Native Americans in such schools for speaking their native languages, discussion of the challenges of being a nonnative speaker of English in our country, among other topics, could be effectively incorporated into social studies units on native cultures, although it is typically not.

AREN'T UNWRITTEN LANGUAGES MORE PRIMITIVE?

Many people might think if a language is not written, that that is evidence it is a "primitive" language. However, it is important to understand our biases as a literate society. Our society takes it for granted that to be "educated" is to be literate, so it can be hard to understand the different ideas about education, intelligence, and culture in people such as the Penan (Davis, 1999), the Lardil (Hale, 1992), the Salish, or hundreds of other communities with oral rather than written literary traditions. Many Native American languages were not written down until relatively recently, but the oral traditions in many of these communities is very complex and sophisticated. There is an emerging new study of the literary principles and qualities of oral literature, its narrative structure, and literary patterning, based on examples from many such communities. Such formal analyses show these oral traditions in the context of the world's literary heritage and seek to represent the texts in a way that reflects how the stories were appreciated and understood by members of the cultures from which they came (see Bierwert, 1996 and references cited there).

Also, Mufwene (2003) pointed out that some languages with very prestigious literary traditions, such as ancient Greek and Latin, have nonetheless ceased to be spoken. Mufwene decries the claim that lack of a writing system is a contributing factor to the death of a language at all.

Now, it is unfair to suggest that a culture should remain static. Any living tradition changes. Hale (1992) said, ".It is . . . the development of new traditions which is most consonant with the human purpose. And it is precisely where local languages are viable that new traditions develop. Thus, for example, in the Southwest of the United States, beside the continuing traditions of sung verse, a new tradition of poetry is developing, in Papago, Pima, Yaqui, Navajo, and Hualapai, for example, in the context of the growing use of the written form of these languages" (p. 41). Attempts to preserve and revitalize language do not mean that the community may not adapt, change, or even assimilate, but rather that diversity should be safeguarded.

CONCLUSION

It is my hope that even a brief discussion in the K–12 classroom of some of the issues raised here will begin to result in a "linguistic literacy" for our students. Understanding the forces behind language change and the consequences of language death can help students to better understand and appreciate our multilingual, multidialectal, and multicultural society.

IMPORTANT ONLINE RESOURCES AND LINKS

- http://ourworld.compuserve.com/homepages/JWCRAWFORD

  James Crawford's website contains information on endangered languages, English Only (Official English), language rights, bilingual education, and much more.

- http://archive.aclu.org/library/pbp6.html

  The American Civil Liberties Union (ACLU) briefing paper on English Only answers questions frequently posed by the public about "English Only" issues.

- http://www.cal.org

  The Center for Applied Linguistics' (CAL) website contains a wide range of linguistic information. "CAL is a private, non-profit organization: a group of scholars and educators who use the findings of linguistics and related sciences in identifying and addressing language-related problems. CAL carries out a wide range of activities including research, teacher education, analysis and dissemination of information, design and development of instructional materials, technical assistance, conference planning, program evaluation, and policy analysis."

- http://memory.loc.gov/ammem/ndlpedu/lessons/01/indian/resources.html

  The Library of Congress's Learning Page website on "Indian Boarding Schools: Civilizing the Native Spirit" includes many links to other sites and papers as well as to lesson plans.

- http://www.fathom.com/feature/122144,
  http://www.fathom.com/course/21701718

These two online seminars "Lost Tongues and the Politics of Language Endangerment" and "Creoles, Pidgins and the Evolution of Languages" respectively, are by linguist Salikoko Mufwene of the University of Chicago. Mufwene's "Goodies" link also has other useful information on pidgins and creoles and language endangerment: http://humanities. uchicago.edu/faculty/mufwene/goodies.html

REFERENCES

Bierwert, C. (Ed.). (1996). *Lushootseed texts: An introduction to Puget Salish narrative aesthetics*. Lincoln: University of Nebraska Press.

Davis, W. (1999). The issue is whether ancient cultures will be free to change on their own terms. *National Geographic, 196*(2), 64–89.

Denham, K. (2003). Linguistics first, then grammar. *Proceedings of the 14th Annual Conference of the Assembly for the Teaching of English Grammar*. State College, PA: Penn State University.

Hale, K. (1992). Language endangerment and the human value of linguistic diversity. *Language, 68*(1), 35–42.

Krauss, M. (1992, August). The language extinction catastrophe just ahead: Should linguists care? *Proceedings of the XX International Congress of Linguists, Oslo, Norway*, 43–46.

Mufwene, S. (2003). Language endangerment: What have pride and prestige got to do with it? In B. D. Joseph, J. DeStefano, N. G. Jacobs, & I. Lehiste (Eds.), *When languages collide: Perspectives on language conflict, language competition, and language coexistence* (pp. 324–345). Columbus: Ohio State University Press.

Pyles, T., & Algeo, J. (1982). *The origins and development of the English language*. New York: Harcourt Brace Jovanovich.

SUGGESTED READING

Crawford, J. http://ourworld.compuserve.com/homepages/JWCRAWFORD

Crawford, J. (1998). Endangered Native American languages: what is to be done and why? Reprinted in T. Ricento & B. Burnaby (Eds.), *Language and politics in the U.S. and Canada: Myths and realities*. Mahwah, NJ: Lawrence Erlbaum Associates.

England, N. (1992). Doing Mayan linguistics in Guatemala. *Language, 68*(1), 29–35.

Fishman, J. (2001). *Can threatened languages be saved? Reversing language shift revisited: A 21st century perspective*. Tonawanda, NY: Multilingual Matters.

Hale, K. (1992). On endangered languages and the safeguarding of diversity. *Language, 68*(1), 1–3.

Hinton, L., & Hale, K. (Eds.). (2001). *The green book of language revitalization in practice*. San Diego: Academic Press.

Hymes, D. (1992). Use All There Is to Use. In B. Swann (Ed.), *On the translation of Native American literatures* (pp. 83–124). Washington, DC: Smithsonian Institution Press.

Jeanne, L. M. (1992). An institutional response to language endangerment: A proposal for a Native American language center. *Language, 68*(1), 24–28.

Krauss, M. (1998). The condition of Native North American languages: The need for realistic assessment and action. *International Journal of the Sociology of Language, 132*, 9–21.

Krauss, M. (1992). The world's languages in crisis. *Language, 68*(1), 4–24.

Ladefoged, P. (1992). Discussion note. Another view of endangered languages. *Language, 68*(1), 809–911.

Mufwene, S. (2001). *The ecology of language evolution.* Cambridge, England: Cambridge University Press.

Tedlock, D. (1983). On the translation of style in oral narrative. In B. Swann (Ed.), *Smoothing the ground: Essays on Native American oral literature* (pp. 57–77). Berkeley: University of California Press.

Watahomigie, L. J., & Yamamoto, A. Y. (1992). Local reactions to perceived language decline. *Language, 68*(1), 10–24.

13

Language as a Reflection of Our Social and Physical World: What Students Can Learn From Metaphor

Janet M. D. Higgins

In order to become aware adults, children need to develop critical strategies. They need to be able to critically evaluate the information presented to them through the media, by politicians, by corporations, and by various interest groups.

Linguistics can contribute to developing such skills through the application of critical discourse studies within the school curriculum. By critical discourse study I mean linguistic analysis directed toward examining the values implicit in linguistic usage (Fowler, 1991). Working with metaphor leads to a direct examination of such values. It leads to an examination of the nature of common, everyday linguistic expressions and the metaphorical concepts which underlie them. Working with students to raise their awareness of metaphorical usage helps develop their critical thinking strategies. Through recognizing that these concepts are indeed not truths but are constructions, that are partial despite being systematic, and that highlight certain aspects of experience but hide others, students can become more critical thinkers.

This chapter provides an outline of some aspects of metaphor and links these to classroom activities that can be used to develop critical thinking.

When we say we are "feeling down," that our minds are not "working properly," we are "running out of time," can't "get our ideas across," or that we are "crazy about someone," we are using expressions which reveal, through the symbolic system of language, the metaphorical basis of our conceptual processes.

The cognitive approach to the nature and organization of the conceptual system "takes the imaginative aspects of reason—metaphor, metonymy, and mental imagery—as central to reason, rather than as a peripheral and inconsequential adjunct to the literal" (Lakoff, 1987, p. xi). Grounded in our bodily and physical experience as human beings, metaphor provides us with the means to think and talk about abstract concepts such as peace, love, argument, time, inflation, happiness, and anger.

Lakoff (1987) described metaphors as mapping domains onto other domains (p. 110). That is, we take the characteristics of objects in our physical and social world and map, or apply, these to abstract concepts. This process enables us to deal with abstract concepts as if they were entities, substances, persons, and containers. We can then refer to, group, categorize, and measure them. We can talk about time, for instance, as if it were a commodity or a journey. We can talk about anger as if it were a substance that boils or is under pressure. We can talk about illness as personified as an enemy to be fought.

Metaphorical thinking is natural and is not bad or good but "simply commonplace and inescapable" (Lakoff, 1991, p. 1). But metaphors are constructed through the selection of parts of experience. Metaphors highlight some parts of our experience and hide others. What we need to become aware of is the selective nature of metaphors. We become so used to a concept being talked about in terms of a certain metaphor that we may take this way as normal, natural and, indeed, even true. Yet by different cultures and in different times, concepts are and have been talked about in very different ways. Exploring the metaphorical bases for common, everyday concepts can help us to become more aware and critical of the dominant thinking in the society in which we live. And more than this, it may help us to find alternative ways to think about the world.

It is surely important for students to learn about their conceptual systems. They should be aware of the metaphorical basis of thought; understand how we use the strategy of metaphor to make abstract concepts into more concrete entities which we can then refer to in various ways. They need to be aware of the dominant metaphors in their society and be able to critically examine the way these metaphors are structured. They need to see how metaphorical concepts are systematic and cohere. They need to understand how metaphors highlight and hide parts of our experience. They need to know how complex metaphors are structured. And they need to be able to identify personification. If we want to develop critically thinking students who can see beyond the surface of political rhetoric, advertising jargon, and cultural stereotyping, this body of knowledge and these skills are important.

I have two interlinked goals for this chapter. One goal is to briefly explore the nature and structure of a number of different kinds of metaphor.

The other is to make suggestions for classroom activities based upon this exploration. The classroom activities are aimed at raising awareness and developing critical thinking. First, students have to recognize what metaphors are and how they are systematic and coherent. They require a methodology for identifying metaphors. Then they need practice in critically examining how metaphors are used in spoken and written language. Going on from there, they can then creatively work on developing alternative metaphors that fit with their own or others' life experiences.

For the basic activities, the method will be to examine expressions used in students' own speech and in that of their peers, family members and in songs, radio, TV, magazines, newspapers, and so forth. For the more advanced tasks, students can use spoken and written texts that are at an appropriate level of interest and language. Texts from course books in other areas of the school curriculum can be an interesting source.

EXPLORATION OF METAPHOR AND CLASSROOM ACTIVITIES

"The essence of metaphor is understanding and experiencing one kind of thing in terms of another" (Lakoff & Johnson, 1980, p. 5), so let's begin with a group of metaphors in which experiences are identified as entities, containers, and substances.

Ontological Metaphors

As human beings we are separated by our environment by a discrete surface. It seems we are partial to boundaries. Boundaries define entities. We tend to give even physical phenomena which are not exactly bounded, discrete boundaries—mountains and corners, for instance. We do the same with activities and emotions. We use the entity *inflation* to identify our experience of rising prices. We can then refer to this entity—"inflation is hurting us"; quantify it—"20% inflation," "too much inflation"; take action against it— "fight inflation," identify aspects of it—"the pace of inflation"; set goals—"we must act to reduce inflation"; assign cause/effect—". . . due to inflation." By conceptualizing this complex social experience metaphorically as an entity we call *inflation*, we can refer to the experience in a variety of ways.

Concepts, once identified as entities, can be further elaborated. The *mind*, for instance, is conceptualized as both a machine and a brittle object. That this is so can be seen by the range of expressions we can draw up for each; we talk about the mind breaking down and snapping, cracking, or shattering.

The activity for students here is to identify abstract concepts that are talked about as entities and then explore how we refer to them, measure them, and so forth. The first activity must help them understand what an abstract concept is, how it differs from a concrete object, and how the abstract concept is "made into" an object through metaphor. Some examples they could begin with are: peace, political power, fame, happiness, and health, but they should then identify their own examples. They then draw up lists of everyday expressions that are used to refer to the concept by themselves, their peers or relatives, or in spoken and written sources. From these they systematically examine the different purposes the metaphors are used for, as exemplified earlier—referring, measuring, identifying aspects, cause/effect, and setting goals.

Further variants of this group of ontological metaphors are the container and substance metaphors. Human beings are containers with surfaces that separate them from the environment. We have an inside and an outside and we apply this principle to not only physical things like rocks, but to abstract concepts like the mind, (*in* my mind/*out of* mind), the visual field (*in* sight/*out of* sight, *coming into* view) and states such as love (I'm *in* love), trouble, shape, and depression. Substances can be viewed as containers; you can jump into the swimming pool—a container object—and also into the water—a container substance. Activities are often characterized metaphorically as substances—running (*a lot of* running).

Emotions are commonly talked of as if they were substances. The body is a container filled with emotions; we are "filled with" excitement or anger for instance. These emotions are conceived of as acting like fluids—we "boil with anger," we "keep cool" and "calm"—and like solids—we "burn" with love or anger or shame. Lakoff and Kövecses (Lakoff, 1987) have looked in detail at the conceptualization of anger, and this would be an interesting case for students to study. Anger can be a destructive emotion in society, with children being among other groups who sadly experience direct effects of it. Uncontrolled anger can affect the ability to carry out a job or maintain stable relationships. Dealing with anger is a task all children have to learn.

The physical manifestations of anger include bodily heat, changes in face color, increased blood pressure, and impaired perception. As anger increases so do the physical effects. If we look at the expressions we use to refer to anger we find that they reflect these physical effects quite clearly: "let off steam," "blow up," "go red in the face." Students can draw up lists of expressions like these referring to anger. One thing they will notice is that the physical effects of anger are used to "stand for" anger. That is, there are groups of common metonymies for anger. These include body heat (a "hothead"), internal pressure ("burst"), redness of the face, agitation ("quivering" with rage) and impaired perception ("see red," can't "see straight").

The basic metaphor for anger is heat—ANGER IS HEAT; the heat of a fluid substance and heat of a solid substance in the container of the body. Looking through their lists of expressions, or adding more to them, students can divide them into groups showing those that refer to elevation; for instance, as anger rises the fluid rises (anger "building up," "rising"), how extreme anger creates steam, how intense anger creates pressure on the container, how when the anger becomes too extreme the container bursts, how then the substance inside comes out of the container, and so forth.

Such an analysis will demonstrate how a wide range of expressions, though apparently random, are systematically linked through the basic metaphor in the system.

One more type of ontological metaphor is personification. Here the entity is characterized as a person. As a person, we can then talk about the entity in terms of human activities. Just as persons differ in character, so too can personified entities. Thus we can talk about an entity being a friend or an enemy, being sly or treacherous, being a mother—life *cheating* us, an experiment *giving birth to* a new idea, an illness *defeating* a person. Students can have a lot of fun identifying personification. In the first task they draw up a list of personified concepts, with examples from their own experience or collected; in the second task they show, through the list of expressions, what kind of personality/ies is/are attributed to the concept. Based on their previous exploration of the emotion of anger, students can complete a further task. They can examine how anger is personified as an opponent, which we "fight," or a dangerous animal ("growling" with rage, "biting my head off").

Orientational Metaphors

The next group are orientational metaphors, in which one metaphorical concept "organizes a whole system of concepts with respect to one another" (Lakoff & Johnson, 1980, p. 14). They are mainly concerned with orientation: up/down, in/out, front/back, on/off, central/peripheral. These metaphors are likely to have arisen from the physical characteristics of our bodies—that we stand upright, when we are ill or asleep we lie down, we have an outer surface that separates us from the surrounding environment—or from the natural environment—when there is more of something in a pile or a container, the level rises—or from our cultural experiences.

Examples we could use with up/down are: HAPPY IS UP; SAD IS DOWN (e.g., I'm feeling *down/low/depressed*), CONSCIOUS IS UP; UNCONSCIOUS IS DOWN (e.g., wake *up*), GOOD IS UP; BAD IS DOWN, RATIONAL IS UP; EMOTIONAL IS DOWN, VIRTUE IS UP; VICE IS DOWN, MORE IS UP; LESS IS DOWN, HEALTH IS UP; ILLNESS IS DOWN.

We can see that there is a consistent system—UP is coherent between happy, healthy, status, more, and so forth. There is, however, a priority among the metaphors. MORE IS UP has priority over GOOD IS UP. Hence, despite the fact that inflation and death rates are negative concepts, we can talk about inflation *rising* and death rates *rising*.

Students can explore these metaphors by taking any pair and drawing up a list of expressions demonstrating them. Another activity is to reverse the pair and see if they can find any expressions for these such as: HAPPY IS DOWN; UNHAPPY IS UP. A further activity is to examine new developments. Subcultures and alternative ways of thinking may appear to reverse the orientations. SMALL IS BEAUTIFUL runs against the MORE IS UP metaphor. However, it is still consistent with GOOD IS UP, since the proponents of this idea believe small is good. Subcultural metaphors may reverse the dominant metaphors but they are likely to cohere with the fundamental values in a society (Lakoff & Johnson, 1980, p. 23). An interesting activity would be for students to look specifically at youth language to see how the metaphorical concepts diverge or cohere with dominant cultural values.

The multicultural classroom provides an excellent opportunity for examining the cultural basis for these metaphors. Students from other cultures can be asked to compare lists of expressions for English and their native language. As Lakoff and Johnson note, other cultures do not necessarily give priority to the UP–DOWN orientation; for some, balance and centrality are more important. Western societies often have the orientation ACTIVE IS UP and PASSIVE IS DOWN as dominant; other cultures reverse this (Lakoff & Johnson, 1980, p. 24). Sharing the results of such analyses is extremely important. Raising awareness of fundamental value differences between cultures as clearly demonstrated in everyday linguistic expressions, should greatly help students from different cultures learn about, and hopefully become more understanding and empathetic of, different values.

Structural Metaphors

Structural metaphors are metaphors in which one concept is metaphorically structured in terms of another. Hence, in ARGUMENT IS WAR, the concept of argument is structured in terms of the activities carried out in conducting war (to *attack* a point, to *defend* a position, to *win/lose* an argument). Metaphors influence the way we perform in daily life. In conducting an argument we perform verbal activities like threatening, attacking, belittling, evading, defending, and bargaining, which originate in fighting and war (Lakoff & Johnson, 1980). In this way, the metaphor structures our actions. Moreover, the activities and linguistic expressions are systematically related to battle and war. Systematicity is an important characteristic of the structure of a metaphor.

Students can choose any metaphorical concept and draw up a list of expressions commonly used to refer to it. Drawing up a list of expressions referring to *ideas*, for instance, students can then be asked to group the expressions into categories. They might come up with groups that illustrate the following metaphors: IDEAS ARE FOOD, IDEAS ARE PEOPLE, IDEAS ARE PLANTS, IDEAS ARE PRODUCTS, IDEAS ARE COMMODITIES, IDEAS ARE FASHIONS (Lakoff & Johnson, 1980, pp. 46–48). This activity demonstrates that we often use a number of metaphors for the same concept. Which ones we select to use at any given time depends on our experience, purpose, and the particulars of the situation. Students can discuss what purposes users may have in mind when they select one metaphor over another. Raising their awareness of the variety or paucity of metaphors used for the same concept and the purposes of their use, can help make students less gullible to political, economic, corporate, or religious rhetoric.

A further activity is to examine a source, such as a teen magazine or a group of songs, for all expressions referring to a selected concept. Choosing *love*, students might find groups of expressions referring to LOVE IS MAGIC, LOVE IS A WAR, LOVE IS A PATIENT, or LOVE IS MADNESS. Students can discuss which metaphors fit with their experience (personally or observed). They can then, more critically, discuss what types of behavior people may exhibit if living by a metaphor such as LOVE IS WAR, LOVE IS A GAME, or LOVE IS A COOPERATIVE UNION.

Case Studies

In this last section I briefly summarize two examples of metaphorical analysis and refer to one other source.

Metaphors of Health and the Body. There is a body of research that has examined the metaphorical concepts underlying discourse on illness (e.g., Sontag, 1989; and Stibbe, 1996, 1997). Stibbe (1997) examined the discourse on cancer among doctors and patients in a corpus collected in a hospice in England, examining not only the metaphorical content but also the effect this had on patients' and doctors' morale. The dominant metaphors in the discourse on cancer were those of warfare and fighting. Aspects highlighted included camaraderie, (bolstering each other up), bonding (patients and staff having close bonds), having knowledge of the enemy (knowing details about the illness), fighting not relaxing, for fighting you need to be strong and be active and not feel sorry for yourself, and when there is still fighting there is still chance for victory. What was hidden was the pain involved in fighting, the possibility of injury, and the prospect of losing. The focus on patients' fighting had positive benefits in that patients were encouraged to take an active part in their own healing. For those for whom the treatment proved a failure, however, the fighting metaphor was disadvantageous; there was a feeling of failure and guilt, time was empty, they had no alternative image for living with a terminal disease. The effort putting into fighting and the pain involved seemed to be in vain because the emphasis was on winning not on any other goals. Stibbe (1997) concluded, "the optimism that the fighting metaphor encourages can turn to anger and disappointment when the doctor tells the patient their cancer is terminal" (p. 61). Metaphorical discourse is not just a way of describing reality. It structures ways of understanding and action. Hence in the discourse of cancer, the selection of the warfare metaphorical concept "affects how doctors and patients think and reason, and hence has an impact on clinical and other health-related decisions" (Stibbe, 1997, p. 65).

In his analysis of the metaphorical concepts used to talk about illness in Chinese culture, Stibbe (1996) noted that there is virtually no talk of warfare in relation to illness in traditional Chinese medicine.

The body is conceived as a network of channels through which vital energy flows to all parts of the body, mind and spirit; the basic metaphor here is THE BODY AS AN ENERGETIC SYSTEM (Stibbe, 1996, p. 178). Illness is when these channels are blocked.

The central metaphor in traditional Chinese medicine is BALANCE. Equilibrium is good health and imbalance bad health. The experiential basis is two pivoted weights, balanced when equal. The metaphorical concepts are the yin and yang. Health is a series of balances, soft–hard, cool–hot, and imbalance is caused by a lack or excess of one or both of the yin/yang elements.

If, as Stibbe (1997) suggested with regard to cancer treatment, the Western metaphor, CURING ILLNESS IS A FIGHT, is unhelpful when the disease becomes terminal, invoking the traditional Chinese metaphor, ILLNESS IS AN IMBALANCE, may be beneficial. Looking at illness through this very different metaphorical lens may lead to finding ways to improve physical and spiritual balance and to improve the patient's quality of life.

These case studies illustrate once again how metaphor highlights and hides parts of experience, and how becoming aware of alternative "ways of looking" can be enriching.

Students can take a concept like illness and examine for themselves the metaphors used to define it. In the multicultural classroom, students can contrast the results of analysis for English and their native language. They can then discuss the possible effects of living and working by that metaphor, and consider alternative metaphors. And finally they can then be given case examples such as those of Stibbe (1996, 1997) with which to compare their findings.

Political Rhetoric. I briefly mention here Lakoff's work on political discourse. He has examined at length the complex of metaphors that have been used to justify the Gulf War (1991). Advanced students might be interested in examining his case study. Newspapers are an excellent source for studying political discourse and the metaphors used in it. An appropriate text can be selected and students can identify the metaphors invoked. They can then discuss alternative ways the arguments could be presented through the use of alternative metaphors.

REFERENCES

Fowler, R. (1991). *Language in the news*. London: Routledge.

Lakoff, G. (1987). *Women, fire and dangerous things. What categories reveal about the mind*. Chicago: The University of Chicago Press.

Lakoff, G. (1991, January). *Metaphor and war: The metaphor system used to justify war in the Gulf*. Mimeo. Paper presented to an audience at Alumni House, University of California, Berkeley.

Lakoff, G., & Johnson, M. (1980). *Metaphors we live by*. Chicago: The University of Chicago Press.

Sontag, S. (1989). *AIDS and its metaphors*. London: Penguin.

Stibbe, A. (1996). The metaphorical construction of illness in Chinese culture. *Journal of Asian Pacific Communication, 7*(3&4), 177–188.

Stibbe, A. (1997). Fighting, warfare and the discourse of cancer. *South African Journal of Linguistics, 15*(2), 65–70.

Suggested Reading

Reddy, M. (1979). The conduit metaphor. In A. Ortony (Ed.), *Metaphor and thought*. Cambridge, England: Cambridge University Press.

Semino, E., & Masci, M. (1996). Politics is football: Metaphor in the discourse of Silvio Berlusconi in Italy. *Discourse & Society, 7*(2), 243–269.

van Teeffelen, T. (1994). Racism and metaphor: The Palestinian-Israeli conflict in popular literature. *Discourse & Society, 5*(3), 381–405.

14

Contrastive Analysis and Codeswitching: How and Why to Use the Vernacular to Teach Standard English

Rebecca S. Wheeler

Teacher education students hold firm convictions about the worth of dialects and their speakers, believing with remarkable consistency that when a student writes or says "I be playing basketball" or "I have two sister and two brother" that student is using "poor English," or "bad grammar," and has "problems with verb agreement" or "doesn't know how to show plurality." Having diagnosed problem and deficiency, educators "correct" the student's writing, showing him or her the "right" way. This is the correctionist, red pen approach to student language. However, linguistics offers a fundamentally different analysis, revealing that the student is not making errors in Standard English but instead is correctly following the language patterns of the home and community. This distinction is crucial to the school classroom.

If the child is not making errors, but is writing and speaking in a systematic language variety, then a different response from the teacher becomes appropriate—a response informed by dialect awareness, drawing on the tools of Contrastive Analysis and codeswitching. From this vantage, the teacher can use techniques of critical thinking to *contrast* the grammatical patterns of the child's language variety (home speech) to the grammatical patterns of school speech, thus making the language contrasts explicit to the child and available to their conscious awareness. As we *add* another linguistic code, Standard English, to the child's linguistic toolbox, the child learns to codeswitch between the language of the home and the language of the school as appropriate to the time, place, audience, and communicative purpose.

CONTRASTIVE ANALYSIS IS A MORE EFFECTIVE
WAY TO TEACH STANDARD ENGLISH

Research in linguistics suggests that Contrastive Analysis is a potent tool for helping students who speak vernacular, or nonstandard, varieties of English more successfully learn Standard English. A study from urban Chicago is particularly revealing. There, Hanni Taylor, a college professor, tested two approaches with her African-American students in English composition. After finding that many of her African-American students were turning in papers with considerable use of vernacular features in their writing, Taylor decided to try an experiment. With one class, she taught English with traditional correctionist techniques, telling students that they were missing this or that letter, or getting the Standard wrong, and showing them how to "correct" it. In the experimental group, she used Contrastive Analysis, "specifically drawing their attention to the points on which Ebonics and Standard English were different" (Rickford, 1999, p. 339). The performance of the two classes was strikingly different.

After 3 months "the *experimental* group showed a 59% reduction in the use of Ebonics [African-American English] features in their SE [Standard English] writing, while the control group, using traditional methods, showed a slight INCREASE (8.5%) in the use of African-American features." Explaining these results, Taylor observed that students "were not aware of the grammatical [AAE] features that interfere" in their Standard English writing (Taylor, 1991, p. 149). So, contrasting the two systems helped students "limit AAE intrusions into their SE usage" (Rickford, 1997).

Such an approach—but focusing on speech rather than writing—has also been demonstrated to be successful with elementary students. Teachers in DeKalb County, Georgia (just outside Atlanta) help young speakers of minority dialects explicitly contrast their home speech with school speech. Thus, when a fifth-grader answers a question with a double negative ("not no more") the teacher prompts the student to code-switch, to which the student replies, "not any more." *The Atlantic Constitution* has reported that in this "Bidialectal Communication" program, the children learn to switch from their home speech to school speech at appropriate times and places, and that "the dialect they might use at home is valuable and 'effective' in that setting, but not for school, for work—or for American Democracy" (Cumming, 1997). This program has been designated a "center of excellence" by the National Council of Teachers of English (Wheeler, 1999).

Kelli Harris-Wright, coordinator for assessment and accountability for DeKalb County public schools, employed a codeswitching model to address "an achievement gap that threatened to widen as DeKalb County's demographic shifted from a majority of white to black students and faced a booming immigrant population" (Lenz, 2003, p. C1). Georgia students showed a "25-point improvement in literacy after just one year of the program" (p. C1).

In sum, as Rickford (1997) reported to the U.S. Senate, "teaching methods which DO take vernacular dialects into account in teaching the standard work better than those which DO NOT." Rickford (1999) referred to the approach as "using the vernacular to teach the standard" (pp. 329–347). (See also Baugh, 1999; Cumming, 1997; Rickford, 1998; Taylor, 1991; Wheeler, 2001, Wheeler & Swords, 2004.)

PRACTICING CONTRASTIVE ANALYSIS

In what follows I provide some examples of how I teach pre-service and in-service teachers to practice Contrastive Analysis in their classrooms.

In response to certain patterns in student writing (such as *My goldfish name is Scaley. Then the dogs was barking at the turkey*—see Figs. 14.1 and 14.2), pre-service and in-service teachers in my classes consistently comment that the writers should "learn English" so that they won't sound "lazy" and "uneducated." The unanimity of response might be understandable were its diagnosis correct. But what's remarkable is that this negative appraisal of student writing is fundamentally flawed, resting as it does on central misunderstandings of the nature of language. Not recognizing the pattern in student performance, teachers have diagnosed error and omission and have attempted to correct accordingly. Yet Christenbury (2000) observed, "telling or teaching students that their language is *wrong* or *bad* is not only damaging, but *false*" (p. 203). Doing so presupposes that only one language form is correct in structure and that that form is "good" in all contexts.

Linguistics gives us the tools to systematically describe language variation (e.g., the variation between home and school speech) and to help children transition back and forth between different language varieties to suit the occasion. Linguistics will enable us to see that language varieties (or usages) follow a regular pattern. This makes all the difference in how we, as educators, respond. If students are choosing a particular pattern of language, and are not making *mistakes* in the Standard English target, then a very different response becomes appropriate in the classroom (Pullum, 1999).

STANDARD AND VERNACULAR LANGUAGE

"Standard" English is often called "good" while "nonstandard" English is considered "bad." But to speak simply in terms of *good* and *bad* seems to imply that our judgment has something to do with the language forms themselves. Nothing could be further from the truth. Such normative judgments reflect not linguistic facts but sociopolitical considerations. Thus, the so-called *standard* is the language variety "associated with middle-class, educated, native speakers of the region" (Wolfram & Schilling-Estes, 1998, p. 284). The public judges this variety as good because they regard its speakers highly, but this judgment has nothing to do with an inherent structural superiority of so-called Standard English. As we see the speakers, so we see their language. (See also Lobeck, chap. 8, this volume.)

Vernaculars are those "varieties of a language which are not classified as standard dialects" (Wolfram & Schilling-Estes, 1998, p. 13). They contain socially stigmatized features such as the so-called English double negative (*I ain't got none*) or irregular verb forms (*I seen it*). The public holds vernaculars in low regard because it typically views their speakers with disdain. The judgment that vernaculars are inadequate reflects sociopolitical considerations and has nothing to do with the grammatical structure of a vernacular.

Finally, speaking of "Standard" English is misleading, implying that only one standard exists. Yet, in American English we see a range of standards, from Formal Standard English (Written Standard English of grammar books, reference works, and the most established mainstream authors), Informal Standard English (a spoken variety defined by the absence of socially stigmatized structures), as well as Regional Standards (the accepted variety of English in a particular geographic area) (Wolfram & Schilling-Estes, 1998).

POSSESSIVE PATTERNS IN STANDARD AND VERNACULAR ENGLISH

After introducing my students to the linguistic definitions of vernacular and Standard English, and to the concepts that difference is not deficit, and that variation is natural, I ask students to offer a neutral description of the language data before them (see Figs. 14.1 and 14.2).

a. My *goldfish name* is Scaley.
b. I go to *Justin house.*
c. The *dog name* is Bear.
d. Did you see the *teacher pen*?
e. *Michael birthday* is in March.

Students often reply, "the writer left off the 's" or the writer "should have added 's," a response presuming only one way exists to signal possession and that the writers of a–e are making omissions and mistakes.

I ask students to look for some pattern that each sentence has in common. After a few moments, someone will observe that the *possessor* precedes the *possessed* noun. We go on to contrast this pattern with the written Standard pattern of possessive formation of *possessor* +'s = *possessed*. Together we make a chart of both varieties that looks like the following:

Possessive Patterns

Variety X   *Variety Y*

My goldfish's name is Scaley.   My goldfish name is Scaley.

I go to Justin's house   I go to Justin House

The dog's name is Bear.   The dog name is Bear.

Did you see the teacher's pen?   Did you see the teacher pen?

What is the rule for possessive in Variety Y (vernacular)?

possessor + possessed = possessive

What is the rule for possessive in Variety X (Standard)?

possessor + 's + possessed = possessive

FIG. 14.1. Possessive patterns across two language varieties.

Through this exercise, we have begun discovering the grammatical rules of one vernacular language as they appear in writing, and have begun the process of Contrastive Analysis that will allow us to more successfully teach written Standard English to vernacular speaking students.

In my education classes, students work with a packet of more than 100 student essays I've collected from local urban elementary and middle school writing, each of which shows one or more vernacular structures. Education students make "grammar translators" like the one in Fig. 14.1, rendering the systematic patterns characteristic of vernacular and Standard English. These tools then become useful for the student as they move into or return to their own public school classrooms.

SUBJECT–VERB AGREEMENT PATTERNS IN STANDARD AND VERNACULAR LANGUAGE

Let's now see how to use Contrastive Analysis to investigate another grammatical pattern frequently found in vernacular writing—subject–verb agreement, as shown here.

a. She *help* people when they are in trouble.

b. My Mom *deserve* a good man like he is.

c. He *play* ball right now.

The conventional, correctionist response to examples a–c assesses the child as "lacking verb agreement." However, subject–verb agreement simply means that form of the verb correlates in a predictable fashion with the form of the subject, reflecting person and number. For example, a regular verb in Standard English takes an '-s' ending with third person singular subjects (*he/she/it—he runs, she runs, the child runs*, etc.), but otherwise, the verb is the unmarked dictionary form, the form that one would see in a dictionary heading (*I run, you run, we run, they run*). Figure 14.2 represents the patterns of two language varieties in a balanced way and allows students to see that a *rule of grammar* is simply a statement of the pattern that the language follows.

Agreement Patterns

Variety X	*Variety Y*
I run	I run
You run	You run
She/he/it run	She/he/it runs
We run	We run
You run	You run
They run	They run

What is the pattern for agreement in Variety X (vernacular)?

All persons and numbers of subject have bare dictionary form of verb.

What is the pattern for agreement in Variety Y (Standard)?

He/she/it (3rd person singular) words pair with verbs showing –s ending.

Remaining persons and numbers of subject show the bare dictionary form

of verb with no ending.

FIG. 14.2. Subject-verb agreement patterns across two language varieties. Adapted from Green (2002), *African American English* (p. 36).

When a teacher finds a student writing *He run with his dog all day*, the teacher can understand that the student is correctly following the agreement patterns of their home language, their vernacular. The teacher can collect samples of student writing to build their own Contrastive Analysis charts for use in mini-lessons relevant to his or her own students. Thus, the appropriate and effective response is for the teacher to help the students do Contrastive Analysis across the two language varieties, the language of the home and school, and then to help the student choose the language code that is appropriate to the time, place, audience, and communicative purpose.

A story from my collaborator, Rachel Swords', classroom proves illustrative (for more discussion, see Ezarik, 2002; Lenz, 2003; Wheeler & Swords, 2004). After implementing Contrastive Analysis and codeswitching in her racially and dialectally diverse urban classroom on the Virginia peninsula, one of Rachel's students, David, began writing a series of stories. Upon reading *Spy Mouse and the Broken Globe*, Rachel was initially concerned—the story continued to show vernacular language features despite the fact that the class had spent considerable time contrasting vernacular and Standard language patterns in writing, and making charts that they display on the classroom walls. Rachel spoke to David about the presence of vernacular language in his work. David explains, "Why Mrs. Swords, I know about the different between informal and formal language, but Spy Mouse doesn't." While Spy Mouse had used vernacular forms in his dialogue, David's Author's Note had been written fully in Standard English. Clearly, David showed a sophisticated awareness of language and voice, notable for any student, but particularly impressive for a third grader.

Codeswitching and knowledge of language varieties also serve children during the writing process. As children construct story narrative, they choose a range of language styles to enhance character. When the task is to produce Standard English, they make editing into a game. After students have completed the substantive content of their reports, children use colored highlighters during the editing process to highlight their successes in matching Standard English patterns. If students find a sentence still in vernacular patterns, they change it to Standard English, and then highlight the sentence. Students are enthusiastic about noting their grammar successes.

Literature is a powerful way to foster student engagement with diverse language varieties and cultures and allows students to discover how language variety is necessary to create authentic voice and literary character. For example, the children's book *Flossie and the Fox* (McKissack, 1986) allows students to role-play, switching between the speaking roles of Flossie who speaks vernacular English, and the Fox, who speaks Standard English. (*Nappy Hair* [Herron, 1998] can also be used for this kind of exercise.) Middle and high school students can discover that sometimes the grammar of their writing matches that of characters in the works of fine authors such as Maya Angelou, Toni Morrison, or Langston Hughes, and they can discuss the rhetorical effects of different language varieties.

CONCLUSION

Basic insights from linguistics tell us that the spoken language varieties children bring to the classroom are not error-filled attempts at Standard English but are instead, regular and rule-governed language systems in their own right. Once teachers recognize that all language varieties are patterned, they can transform classroom practice, moving from correction to contrast. In doing so, teachers move away from the mind-numbing error-hunt, into skills of critical thinking beneficial to *all* students. Recognizing pattern, the teacher leads class discussion as children observe language data, note and describe patterns, and make and test predictions about how various meanings are signaled in different language varieties.

For students who come to school speaking a vernacular language, Contrastive Analysis and codeswitching have been demonstrated to be far more successful than traditional approaches in fostering Standard English mastery and improving performance on standardized tests, which are written in and expect responses in Standard English. Given the pernicious and longstanding achievement gap in American public schools, I believe it is time we turn to approaches that work—the linguistically informed, dialectally aware approaches of codeswitching and Contrastive Analysis.

REFERENCES

Baugh, J. (1999). *Out of the mouths of slaves: African American language and educational malpractice*. Austin: University of Texas Press.

Christenbury, L. (2000). *Making the journey: Being and becoming a teacher of English language arts* (2nd ed.). Portsmouth, NH: Boynton/Cook Heinemann.

Cumming, D. (1997, January 9). A different approach to teaching language. *The Atlanta Constitution*, p. B1.

Ezarik, M. (2002). A time and a place [Electronic version]. *District Administration: K–12 Education Leadership, Curriculum, Technology & Trends*, May, 2002, 38–42. Retrieved July 24, 2002, from http://www.districtadministration.com/page.cfm?id=205

Green, L. (2002). *African American English: A linguistic introduction*. Cambridge, England: Cambridge University Press.

Herron, C. (1998). *Nappy hair*. New York: Random House.

Lenz, K. (2003, February 7). Cracking the Code: The way we speak—Teacher hopes language bridge helps span achievement gap. *The Daily Press*, Newport News, VA.

McKissack, P. (1986). *Flossie & the fox*. New York: Dial Press.

Pullum, G. (1999). African American vernacular English is not standard English with mistakes. In R. S. Wheeler (Ed.), *The workings of language: From prescriptions to perspectives* (pp. 39–58). Westport, CT: Praeger.

Rickford, J. R. (1997, January 22). *Letter to Senator Specter, Chairman, U.S. Senate Subcommittee on Labor, Health and Human Services and Education*. Retrieved December 17, 2002, from http://www.stanford.edu/~rickford/ebonics/SpecterLetter.html

Rickford, J. R. (1998, March 25). *Using the vernacular to teach the standard*. Paper presented at the 1998 California State University Long Beach [CSULB] Conference on Ebonics. Retrieved June 11, 2002, from http://www.stanford.edu/~rickford/papers/VernacularToTeachStandard.html

Rickford, J. R. (1999). Language diversity and academic achievement in the education of African American students: An overview of the issues. In C. Adger, D. Christian, & O. Taylor (Eds.), *Making the connection: Language and academic achievement among African American students* (pp. 1–30). Arlington, VA: Center for Applied Linguistics.

Taylor, H. U. (1991). *Standard English, Black English, and bidialectalism: A controversy*. New York: Peter Lang.

Wheeler, R. S. (1999). Home speech as springboard to school speech: Oakland's commendable work on Ebonics. In R. S. Wheeler (Ed.), *The workings of language: From prescriptions to perspectives* (pp. 59–66). Westport, CT: Praeger.

Wheeler, R. S. (2001). From home speech to school speech: Vantages on reducing the achievement gap in inner city schools. *The Virginia English Bulletin, 51*, 4–16.

Wheeler, R. S., & Swords, R. (2004). Codeswitching: Tools of language and culture transform the dialectally diverse classroom. *Language Arts, 81*(6), 470–480. See also http://users.cnu.edu/~rwheeler/professional/gap.html

Wolfram, W., & Schilling-Estes, N. (1998). *American English*. Oxford, England: Basil Blackwell.

15

English LIVEs: Language In Variation Exercises for Today's Classrooms

Kirk Hazen

The study of dialects offers an innovative and engaging opportunity to learn about language. Ideally, by learning about the variations of language, students will come to understand at least three basic facts: languages change over time; languages always have variation; social identity influences language. From this knowledge, teachers and students can begin to understand that their languages, regardless of the social stigmas stacked against them, are beautifully complex, rule-governed systems. One kind of language variation, dialect diversity, reflects the fact that languages change over time and that people who live in the same geographical area or maintain the same social identity share language norms; in other words, they speak the same dialect. Although dialects differ geographically and socially, no dialect is better linguistically than another. While many people believe there to be only one correct form of a language, what is standard actually varies from dialect to dialect. For example, a common Southern pronunciation of the word *pin* does not differ from the pronunciation of the word *pen*. But because other dialects make a distinction between the vowels of *pin* and *pen* preceding the nasal sound /n/, speakers of those dialects may assess the Southern pronunciation as incorrect instead of simply different. Judging someone's pronunciation (or grammar or word choice) as wrong may lead to unwarranted judgments about their intelligence or ability.

Such dialect discrimination is widely tolerated in the United States, but if people had a better understanding of how language works, they would probably be less inclined to make negative judgments about speakers of different dialects. Knowledge about how language works is fundamental to understanding human communication in the same way that knowledge of biology leads to a better understanding of how the human body works.

Following, we look at dialect diversity and historical language change in more detail, and we explore variation in our own daily speech patterns.

DIFFICULTIES IN TEACHING ABOUT DIALECTS

In teaching about dialects, teachers may encounter certain challenges, including widespread misperceptions about how language works and intolerance toward disempowered groups. Teaching about language variation may mean questioning some widely held views about language, what most people view as "common sense." Although popular views are not always inaccurate, they may need to be re-examined. For example, blood-letting was widely perceived as a cure for certain diseases when the body was believed to have four primary humors that controlled health. Since then, advances in medicine have led people to change their view of blood-letting. In the same way, many people believe that there is a single "thing" that is "Correct" English, but linguistic science shows that what is considered standard in one part of the country is different from what is considered standard in other parts of the country and from what is considered standard in other parts of the world. Debate about what is *correct* can become a moral battlefield where individuals argue the merits of language use and language instruction according to absolute standards of right and wrong.

Attitudes about various dialects may also be influenced by a continuing intolerance toward different ethnic and cultural groups. Teachers with foundational training in linguistics can directly address implicit or institutionalized discrimination that shows up in language (e.g., "the lady doctor" vs. "the doctor") or in attitudes toward language. The extent to which the teacher is responsible for changing attitudes about other people is a difficult question, but an open examination of language attitudes can provide opportunities to discuss broader social issues. One way to begin such a discussion and raise language awareness in productive ways is for the teacher to engage the students in a dialogue about basic assumptions of language. Teachers might start with a series of true-or-false questions, such as the following:

1. Language change is a process of decay.
2. Some dialects are "better" than others.
3. Grammar books used in schools cover most of the rules and processes of English.

4. Writing and speech are essentially the same thing.

5. Children require detailed instruction to learn language.

A class discussion about the falsity of the foregoing assumptions can bring the linguistically informed teacher and the students into an awareness of how there are many common misperceptions about language and of how certain language-related terms, such as *rules, dialect*, and *language*, may be used in different senses. Definitions of such terms can be found in introductory linguistics texts such as that by Fromkin, Rodman, and Hyams (2002).

IDENTIFYING LANGUAGE PATTERNS

Another useful strategy for teaching about dialects involves looking for patterns of language variation. The teacher should guide the students in examining language samples to find linguistic explanations for the patterns they note. A second set of language samples can be used for testing the students' hypotheses. In this manner, the students are following the scientific method: observation (i.e., looking for patterns), hypothesis development, and hypothesis testing. A good way to begin is to examine nonstigmatized data first in which variation is considered perfectly acceptable and correct for your particular group of students, as in the following exercise.

Sounds are either voiced or voiceless. The /t/ in *time* is voiceless, and the /d/ in *dime* is voiced. This vocal fold vibration of the voiced sound /d/ is the only difference between the /t/ and /d/. Ask students to say these words out loud (not whispered) to test this feature (and to try it with voiceless /s/ and voiced /z/ to better feel the vibration of the vocal folds with their hands on their throats). This voicing distinction will help students understand the exercise described below. Also, it should be noted that this exercise is designed for speakers of dialects in which the past tense suffix is pronounced.

The following words are all regular verbs, but the past tense marker <-ed> that is attached to them comes in three different phonetic forms: /t/, /d/, and /ɪd/.

1. hop	5. stretch	9. need
2. score	6. bag	10. side
3. knit	7. bat	11. flex
4. kick	8. explain	12. burn

Have students say each of these verbs aloud in the past tense (e.g., *Yesterday, the rabbit _____ (hop) over the fence*). Note the sound of the past tense marker for each of them. Sort the verbs into the following three columns according to which past tense marker attaches to them. The first three are completed for an example.

/t/	/d/	/ɪd/
_____ hop[t] _____	_____ score[d] _____	_____ knit[ɪd] _____
_____ _____	_____ _____	_____ _____
_____ _____	_____ _____	_____ _____
_____ _____	_____ _____	_____ _____

This exercise helps students see that there is more than one way to pronounce the past tense marker represented by the written form <-ed>, and the choice follows a pattern: If the root word ends in the sounds [t] or [d], the <-ed> ending is pronounced [ɪd]. If the root word ends in a voiced sound other than [d], the <-ed> ending is pronounced [d]; if the root ends in a voiceless sound other than [t], the ending is pronounced [t]. With this background, students can move on to analyze other data involving historical language change and dialect variation.

PUTTING THE PAST UNDER A MICROSCOPE

The past tense in English is not all regular <-ed>s. Some of the most frequent verbs are irregular, such as *to be*. Centuries ago, irregular verbs used to be more common in English, but their numbers have dwindled. Many formerly irregular verbs have been made regular: They now take an *-ed* form, as in *Yesterday, I worked* (the old form was *wrought*). In the following exercise, students explore not only some of the patterns of irregular verbs, but they also investigate how verbs change from irregular to regular.

Each student should take a moment to individually fill out the blanks below. The class as a whole then can participate as the teacher reads the sentences out loud. This format allows the students to recognize different answers the class gives. In a way, this exercise is a survey: The different answers might have social evaluations but remain normal instances of language variation (e.g., *sneaked* vs. *snuck* in G below).

Historical Accidents:

A. *Find*: I don't know where she lost it, but she _____ it by the sofa.
   Mind: I don't *mind* if it makes noise now, but last night I certainly _____ all the noise it made.

B. *Teach*: He was a teacher who *taught*.
   Preach: She was a preacher who _____.

   C. *Sink*: The boat was about to *sink* when he fell off; it eventually ____.
      Think: The professor had a lot to *think* about. Eventually, she ____ about all of it.
      Wink: She thought about *winking* at him, but eventually, he ____ at her.

   D. *Speak*: Yesterday, she ____ to me.
      Leak: Yesterday, the seal on the window ____.
      Seek: For years, I ____ the desires of my heart.

   E. *Steal*: Last week, I ____ second base.
      Kneel: Before I bought the stool, I ____ to weed the garden.
      Feel: Yesterday, he ____ the avocado before buying it.

In this first set of verbs, many students form a consensus on the past tense form. However, some of them may vary: Both *kneeled* and *knelt* are common today. For the following verbs (F–H), widespread variation used to be normal. The three verbs were previously <-ed> forms, but for many U.S. speakers, they are now irregular forms. These verb forms illustrate that what is "correct" varies from area to area and from speaker to speaker. It is impossible to claim that the original form was the best, since for many verbs, the modern, socially approved form is not the original form. Essentially, matters of correctness are contemporary social choices, not linguistic ones.

   Past Fluctuations:

   F. *Catch*? Yesterday, I ____ the ball.
      (*catched* or *caught* on the analogy *teach~taught*?)

   G. *Drag*? Yesterday, I ____ the body to the grave.
      (*dragged* or *drug* on the analog of *dig~dug*?)

   H. *Sneak*? Last time, I ____ into the game.
      (*sneaked* or *snuck* on the analogy of *stick~stuck*?)

For some of these forms, social values may be attached. Some students argue that *snuck* is an ignorant form, only to be contradicted by other students who argue that *sneaked* is much worse. The form *snuck* appears to be predominantly a U.S. form which appears to have come about in the 19th century, but across even the United States, the original form of *sneaked* is still holding its ground. There is no linguistic argument for one over the other (both are fine), and the determination of "correctness" is based on usage and fashion.

   The following verbs (I–K) are currently undergoing variation between an <-ed> form and an irregular form. Some of these verbs have been in variation for centuries.

Fluctuations Today:

I. *Strive*: By the end of the game, she ____ to score a goal.

J. *Hang*: Last month, Texas ____ three men. Last week, I ____ ten pictures.

K. *Dive*: At the pool, she ____ five times in a minute.

The paths of these three verbs to their current variation are most likely different. The verb *strive* is not a commonly used verb today, and students who conjugate it in the past tense in this exercise may be doing it for the first time. As with any unfamiliar or nonce verb, English speakers default to the <-ed> form, *strived*. The verb *hang* has developed two accepted past tense forms after more than 1,000 years of variation: Often, *hung* is used for inanimate objects such as pictures and doors but *hanged* is used for people being executed (e.g., *They hung the picture but hanged the criminal*). The verb *dive* had the form *dived* for a few centuries, and this form is still normal in some English dialects, but for most of the United States, the more normal form is *dove* (created by analogy with *drive/drove*).

Some of the irregular past tense forms only exist today as fossils in other parts of speech. Some adjectives, like the ones in L and M, are the original past forms of the verb, even though the verbs are now formed with <-ed> endings today.

Fossils:

L. *Work*: Last week, I ____ hard to learn to be a blacksmith; I made a *wrought* iron gate.

M. *Melt*: The ice ____ in the spring, and then the volcano threw *molten* lava everywhere.

Students need to realize that this kind of variation over time is normal for language. It also continues today with other irregular verbs.

EXAMINING STIGMATIZED FORMS

The next step in teaching about dialects is to introduce stigmatized data; in other words, a linguistic pattern that is socially evaluated negatively: perhaps a-prefixing from Appalachian English (e.g., "She went a-hunting"), habitual *be* from African American Vernacular English (e.g., "Tuesdays, we be bowling"), or the Southern vowel merger (e.g., pronouncing *pin* and *pen* the same; see Wolfram, Adger, & Christian, 1999). It may be best to choose patterns that students are already familiar with. On the other hand, if teachers want to avoid evoking the students' language prejudices, they may prefer to use examples of language patterns that are not familiar to the students. For example, in N below, although the <-ed> form of the verb *know* is often stigmatized, it is following the same patterns as *work* and *melt*. It is beginning to follow the regular pattern, a trend begun in the 19th century. Students a century from now may look on *knowed* the same as our students look on *worked* and *melted*.

Future Change:

N. *Know*: Before I took the test, I thought I ____ the answer.

Another example comes from African American Vernacular English. AAVE speakers typically devoice (or "drop") the final consonant in a cluster. The past tense [t] or [d] or [ɪd], when attached to a verb that ends in a consonant, will therefore give rise to a cluster: *burn = burn + [d]* that is then reduced to a single consonant. This reduction gives rise to pronunciations such as *miss* and *burn* in the sentences *I burn my hand* or *I miss the bus*, rather than *I burned my hand* and *I missed the bus*. Though patterned and regular, AAVE is often socially viewed as "substandard" or even "incorrect." Analyzing data from this language variety provides an opportunity to discuss how social values that are not based on linguistic fact can be attached to dialects spoken by marginalized groups.

The general pedagogical approach suggested here is to guide the students from considering unstigmatized variation in English to considering stigmatized variation. The goal is to have them understand that stigmatization is a social judgment, not a linguistic matter. Language variation is neither bad nor good. But because discussion of "correct" English is sure to arise, it is best to address that topic directly. The following definitions are useful.

CORRECT ENGLISH DEFINED

In commenting that a segment of talk or writing is good or correct, nonlinguists may have in mind the kinds of criteria for what we would call *Prescriptively Correct English*. Prescriptions can be found in grammar books, books on writing style and usage, and in schools and other institutions. The following assumptions underlie Prescriptively Correct English (PCE):

- Some forms of the language always work better (linguistically) than other forms of the language. For example, "She is not home today" always works better than "She ain't home today."

- English is a single entity that should be protected from corrupting influences that would cause further decay in its form. English has already been corrupted by slovenly use and should be reformed to the standards of yesteryear.

But linguists and others are also concerned with using language in ways that are appropriate for the situation. We can call this *Rhetorically Correct English* (RCE), and it is associated with the following assumptions:

- Some forms of the language work better than others in certain contexts. For example, there are some contexts in which "She ain't home today" will work better than "She is not home today."
- No institutionalized authority exists to govern the production of English. Appropriate language production is governed by the speaker's intention, the audience, and the context (i.e., rhetoric).

Because change is a fundamental feature of human language, the Rhetorically Correct English of any particular context will most likely be different from, but neither inferior nor superior to, the Rhetorically Correct English of yesteryear. Discussing different views of correct English helps students gain a more scientific understanding of language. The goal is for students to see that language variation is fundamental to human language.

CONCLUSION

Language variation is an engaging topic for learning about language. It helps students understand that language has changed and that it continues to be shaped by geographic, historical, social, and ethnic factors. In addition, learning about language variation allows them to examine their views about what constitutes correct English and to evaluate intolerance toward certain varieties of English. Through the study of language variation, they are better able to understand the dynamics of language and its role in society.

ACKNOWLEDGMENTS

This work has been inspired by the work of Walt Wolfram. This chapter is based on an ERIC Digest: Hazen, K. (2001). *Teaching about dialects*. Washington, DC: ERIC Clearinghouse on Languages and Linguistics. http://www.cal.org/ericcll/digest/0104dialects.html. The author would like to thank Carolyn Adger, Erik Thomas, and Jeannie Rennie. Support for research knowledge incorporated in this chapter comes from the Eberly College of Arts and Sciences and the Department of English at West Virginia University.

REFERENCES

Fromkin, V., Rodman, R., & Hyams, N. (2002). *An introduction to language* (7th ed.). Boston: Heinle.
Wolfram, W., Adger, C. T., & Christian, D. (1999). *Dialects in schools and communities*. Mahwah, NJ: Lawrence Erlbaum Associates.

16

Developing Savvy Writers by Analyzing Grammar Rants

Patricia A. Dunn
Kenneth Lindblom

When students write, their writing is not read like that of other writers. Ordinary writers are read for meaning. Student writers are read for correctness. By "ordinary writers," we mean adults who use writing (letters, memos, reports, e-mail, grocery lists, etc.) to carry on the ordinary business of their personal or professional lives. These ordinary writers are assumed credible; student writers, however, are assumed noncredible. Ordinary writers write for particular purposes in which they are invested; student writers write for the purposes of teachers and examiners, and they are usually 1 of 20 or more writers writing the same thing. There is very little—if anything—about the typical school writing scenario which accurately reflects the non-school writing situation. In short, student writers are subjected to artificial and unfair standards to which ordinary writers are not.

Much research over the past several decades supports these claims. Joseph Williams (1981) demonstrated how handbook writers very often break their own rules without ever receiving the consequences student writers are immediately subject to, and that "error" is very often a construction of a reader's institutional power over a writer. When the writer is more powerful than the reader, many fewer errors are noticed. Patrick Hartwell (1985) described how people use the word *grammar* in very different ways, confusing the issue further. He did a meta-analysis of research, concluding that direct teaching of formal grammar does not help students write better, and that more research into this question may not help, because people tend to read such research results through a pro or con grammar lens, making the results almost irrelevant. Very recently, Nancy Mann (2003) and Barbara Schneider (2002) reported research that makes clear that readers treat professional writers and student writers very differently. Mann's research on punctuation suggests that "real punctuation decision rules are very different from and probably much simpler than the rules we teach" (p. 360). Schneider's work seeks to answer why professional writers can use nonstandard quotes with impunity, while the same strategy used by student writers "marks the texts of students as novices" (p. 189).

We hope that this volume on integrating linguistic knowledge into the schools can change conversations in schools and society regarding writing, language, power, and grammar. At stake are student self-esteem and identity, as well as teacher knowledge and theoretical sophistication: that is, having a clear idea why some things are emphasized in teaching and not others. Also at stake is developing a more informed citizenry: more savvy readers and writers, able to not only use language with a heightened consciousness of how their word choice, style, and editing as writers will "play" with particular audiences, but also how the texts they read use language and cultural commonplaces to "play" them as particular readers.

WHAT'S A TEACHER TO DO? DEFINING THE "SAVVY WRITER"

Whereas we have taken up elsewhere the mistreatment student writers regularly receive from their teachers (Dunn & Lindblom, 2003), here we seek to take the next step by discussing what student writers and sympathetic writing teachers can do in the face of unfair and oppressive systems of assessment. Our answer is this: Aim for students to become what we call "savvy writers." Savvy writers are aware of the ways in which they are judged by different audiences. Savvy writers know that some audiences are prejudiced against them, so they write in ways that attend to those prejudices. Savvy writers are aware of different conventions that determine and predetermine how they are read, and they manipulate those conventions toward their own ends. They understand that when they write from a lower position of power to a higher position of power, they must appear to subscribe to the conventions of those powerful readers. Savvy writers also know that the conventions of those more powerful readers are no more "correct" than the conventions that operate in other communities of writers and readers. These writers realize that even though many teachers demand that students write in "Standard English," what counts as "standard" for each teacher is different. Savvy writers are aware that there are many standardized Englishes to choose from, as the different style books available evidence (e.g., APA, MLA, *The Chicago Manual of Style*, etc.), and that not all powerful readers are aware of these many choices. Savvy writers know that powerful readers assume their own correctness and do not take kindly to being corrected themselves. In other words, savvy writers know their place in the pecking order.

There is an argument to be made that school systems already indirectly teach students to be savvy writers. Students ordinarily write for four to seven teachers at the same time, and many of those students are well aware that each of those teachers uses a different set of standards to determine what counts as correct. Some teachers do not even use a consistent set of standards but simply mark papers based on their sense of style at the moment. But we believe this indirect learning is not fair to students. We suggest instead that writing teachers put on the table that there is no such thing as a single, correct English. We suggest immersing students in the controversial aspects of standardized Englishes so that they can develop a savviness regarding the ways in which they are read as student writers. Such savviness will carry over to their non-school writing, the writing in which they are not judged as students. If we simply continue to teach students that there is such a thing as a single, correct English, we continue to perpetuate a myth that is harmful to students and their potential as writers.

As Rebecca Wheeler (2001)[1] and others (Pinker, 1994; Sledd, 1996; Smitherman, 2000) have argued, conversation about language use shouldn't be about "good" and "bad" writing, "correct" or "incorrect" grammar, or "proper" or "improper" English. Wheeler said it should be about appropriateness, being able to judge what tone and style are appropriate in different situations.[2] This is what we're calling savviness. A savvy writer is able to step back from a particular writing task and make informed judgments about who will be reading this piece, the position of the person writing it, the power relationship between them, what the purpose of the task is as well as the available means of addressing that purpose in the particular context.

If, for example, students think there should be more parking spaces available at school, and they want to persuade readers to make more spaces available, they of course need to proofread and copy edit their argument. But first they need to be savvy about who might be able to change that situation, what specific means of persuasion might convince those people, when might be the best time to make the case, where to make it, and who might be in the best position to do so. Certainly editing and proofread-

---

[1]We are grateful to our colleague, Susan Burt, for telling us about Rebecca Wheeler's work.

[2]Rosina Lippi-Green (1997) maintains that "appropriacy arguments" are "schizophrenic" in that they inevitably carry a contradictory message: "appreciate and respect the languages of peripheral communities, but keep them in their place" (p. 109). In other words, the advice to use "appropriate" language for each situation, while better than "proper" or "correct," continues to give students the message that their home language is not "good" enough to be used in academic or formal settings.

ing are critical, but there is much more to writing an effective argument than what gets called "proper grammar."

We think the aim of a writing course should be to produce not "correct" writers (correct for what? doesn't it depend?) but to produce "savvy" writers: a task that is both much more complicated and challenging but also much more able to tap into what students already know about language, power, and life.

A TEACHING STRATEGY FOR DEVELOPING SAVVY WRITERS: ENGAGING STUDENTS IN THE CONTROVERSY

We once taught an English Education major who remarked that she wanted to be an English teacher because she has always enjoyed correcting people's grammar, that it made her feel smarter than other people. This young woman's unsettling honesty prompted us to think about the reasons some people enter the teaching profession and the ways in which their views of language correctness, even when well intentioned, can be quite harmful. Evaluating student writing reminds writing teachers constantly that they have power, and it invites them to use and enjoy that power. And let's face facts. We are not going to change these discriminatory attitudes any time soon. Many people are too invested in them. In fact, in their popular writing textbook Crowley and Hawhee (1999) claimed that "usage rules are the conventions of written English that allow Americans to discriminate against one another" (p. 283).

Rather than accept this fact and teach our students "the rules of correct grammar" (as if such static entities actually existed), we suggest immersing high school writing students in these controversies themselves. Let's help student writers see how writing is judged and upon what those judgments are often based. There are many, many published examples of what we call "grammar rants": highly dramatic, passionately written texts that present students with the perfect opportunity to critically analyze notions of "correctness." In the next section of our chapter, we reference many such pieces and suggest the kinds of analysis that teachers and students can take on together. We believe engaging students—of all levels—in such analysis will not only help them to understand the haphazard ways in which writing is judged, but will also help them develop a savviness regarding their own audiences, purposes, and contexts for their writing. Engaging students in these controversies will also make students more attentive to the ramifications of error and perceived errors. In other words, students will come to understand the ways in which errors that can be pointed out in their writing will hinder their own ability to get what they want in their writing. Many students already have a political and social savvy; our teaching method harnesses that savvy for the benefit of their writing, whether for creative, academic, personal, or professional purposes.

SAMPLE LINGUISTIC ANALYSES OF "GRAMMAR RANTS"

Journalists, teachers, politicians, and many others complain often and in print about the state of the teaching of grammar, spelling, writing, and speaking. Such rants go back as far as ancient Greece and appear frequently to this day in local newspapers. In these artifacts, writers reveal the political, social, and economic assumptions that underpin their views. Linguistic analyses of these rants and the texts about which they are ranting can help teachers and students analyze not only the technical blips in texts that get so many commentators upset, but that analytic work itself is a concrete, specific way to help students avoid those blips most likely to send readers into a tizzy. But more importantly, sociolinguistic and rhetorical analysis, such as we demonstrate here, can help teachers and students analyze the reasons readers get into a tizzy in the first place. We see at least three reasons:

1. Error has a perceived moral component. People who make errors are often thought of as lazy, tasteless, and contemptuous of authority. In his critique of the "folk sentiment" (p. 17) that surrounds common knowledge regarding language, Edwin Battistella (1999) said, "Traditional grammar is also to a great extent a surrogate for traditional values and morality." (p. 16)

2. Error reflects a change in language. Some people see themselves as guardians, knights of the language realm and therefore view new words as interlopers and shifts in usage as attacks on the castle's foundation. Rants against change are often post lapsarian laments, recalling the good old days when presumably everyone used "proper grammar." As any linguist will note, language is an organic entity that changes and grows with a culture; therefore, attempts to stop it are wrongheaded, silly, and doomed to failure. As Rei Noguchi (1991) has shown, readers tend to have the strongest negative reaction to errors that mark "the writer's social status." (p. 24)

3. What counts as error is non-prestigious language. The prestige dialect, that is the dialect of the upper classes, is thought of as "correct." Those who rant against non-prestige dialect use make arbitrary value distinctions between upper-class dialects and lower- or working-class dialects. There is no

linguistic basis for these distinctions, but there are real consequences for those who fail to recognize them.

In the following paragraphs we demonstrate how these assumptions play out in texts we have found. We suggest that students and teachers can use these analyses as models for their own. Here we make only brief references to texts because space in this collection does not allow us to quote at length. We encourage our readers to find the complete texts and analyze them with their students. Suggestions for a "Grammar Rant Archive" may be found in the appendix to this chapter.

In our local newspaper, there is a daily feature called "FunnyFiles," where story snippets are taken from the Associated Press and used for filler inside the front page. In one piece with the headline, "W.Va. Candidates Misspell Party Name" (2003), the lead read, "Spelling isn't a priority for several candidates in city elections." The piece went on to describe how a number of both Republican and Democratic candidates for city elections in Charleston, West Virginia, misspelled their respective parties' names on filing forms. The candidates, when asked about the misspellings, responded variously that they were in a hurry to beat filing deadlines and didn't have time to think about spelling. The journalist who ran the filler seemed to believe that readers would share a chuckle and a bit of head shaking at the idea that people running for city council would write "Democrate" or "Repbulican" on the form. On some level, perhaps some find it mildly amusing. We think, however, this little news story illustrates a common theme in the print media: that a person who misspells something is fair game for ridicule and that the person who discovers the "gaffe" (as it is called in the story) is entitled to some self-righteous giggling. What's not brought out is that the very journalists who are making fun of other people's spelling errors themselves have both electronic spell checkers and paid copy editors to proofread their tee-heeing about the misspellings of others, people who in this case were rushing, on deadline, to fill out by hand their own paperwork involved in participating in public service. Our rant about "FunnyFiles" may itself be called nitpicking, but we think this filler-writer's smug attitude about language represents a typical assumption in American society: "People who make spelling errors are stupid," an assumption that can be quite harmful to students learning to write.

Negative assumptions associated with language use abound. In a rant against Eminem (and basically all rap artists), conservative syndicated columnist Bill O'Reilly (2003) argued against anything he can think of that "demeans our basic values":

> If a working-class or poor child rejects education, does not learn to speak properly, does not respect just authority and does not understand that having babies at age 14 is a ticket to ruin, then that child's life will likely be tragic.

What are the assumptions behind such a statement? What does he mean by "to speak properly," and how is failing to do so equated, by implication, with a "ticket to ruin" and a "tragic" life? Granted, in a hypersensitive society given to hypercorrectness and to making sweeping, unfounded, cruel assumptions about what a person's language use indicates about his or her character, perhaps what O'Reilly means is that not speaking "properly" will cause others to unfairly discriminate against such a speaker. In other words, it's possible O'Reilly means his phrase as a critique of society's ignorance in this regard.

However, there is another, more likely, interpretation of that remark that we think is more consistent with mainstream society's view of language: that "proper" speech is somehow an indicator of being a "better" person: more affluent, more academically educated, and more moral (the really harmful part). We might ask our students: What do you think O'Reilly means by speaking "properly"? From his perspective, who speaks "properly" and who does not? Who gets to define what is deemed "proper"? Whose voice about what is, or is not, "proper" is the loudest and has the biggest platform for proclaiming such a judgment? Is it really "tragic" to speak in a way Bill O'Reilly categorizes as not "proper"? What might it mean that he has put "does not learn to speak properly" in the same string of "tragic" mistakes as not respecting authority, rejecting education, and having a baby at fourteen? Students reading this column, which is, granted, mostly a critique of Eminem's sometimes misogynist, homophobic lyrics, will probably want to get into a debate about the pros and cons of Eminem and/or other rap musicians. However, O'Reilly's casual linking of these purported sins of a hypothetical "working-class or poor child" reveals not only O'Reilly's ignorance of linguistic deconstructions of "proper"—as we've unpacked them above—but also plays to what O'Reilly obviously believes is a shared assumption with his audience: that a failure to speak "properly" is a moral flaw equal to the other behaviors leading, in his view, to a "tragic" life.

Lest readers think O'Reilly's column is atypical of published views of proper/improper, rightness and wrongness, here are some more snippets, representative of this self-righteous lecturing.

The following distress signal is from a web page called "Home School Curriculum Plus" (2002), on a link called "Grammar Basics": "The English language is in serious danger. Lack of proper English grammar education contributes to the downfall of this illustrious language. Don't let your child be part of its demise!" In other words, the authors of this site see "the English language" as something that should not change. Change is "downfall." (See Denham, chap. 12, this volume.) The authors of this site also seem to view grammar as a subject, something to be learned like the alphabet or multiplication tables, and that this memorization of "grammar basics" will somehow lead to "good writing skills." They go further to claim: "A comprehensive understanding of English grammar will help your child understand anything they [*sic*] must read in life; from college text books to tax forms."

As Steven Pinker (1994) pointed out, it is in the nature of language to change. Change is not downfall but dynamics. What teachers need to understand is what a study of linguistics could tell them: languages change. In fact, Pinker has written much about the failure of self-proclaimed "language mavens" such as William Safire to understand this basic feature of language. Pinker takes on Safire's columns, where Safire criticizes what he perceives as alarming breakdowns of the English language. Pinker, however, critiques Safire's criticism itself, arguing that Safire is clinging to older forms of usage, not realizing that language changes and that the average speaker rapidly picks up on this fact:

> The foibles of the language mavens, then, can be blamed on two blind spots: a gross underestimation of the linguistic wherewithal of the common person and an ignorance of the science of the language—not just technical linguistics, but basic knowledge of the constructions and idioms of English, and of how people use them. (p. 26)

Drawing students' attention to how Pinker corrects the "correction" performed by Safire would not only alert them to what language mavens typically prowl for. More importantly, it would help students make linguistically informed decisions concerning which terms to use in what circumstances; that is, are they writing to a "Pinker" or to a "Safire"?

Another rant comes from Peter Kalkavage (1998) in *Education Digest* (in an article condensed from *Basic Education*). First, he says, "The student's train of thinking very often does not make it to the page." We agree. Then he contradicts himself by referring to "the unbreakable bond that exists between writing and thinking." Here he makes the common error of reading a student's sentence as an absolute snapshot of the student's thinking. But our concern here is not Kalkavage's confusion regarding his own thoughts about writing and thinking, but rather his hyperbole regarding the "run-on sentence":

> The infamous "run-on sentence" is a case in point. No other error in writing is more instructive of the unbreakable bond that exists between writing and thinking. In the run-on sentence, the mere juxtaposition of clauses replaces the spelling out of a logical connection. A transition is implied but not expressed. *The run-on sentence is thus the very picture of intellectual hiatus.* (italics added, p. 59)

Leaving out a comma or conjunction or a semicolon equals "intellectual hiatus"? Furthermore, if "a transition is implied," can't most readers simply add the "but" or "and" implicitly as they read? We're not arguing that students shouldn't know how to edit for commas and semicolons. In fact, after students have read Kalkavage's rant about run-ons would be an opportune time to show them some of these reputed villains, show them how to fix them or at least how they can make them less offensive to the run-on bounty hunters, and then ask students their opinions regarding whether a particular run-on is, indeed, proof of "intellectual hiatus" on the writer's part. If yes, why? If no, why do some people think it is? If "run-ons" could be found in published, prize-winning writing (as they are, for example, in Annie Proulx's (1994) Pulitzer Prize-winning novel, *The Shipping News*), those findings would contribute to the savvy-learning opportunities in this lesson. In other words, are some writers pounced upon more than are others for a misplaced comma? Are "run-ons" always defined the same way, for all writers, in all genres? And finally, such a discussion of "run-ons" and the furor they stir might also clear up the misconception among many students that a "run-on" is any sentence more than three lines long.

Here is more hyperbole, this too from *Education Digest*, also condensed from *Basic Education*. David H. Lynn (1993) wrote: "Unless writers understand the crucial distinction between *its* and *it's*, for example, the readers they are writing for will be baffled and tripped and eventually annoyed into giving up altogether" (p. 69). Baffled? Tripped? Granted, Lynn's rant itself demonstrates the annoyance at least one reader feels when encountering an *its/it's* mix-up. However, it is difficult to imagine readers being hopelessly confused by "The dog wagged it's tail" or "Its a nice day."

David Lynn's (1993) scolding regarding *its/it's* is mild compared to Alvin Brown's (1997) campaign to eradicate apostrophes from possessive pronouns. His solution (also, by the way, from *Education Digest*) is worth quoting at length. Keep in mind that Brown is making people aged 17–22 perform the following lesson:

> Possessive pronouns will be the first part of the new material. Even at this present level of education, many students still employ some form of the apostrophe in their writings. Yet, I'm sure every member of the class has been taught countless times that possessive pronouns do not have apostrophes. They just don't remember, so I introduce a memory aid to remedy this woe.

The 5 Po's

> With fanfare I announce the concept of the 5 Po's while printing in large letters this memory aid on the blackboard with accompanying underlining: "Possessive Pronouns Positively Prohibit 'Postrophes." Students then look at all the possessive pronouns listed in their books just to check out this rule. Yes, sure enough, the statement is true; it has no exceptions. *All together, the class loudly chants this slogan as they write it while properly underlining the 5 Po's.*
>
> *Meanwhile, I'm keeping cadence by striking a ruler against the desk as the students speak.* If not by the end of this lesson, then after the next review, each per-

son will forever understand that possessive pronouns omit apostrophes. I
guarantee it. (italics added, p. 68)

Believe it or not, this article was condensed from a 1996 *English Journal*.
Granted, there is no question that Brown is using multisensory strategies,
and we support their intelligent use if they are helping students to learn important concepts or ideas. But how can Brown justify spending his adult
students' class time having them scream this chant while he bangs a ruler
in time against a desk?

Using these rants from Lynn and Brown as artifacts for discussion in a
classroom would not only demonstrate to students something important
about some teachers' reactions to misplaced apostrophes. Certainly, savvy
writers should be aware of this over-the-top reaction to writing *it's* when the
writer means *its* and vice versa. Putting these curious reactions to minor errors on display will draw attention in a dramatic way to the difference between *its* and *it's* and indirectly teach students what all the fuss is about.
More outrage regarding similar errors can be found at a website called The
Apostrophe Protection Society (http://www.apostrophe.fsnet.co.uk/), where
the owners have posted many examples of "real life apostrophe abuse!"[3] Students will no doubt pay more attention to their copyediting of these two
forms (*its* and *it's*) after having read Brown's and Lynn's fumings regarding
them, or having visited that web site. Such a discussion can not only help students proofread for such minor errors. It can do so without humiliating them.
It can also demonstrate the histrionics with which some readers react to
such substitutions. This in turn can move to an inquiry of why.

Here is David Lynn (1993) again, also scolding us for run-ons:

> A run-on sentence (also known as a comma splice) blurs connections and
> breeds confusion. Unless used for deliberate effect, incomplete sentences,
> lacking a subject or predicate, can baffle sense altogether. The mangling of
> apostrophes drives me particularly crazy. That we increasingly see examples
> of these flaws even in *The Economist* and *The New Yorker*, erstwhile guardians
> of editorial law, is certainly no reason to be sanguine and believe that gram-
> matical distinctions no longer matter. (p. 69)

Although Lynn admits, earlier in his rant, that languages do change, this
snippet seems to indicate his disappointment that they do so. Lynn seems
to feel especially betrayed by the institution of *The New Yorker* and its perceived role as guardian of "editorial law." However, an article by Ben
Yagoda (1997) in *The Chronicle of Higher Education*, discusses the role indi-

---

[3]We would like to thank Anne Lobeck and Kristin Denham for pointing us to this site, and for
other good suggestions they made regarding this manuscript.

vidual human beings played in *The New Yorker*'s reputed fussiness regarding commas, restrictive and non-restrictive clauses, and *which* and *that* distinctions. Yagoda, who is writing a history of *The New Yorker*, begins by describing the influence editor Harold Ross (who "was seriously into commas") had at *The New Yorker* from 1925 until 1951. Ross's successor, William Shawn, continued Ross's "comma fixation" by relying heavily on H. W. Fowler's *A Dictionary of Modern English Usage* (1926), called by Yagoda "a charmingly cranky collection of prescriptions and opinions" (p. B9). James Thurber and Saul Bellow both made fun of what they perceived as an obsession at *The New Yorker* regarding prescriptive traditions. Ross's persnickediness was continued after he left by Eleanor Gould Packard, who, Yagoda points out, was the "final copy checker" for every sentence and every word. She had been at *The New Yorker* since the 1940s, and as of the 1997 publication of Yagoda's *Chronicle* piece, was still there. Yagoda argues that it has only been since Tina Brown's editorship that copy-editing traditions began to change. Because the new focus at *The New Yorker* on breaking news has required many last-minute story changes, they have not been able to focus so heavily on "the traditional copy-processing protocol—a highly involved and time-intensive enterprise that bears some similarity to a group of Talmudic scholars' hashing and rehashing some particularly thorny piece of rabbinical law" (p. B9).

What this story about *The New Yorker*'s copy-editing history would do for young writers is to demonstrate how individual human beings in positions of authority have much to do with "editorial law" referred to by the likes of David Lynn. Because people looked to *The New Yorker* as a model, a study of its editorial history would show students how one editor, using one particularly picky handbook, could actually influence changes in comma use that were happening in the editorial world beyond *The New Yorker*. In other words, it would show fallible human beings as arbiters of grammar "law," not a god-like authority passing down grammar commandments. The dramatic exchanges about commas and *which's* and *that's* between these copy-editors and the famous authors writing in the journal through the years would, like the meta-cognitive discussions of run-ons, fragments, and *its/it's* confusions, also draw attention to the usage or punctuation disagreement itself, giving students a more interesting reason to be able to articulate and put into practice one tradition or another regarding these disputed demons.

Grammar rants often show up in advice columns. In a piece entitled "Good Grammar Magic to Her Ears," Dear Abby (Phillips & Phillips, 2002), reprints what she calls "basic grammar rules," and she claims, "we can all use this refresher course." Prior to listing the "rules," she explains that the rules come from a call she put out to her readers for "misuse of words and other irritants" and "pet peeves." Before we even read her list, savvy readers will realize that we are not about to read grammar rules, but rather what some readers have found personally annoying. Personal annoyance is cultural and not logical, as we see from her list, which includes the lay/lie distinction; "between you and me" instead of "between you and I"; "over-use" of words like "basically"; using "myself" instead of "me." None of these irritations result in confusion for readers, nor is there any logical reason why any of what is called "correct" is correct other than cultural convention. Also on the list are pronunciation differences: "nuke-lee-er" is correct and "nuke-you-ler" is wrong; "Feb-bru-ary" is correct and "Feb-yoo-ary" is wrong; "fort" is correct and "for-tay" is wrong; "ask" is right and "ax" is wrong. Pronunciations are culturally specific, based on habit. The man who currently has his finger on our nuclear button, President Bush, routinely says "nuke-you-ler," and that doesn't seem to interfere with his power—in fact, to many it makes the old-money millionaire seem charmingly ordinary, but if a student said "nuke-you-ler" in a speech it would most certainly mean points off. And Abby is herself annoyed that the word "irregardless ... has nosed its way into the dictionary," but Abby doesn't seem to mind that the words "inflammable" and "flammable" are synonyms. Abby's rules are not grammar rules at all, but rather distinctions between a prestige dialect and a working-class dialect. And surprise, surprise: The prestige dialect counts as correct while the working-class dialect is wrong. It won't take students long to see what these "grammar" rules are really based upon.

CONCLUSION

Our allegiance is neither to grammar nor to linguistics, but to students trying to write more effectively: to have the effect on readers that the writers wish to have. Sometimes we have to help students think through what that effect might be, especially if they are given a nondescript, generic writing assignment such as "a research paper" with no other purpose than to "give information." Getting good grades will motivate only some students, and only for a while. Perhaps students are bored by lectures on parts of speech because they know, instinctively, that such nomenclature lessons are not going to help them write better. Perhaps it is the teachers who need to have their teaching revised and edited, and their own nomenclature regarding "correctness" corrected.

For student writers, the stakes are much, much higher and more critical. Their writing, unfortunately, is probably not read by readers truly interested in their descriptions or narrations or arguments but rather by readers who want or need to assess students' content knowledge or proofreading skills. That the stakes are so high for our students means, unfortunately, that they need to be hypersensitive to the idiosyncrasies of their teachers or potential employers, even though the set of idiosyncrasies may change from year to year and from teacher to teacher. As we have seen, readers often erroneously connect the textual features of student writing to the character of the students themselves. Sometimes the reader is hypercritical, a reflection, perhaps, of a need on the part of people in authority to feel superior, to exclude, to close the circle of success, all in the self-righteous name of high standards (without bothering to say higher than what). It may also stem from a basic insecurity regarding readers' own writing, which may itself be so mediocre in this regard that they feel a bit better about themselves by calling attention to the tiniest perceived error in the writing of people over whom they have some authority.

Therefore, it is crucial that we work to make more connections between linguistics and education in order to improve the teaching of writing in the schools. What a study of linguistics can do is to make both teachers and students more sensitive to the particular pet peeves of professional and amateur grammar guardians everywhere, making students more careful shapers of language for each rhetorical situation. More importantly, as savvy language analysts themselves, students especially will become more able to defend their egos against explicit or implicit insults to their intelligence or moral character, made by people with more power, but less knowledge of linguistics.

APPENDIX: AN ANNOTATED ARCHIVE OF GRAMMAR RANTS

• Scanning one's local newspaper for several months should yield plenty of points of departure for critical analysis and grammar-savvy building for students. If pressed for time, however, here are some resources in which the writers are either grousing about grammar themselves or are linguists already foregrounding and critiquing grammar rants.

• In one chapter of *Verbal Hygiene*, Deborah Cameron (1995) examines "the great grammar crusade" that took place in Britain in the late 1980s. By citing numerous newspaper articles at that time, she shows how issues related to grammar became tied to a perceived moral crisis. While the chapter itself ("Dr Syntax and Mrs Grundy") might be interesting reading for seniors or honors students, the background provided there is probably most appropriate for teachers. However, the quoted snippets Cameron includes from British newspapers during that era would be enough to spark discussions about verb tenses, split infinitives, drills in identifying nouns and verbs, and so on. Also in Cameron's book is a section teachers could use in conjunction with the story, mentioned in our essay, of how real people at *The New Yorker* prescribed comma rules as well as "which" and "that" dictates for decades.

Parallel to that story is one Cameron tells about Simon Jenkins, a former editor of *The Times* of London, a man who played a similar role at that publication to the role, mentioned earlier, that "Miss Gould" played at *The New Yorker*: resident curmudgeon who almost single-handedly kept change from happening at their respective publications, which in turn affected society's view of what was acceptable.

• In *English with an Accent*, Rosina Lippi-Green (1997) pulls no punches in her critique of how the news media and educational systems both perpetuate myths about language and teach people how to discriminate against one another through these myths. She uses many examples from language arts textbooks, television specials, advertisements, and research results to show how ideology shapes attitudes under the guise of "clear" language use.

• In the early fall of 2002, there was a flurry of news stories and syndicated columns across the country surrounding the publication of an academic article by linguist M. E. A. Siegel (2002) that appeared in the *Journal of Semantics*. This curious reaction to a technical analysis written for academic linguists is explained by the article's subject of research: the word *like*. By itself, the 71-page journal article would be incomprehensible to almost anyone but linguistics scholars. However, the Temple University news release summarizing it generated some language-related drama because the gist of research attributed to *like* the status of a complex "discourse particle," not simply a filler such as "um" and "y'know." The reaction in the media was predictable: writers railing about the perceived decline of the English language to which they believed *like* was a primary contributor. The rants themselves are dramatic enough, but even more interesting is Siegel's answers in interviews to the predictable questions asked about her research. Here is a clip from a story by Eils Lotozo (2002) in the Albany (New York) *Times Union:*

> And to those who see the rise of *like* as an assault on proper English and a sign of the decline of civilization, Siegel has this reply:
> "People have been saying that about new words for centuries." She cites as evidence the introduction to an early diction of English, compiled in 1755 by Samuel Johnson. "He said he was writing the dictionary to refine the language to grammatical purity because we have to listen to the language of the learned. He mentions all the people who speak wrong, and they are porters, herdsmen and girls.
> "The language mavens always say, 'Oh, they're wrecking the language.' And it's always girls and working people. But languages change because they need to change. There are so many more girls and working people than there are language mavens." (D1+).

Here, Siegel rants refreshingly on the ranters, drawing attention to their prejudices about groups of people to which they do not belong. She casts the "girls and working people" as the real experts on how language changes and the self-proclaimed language mavens as those with the misguided view of the nature of language. *Chicago Tribune* columnist Mary Schmich (2002) also takes up Siegel's research on *like*, but she makes fun of Siegel's work, using "discourse popsicle" for Siegel's technical phrase, "discourse particle." It is interesting to note that Mary Schmich is currently the Illinois Writer of the Year, chosen by the Illinois Association of Teachers of English.

An equally dismissive column was written by columnist Joanna Soto Carabello (2002), writing in the *Athens Banner-Harold*. Carabello calls *like* a "hyperactive simile syndrome" and an "ailment." Having students examine these different views of *like* would both show them how the use of that word will be received by mainstream language guardians. However, it will show them this in a way that will not insult users of *like*, and it will also teach them something about class and gender prejudices in this country.

• In the essay, "Standard English: What it isn't," a chapter in Bex and Watt's *Standard English: The widening debate*, Peter Trudgill (1999) argues that there are many styles available to speakers of Standard English. He says the sentence "The old man was bloody knackered after his long trip" is just as "standard" as "Father was exceedingly fatigued subsequent to his extensive peregrination" or as "Dad was very tired after his lengthy journey" (p. 120). Arguing that these sentences display stylistic differences, not grammatical ones, Trudgill's views and examples would be a good way to problematize what "standard" can mean. The first example is especially interesting for students in the United States, since "bloody" is a swear word in Britain, but not in the United States. That fact alone should help students become more aware of context as arbiter of perceived "correctness," not universal rules. Other sections in the Bex and Watts collection is chock full of possible points of departure.

• Bill Bryson's *Mother Tongue* (1990) is a must-read for any teacher concerned with either enforcing "proper" English or critiquing the notion of such a thing. Students themselves should read Bryson's short Chapter 9, "Good English and Bad," for it outlines the quirkiness of individual preferences in the 1800s in England, and how those idiosyncrasies came down through the years as "rules," which they clearly are not. If the school does not have censorship problems, Bryson's Chapter 14 on "Swearing" would be a hoot for students to read. If teachers are fearful of students reading about "swear words" in school, they might simply pass on to students that "Among the Chinese, to be called a turtle is the worst possible taunt" (p. 214). That nugget, plus numerous other inoffensive ones from that chapter, would show students how discourse practices are not universal but local. Besides being very funny, this chapter also demonstrates people's intense emotional reaction, the world over, to words perceived to be the worst.

• In addition to these texts, an almost endless supply of other grammar rants are easily available. There are many language-related columns by Wil-

liam F. Buckley, Jr., and William Safire available now in collections of their
work or online through easy-to-use search engines. For teachers or students
looking for post-modern grammar rants that simultaneously critique themselves—but still remain grammar rants—there is David Foster Wallace's
(2001) essay in *Harper's Magazine*, "Tense Present: Democracy, English, and
the wars over usage." If teachers of high school or middle school want to
bring their students into the grammar debate as carried out by other teachers, they could let their students peruse the special issues *English Journal*
had on grammar: November, 1996, and January, 2003. Even more interesting
would be a class trip into the library's periodical stacks to see what writers
were saying about grammar in the volumes of *English Journal* at the turn of
the 20th century. Such an excursion would demonstrate to students that language changes, as do views of it.

REFERENCES

Battistella, E. (1999). The persistence of traditional grammar. In R. Wheeler (Ed.), *Language alive
    in the classroom* (pp. 13–21). Westport, CT and London: Praeger.
Bex, T., & Watts, R. J. (1999). *Standard English: The widening debate*. London and New York:
    Routledge.
Brown, A. R. (1997). Correct Grammar can—and must—be taught. *Education Digest, 62*, 65–69.
Bryson, B. (1990). *Mother tongue: English and how it got that way*. New York: Avon.
Cameron, D. (1995). *Verbal hygiene*. London and New York: Routledge.
Carabello, J. S. (2002). Carabello: Assault on English language continues, like, unabated. *Athens
    Banner-Herald (OnlineAthens)*. October 5, 1–3. http:www.onlineathens.com/stories/100602/
    opi_20021006093.shtml
Crowley, S., & Hawhee, D. (1999). *Ancient rhetorics for contemporary students* (2nd ed.). Boston,
    MA: Allyn & Bacon.
Dunn, P. A., & Lindblom, K. (2003). Why revitalize grammar? *English Journal, 92*, 43–50.
Hartwell, P. (1985). Grammar, grammars, and the teaching of grammar. *College English, 47*,
    105–127.
Home School Curriculum Plus. (2002). Grammar basics. http://home-school-curriculum-
    plus.com/Grammar-Basics.html, 1–2.
Kalkavage, P. (1998). Student writing and the trouble with grammar. *Education Digest, 63*, 58–61.
Lippi-Green, R. (1997). *English with an accent: Language, ideology, and discrimination in the United
    States*. London and New York: Routledge.
Lotozo, E. (2002). It was, like, a linguistic revelation. *Times Union* (Albany, NY), D1+.
Lynn, D. H. (1993). Are grammarians antiquarians in an information age? *Education Digest, 59*,
    68–69.
Mann, N. (2003). Point counterpoint: Teaching punctuation as information management. *The
    Journal of the Conference on College Composition and Communication, 54*, 359–393.
Noguchi, R. R. (1991). *Grammar and the teaching of writing: Limits and possibilities*. Urbana, IL: Na-
    tional Council of Teachers of English.
O'Reilly, B. (2003). 'People's Choice' Eminem demeans our basic values. *The Pantagraph*
    (Bloomington, IL), January 19, C4.
Phillips, P., & Phillips, J. (2002). Dear Abby: Good grammar magic to her ears. *The Pantagraph*
    (Bloomington, IL), April 9, D2.

Pinker, S. (1994). Grammar puss. *New Republic, 210,* 19–26.

Proulx, A. (1994). *The shipping news.* New York: Simon & Schuster.

Schneider, B. (2002). Nonstandard quotes: Superimpositions and cultural maps. *The Journal of the Conference on College Composition and Communication, 54,* 188–207.

Schmich, M. (2002). Well, additions to linguistic list are exactly right. *Chicago Tribune* (online edition), http://www.chicagotribune.com/news/columnists/chi0209220283spe22,0,25994. column, 1–2.

Siegel, M. E. A. (2002). *Like:* The discourse particle and semantics. *Journal of Semantics, 19,* 35–71.

Sledd, J. (1996). Grammar for social awareness in time of class warfare. *English Journal, 85,* 59–63.

Smitherman, G. (2000). *Talkin that talk: Language, culture and education in African America.* London and New York: Routledge.

The Apostrophe Protection Society (2003). http://www.apostrophe.fsnet.co.uk/

Trudgill, P. (1999). Standard English: What it isn't. In T. Bex & R. J. Watts (Eds.), *Standard English: The widening debate* (pp. 117–128). London and New York: Routledge.

Wallace, D. F. (2001). Tense present: Democracy, English, and the wars over usage. *Harper's Magazine,* April, 39–58.

W. Va. candidates misspell party name. (2003). *The Pantagraph* (Bloomington, IL). Jan 20, A2.

Wheeler, R. S. (2001/November). *Grammar alive: Discovery learning of grammar in the classroom: Code-switch to success, from home speech to school speech in the public school.* National Council of Teachers of English presentation. Baltimore, MD.

Williams, J. M. (1981). The phenomenology of error. *College Composition and Communication, 32,* 152–68.

Yagoda, B. (1997). Language, commas, and the unmistakable sound, of 'The New Yorker.' *The Chronicle of Higher Education,* October 17, Opinion, B9+.

17

Linguistics as a Tool in Teaching Fiction Writing

Donna Jo Napoli

WHY ENGAGE IN CREATIVE WRITING?

Whether we publish our creative writing or not—that is, whether we write for ourselves only or for strangers, as well—we gain much from creative writing. Creative writing allows us to express ourselves in a fuller range of ways than ordinary conversations and ordinary work-related (or, in the case of students and academics, school-related) writing typically does. Such expression can play a part in helping us to understand the world around us and our reactions to it, because it is often only once we've put something in words that we recognize our own concepts in a coherent way. It is no accident that journal writing has become popular in recent years; many disciplines have recognized the value of engaging in a range of writing types.

There is another practical reason to promote creative writing. Writing is a financially cost-free activity; all you need to do is pick up a pencil. So it is a gift you (the teacher) can give yourself, as well as your students, knowing that all of you can indulge in it and benefit from it your whole lives, regardless of your career paths and economic status.

HOW LINGUISTICS CAN HELP
IN WRITING DIALOGUE

Fiction writing consists of both description and dialogue, where by *dialogue* I mean conversation between two or more characters. In order for fictional dialogue to ring true, it must bear similarities to real dialogue. But in order for fictional dialogue not to bore us to tears, it cannot be a simple mimic of real dialogue. In this chapter we focus on ways to build an effective mapping from real to rendered (i.e., fictional) speech.

Perhaps the best known rule of fiction writing is this: Write what you know about. And, judging from which fiction books appear on *The New York Times* bestseller list, we might add that you should have a plot that is complex, perhaps involving the underdog winning against the odds and/or discovering hidden resources within herself. But just as important as the information in your book and the intricacies of your storyline is the language you use. If it is appropriate to the world of your story, it can give the sense that you, the storyteller, are trustworthy. Why pick up a fiction book if the storyteller isn't trustworthy, after all?

And that brings us to a major difference between fiction and nonfiction. Why do we read each of them? Certainly we read nonfiction for information and enlightenment about a given area. If we want to learn about sharks, for example, we head for the nonfiction books about the sea. But why pick up fiction (unless, of course, you have to because it's been assigned in a class)? I contend we read fiction in order to widen our own understanding of the world and ourselves through the vicarious experiences offered in the story. The best stories allow us to climb inside the protagonist's skin and walk his path, breathe his air, feel his joys and sorrows and fears and shocks and ecstasies. We can't do that if we don't believe the storyteller; it's as simple as that.

There are several factors that go into developing language that is appropriate to the world of your story. Let's start with a story set in the present time, in your hometown, in which the protagonist has pretty much your physical and social characteristics. The best guide to good language for such a story is your own ear. Write a scene with lots of dialogue among people who are a lot like you, then another with lots of internal monologue of a person who is a lot like you. Read them aloud, preferably into a tape recorder. If you stumble over any sentence because of its structure (i.e., if you read it, then stop and have to begin again after you realize it should have been read with a different intonation contour), rewrite that sentence. If anything feels strange or stilted, rewrite it. Keep rewriting until the dialogue rings true to your ear. The task might well be harder than you expected.

What makes a dialogue ring true? Maybe the most important thing is that what the characters say should be believable, given their personalities and situations. Those are things I cannot begin to teach you in an essay like this and that I have doubts that anyone can really teach you (or anyone else). But I do have some advice: Put yourself into each character's shoes and bring everything you know about people and about the world to bear on figuring out how the characters would behave and talk. Some people are complex, some people give the appearance of being relatively straightforward.

So some of your characters should be complex, while others should be relatively straightforward. And so on.

But there are other factors that have a part in making a dialogue ring true or not—linguistic factors—including rhythm, phrasing, choice of lexical items (vocabulary). That's what we'll focus on here. And that's why you need to read your own fiction aloud, to sensitize yourself to the oral nature of dialogue. We are definitely playing a game when we write dialogue; there are many things that happen in spoken language that cannot happen in the same manner on the page. The job is not to reproduce spoken language faithfully, but to play the game so well that no one notices the gulf between the written word and the spoken word. Language in a story should not call attention to itself; it should serve the vicissitudes and the necessities of the storyline; it should be the skeleton that allows the body of the story to walk around.

So let's begin with a question: What are the sorts of things that happen in real conversation that cannot be rendered exactly, that is, with a one-to-one correspondence, on the page? You can imagine them for yourself, but it might be instructive to pull out that tape recorder again and record a spontaneous conversation among three or more people. (Warning: In this situation, you are treating the speakers you record as linguistic informants. Be careful to respect their rights. You must inform them that you have recorded them and get their permission to listen to the tape and use the information you learn from it. If they don't give that permission, you must erase the tape without listening to it. This is all quite tricky, however, since if you tell them ahead of time that you are going to record them, you risk getting self-conscious and unnatural conversation.)

Some of the things you will have noticed are the suprasegmentals, that is, the pitch, intensity, and duration of the sounds. We do not mark the suprasegmentals in our alphabet in English, so it's important for us to discuss how to get across such information in our writing. (Other languages with the same basic alphabet, however, may mark duration, as Latin does on vowels and Italian does on consonants. And pitch can likewise be marked in some languages. However, I know of no language that marks intensity alone, although some mark the combination of intensity, pitch, and duration known as stress.)

Another thing you may have noticed is that the quality of the sounds in a given word may vary from one speaker to another, where by *quality* I mean the technical linguistic definition (not any sort of aesthetic judgment). The vowel in the word *mig* differs from the vowel in the word *mug*—and that difference is called a quality difference. We mark that particular quality difference in those particular words by using a different letter. However, we have a standard spelling for words, even though we have multiple pronunciations for them. So if we want to be faithful to the way a given speaker pronounces words, we need to study effective ways to convey in writing information about quality differences.

A third thing you may have noticed is that speech is not necessarily linear in time. Multiple speakers can speak at once. But writing is, per force, linear. How to present this aspect of speech on the page is a challenge.

The last two things we look at in this chapter are differences in syntax between speakers, and the range of our lexicon (our vocabulary) in conversation and in writing. Unlike the other topics covered in this chapter, these elements of language can easily be rendered in writing. The questions here for dialogue, though, are what effect presenting differences in syntax has, and what effect selecting different elements from our lexicon has.

THE SUPRASEGMENTALS

Three of the things that you might have noticed are that speech can vary in intensity (loudness), duration, and pitch. These three factors are called the suprasegmentals ("supra" because in a sense they are additional factors for any sound segment—so, for example, you can say [a] loudly or softly, slowly or quickly, in a low tone or a high tone). English does not mark the suprasegmentals in our writing system; our alphabet tells us nothing about them.

Our fictional conversations, however, often need to convey the suprasegmentals. The duration and/or intensity of an utterance varies with whether a speaker is hesitant or decisive or excited or drugged, or whether there's an echo, or many other factors. Likewise, the intonation of an utterance varies enormously, sometimes being crucial to the meaning of the utterance. So the suprasegmentals are important elements of how an utterance is delivered. Generally, they can be handled relatively effectively on the written page with description.

The speed or dynamics of delivery, for example, can be handled by simply saying explicitly, "he hesitated" or "he spoke haltingly." But it can also be conveyed by giving other descriptive information, as in the following example, where by the time he utters that final question we know that it is going to be slow and halting:

> He looked where she was looking. He took a maddeningly long time doing anything, answering any questions, Dicey thought. "Do you want to hold it?" (Voigt, 1982, *Dicey's song*, p. 186)

It can also be conveyed by repeating letters to show increased duration and by putting dots between words to show halting speech. In this example, we see the rendering of echoed speech:

Jane's voice echoed back across the black water. "Rub a monkeeee's . . . tumm-mmy . . . with . . . yourrr . . . heaaaaaaaaaa . . ." (Sacher, 1995, *Wayside School gets a little stranger*, p. 122)

A dash within a word can tell us about duration and stress. In the following example a monosyllabic word is pronounced as disyllabic:

"It isn't right, Owl," she said, shaking her head at me. "Their own son."
"Daughter," I corrected gently. Dawn was getting mixed up. The strain was clearly too much for her.
"Wha - at? Daughter!" She turned her gaze from me back to Houle. "That," she said, "is a boy." (Kindl, 1999, *Owl in love*, p. 155)

Dashes or elongated hyphens can also tell us the rhythm with which an overall utterance is delivered. In the next example we get words coming with each bounce on the trampoline:

"Bad—Sam! Bad—Sam!" scolded Lana from the trampoline. (Cleary, 1970, *Runaway Ralph*, p. 125)

Emphatic stress can be handled through italics, as in:

I tell her, "They could be lost forever, don't you *know* that?" (Wolff, 2001, *True believer*, p. 159)

Italics like this, though, are tricky. By doing this, you are directing the reader toward a single delivery of the line in terms of sentential stress pattern. But, in fact, if you go to see different productions of a single play, you will find that different actors deliver the same lines in different ways, particularly with respect to sentential stress patterns. And you might enjoy a surprising interpretation of a certain line by a given actor. In the example I quoted here, I believe the italics were effective—because this book is, in my opinion, written in a kind of prose-poetry. The author has a beautiful command of the rhythm of the lines and is justified in leading the reader. But most of the time I believe that readers should be allowed to supply their own emphatic stress, based on their own interpretation of the text.

In contrast to emphatic stress, which picks out a certain word or phrase for prominence, sometimes an entire utterance has to be delivered a certain way with respect to the complex interaction of all the suprasegmentals in order to be properly delivered in the mind of the readers. Tags before or after a direct quotation can be an effective way of conveying such deliveries. Here's an example:

"Next batter," the ump yelled over at Dad. (Gantos, 2000, *Joey Pigsa loses control*, p. 66)

Here we know the intensity of the overall utterance. Other useful tags in this regard involve words like *whisper, yelp, murmur, shout.* Tags can be efficient ways of showing a speaker's emotions, as in:

"Why," he asked accusingly, "why aren't you drinking your tea?"
"Tin—tin—tin," I stammered. (Patterson, 1980, *Jacob have I loved*, p. 71)

I'd like to insert a warning about tags at this point, because a misuse of them can make for annoying reading. When would you ever use a tag like "she said"? We generally assume that people are simply saying things unless we are told otherwise (that they are whispering or whatever). So adding such a tag does not give us information about intonation or any other aspect of delivery. When would you use a tag like "she asked"? A direct question will typically end in a question mark (although in the earlier example it does not), whose job is precisely to tell us that what was said is a question. That question mark gives information about intonation, then. So if we have a question mark, we don't need the tag to tell us intonation. In many instances, then, such tags are superfluous. But in other instances a tag like these can serve to identify who's speaking. Often, though, we don't have to interrupt the flow of the text with an identificational tag. We can identify the speaker simply by putting other sentences around the quote, sentences that describe the speaker doing things, as in these two examples, one involving a quoted statement and one involving a quoted question:

"You gooseberry, that's Lake Michigan." Gramps kissed his finger and put it against Gram's cheek. (Creech, 1994, *Walk two moons*, p. 37)

You could hear Lorraine upstairs for about five minutes. When she came downstairs, she had this picture in her hands.
"Who's this?" (Zindel, 1968, *The pigman*, p. 62)

Now here's another question for you about tags: When would you use a tag like "she replied" or "she suggested" or "she repeated" or "she offered"? We know that something is a reply or a suggestion or a repeat or an offer just from the context of the quotation. These tags typically do nothing but identify the speaker. Eschew them unless they are doing a job that needs to be done. And if the only job is one of identification of the speaker, opt for the less intrusive *say.*

What do you think of the tag in this example (which I've made up):

"Where are you going next?" she giggled.

Say it aloud and follow the instructions in the tag. Can you giggle as you say that question? I bet not. The character here may have giggled before speaking or after speaking, but she sure did not giggle the entire time she produced the utterance, because that's not how people talk. Don't use tags like this. Please. Make your tags true to how your characters really talk.

FAITHFULNESS TO THE QUALITY OF SOUNDS

Another thing that might have troubled you when listening to real conversation is that you aren't sure how to get across the precise way some vowel or consonant was pronounced. The concern here is for faithfulness to the quality of the sounds in a conversation. At least two distinct types of problems come up in this regard. One is that sometimes noises occur which are not lexical items. The other is that we all have different ways of talking, and our pronunciation is generally the part of the grammar that varies the most in this regard. So in one person's speech the word *dog* will rhyme with the word *fog*, but in another person's speech the word *dog* will rhyme with *rogue*. The vowels in the two pronunciations of *dog* differ in quality—the first is a lax vowel, the second is a tense vowel.

Let's start with noises that aren't part of lexical items. They can simply be described, as in "she burped" or "she made a raspberry at him" or "I heard a loud crack." But an author can also try to convey them through (somewhat) phonetic spelling, as in:

> "O-o-o-uggg." Chris's arm flailed the air, his accusing finger pointed here, no, there; it pointed everywhere. (Raskin, 1968, *The westing game*, p. 29)

Variation in pronunciation offers similar choices. I asked you earlier to write a conversation in which all the characters have a similar sociolinguistic background to your own. The point was to show you that even with this kind of simplifying restriction, writing good dialogue is difficult. Of course, though, much of the time a conversation involves people of different sociolinguistic backgrounds—so the various participants in the dialogue will be using somewhat different grammars. An author can simply state that a certain character has, for example, a New Jersey accent and leave it at that. The reader then can assume the job of trying to imagine how that character sounds or not. (And, of course, a reader from Jersey might be frustrated, wanting to know whether we're talking south Jersey, such as Camden, or a little more north Jersey, such as Trenton, or coastal Jersey, such as Atlantic City, and whether the speaker is upper class or lower class, and so on.) Or the author can state that a certain character is only 2 years old and has babyish speech. Then when quotes are given by that character, the reader is left to imagine what *babyish* entails. In the example that follows, the author gives the quotation in ordinary spelling, but then describes how the character speaks:

> "Up here," the voice says, a faint southern accent softening the words. (Cormier, 1977, *I am the cheese*, p. 146)

Alternatively, the writer can try to guide our pronunciation through creative (somewhat) phonetic spelling, as in:

> "Whaddaya think?" (Spinelli, 1982, *Space station seventh grade*, p. 42)

Here the author is letting us know that we should read the whole conversation in an informal register, applying rules of phonology that belong to fast, casual speech. With this spelling, the author is driving home the easiness of the relationships between the characters.

That can be pushed harder, as in:

> "Lissen now, mates. You lot stay in the ditch an' keep yer heads down. As for you scurvy oarpullers, you don't breathe a word, just follow me an' try to look hard done by, haharr, though that shouldn't be too hard. Mind though, if one of you steps out o' line the crew in the ditch'll deal with ye . . ." (Jacque, 1991, *Mariel of Redwall*, p. 178)

Here many of the words have spelling intended to give us alternative pronunciations to the standard.

In the next example, the author uses ordinary spelling in the quote followed by a description of the character's accent, but then adds examples of the character's particular way of speaking using creative spelling:

> "It's chilly, still," she says, in a small, firm voice when she is close enough to be heard, her hands stuffed down deep inside her raincoat. It is a voice I love. In many ways it was her voice I loved first, the sharpened midwestern vowels, the succinct glaciated syntax: Binton Herbor, himburg, Gren Repids. (Ford, 1986, *The sportswriter*, p. 11)

Examples like these are effective. But caution should be your guide in these cases. No two people speak alike. And you cannot get across the range of quality of sounds that occur in speech without actually using the International Phonetic Alphabet (or some equivalent). But if you did that, you'd be bombarding the reader with too much information (if the reader could understand you at all, that is). All you want to do is give enough information about the sounds so that you can make your point to the reader. What is your point? Will it become important to the reader that a certain character is a non-native speaker of English, for example? Then just a small reminder now and then is enough. And notice that it is a lot easier to understand the written version of a foreigner's speech if you use ordinary spelling but arranged in a foreign syntax—allowing the reader to supply the foreign pronunciation. Creative spelling might just lead to incomprehensibility. Here's a nice example of effectiveness in this regard:

> When it was all over, and Billy's fish was squashing all the other fish in the fish box, Sanji reached out and shook Billy's hand. "How you feel, *haole* boy?"
> "Like something Tomi's dog coughed up."
> Sanji laughed and said, "If was me, I cut the damn line, already." (Salisbury, 1994, *Under the blood-red sun*, p. 60)

The foregoing example raises another issue involving not just sound but meaning, as well. Sometimes speakers will introduce words from other languages into their conversation, like *haole* above. The reader may not know what these words mean or how to pronounce them. You, the writer, must ask yourself why you include those words. If it is just to give a flavor of the time and place (in this example, of the cultural mixing in Hawaii), then it may not be necessary that the reader know either the meaning or the pronunciation of the particular lexical items. If, instead, the meaning of a word is essential to the progress of the story, then you might give it in as unobtrusive a way as possible:

> "He must be the son of a *padrone*, one of the bosses." (Woodruff, 1997, *The orphan of Ellis Island*, p. 34)

The Italian word *padrone* means "boss"—as the author has deftly told us. But we don't need to know how the word is pronounced; it simply doesn't matter to the story. Give only the information necessary to make your story go forward (as this author did). Don't get caught up in complications unless they pay off.

This is true in lots of ways. Consider this example:

> Buhlaire swore right in Aunt Digna's face. (Hamilton, 1991, *Plain city*, p. 87)

Here we don't know the words that were said, and we don't need to know them. We know exactly what we need to know: how they were considered by the protagonist. The author didn't get caught up in details that might have derailed the story.

This is fiction you're writing—not linguistics, and not poetry (or not usually), and not a report of reality. Language is simply the vehicle for the story. Let it be useful, but don't let it take over.

LINEARITY OF WRITING VERSUS NONLINEARITY OF SOUNDS

One of the biggest differences between conversation in the air and its representation on the page is that the first need not be linear in time but the second must be. That is, two or more noises can be coincidental in time—a background noise plus a speaker's voice, for example, or two speakers talking at once—but you cannot superimpose one line of text over another (not if you want the reader to be able to read it, that is). Nevertheless, you have to include these realistic elements in your dialogue if you want your readers' trust.

One way to do it, of course, is to state that everyone is speaking at once and then to give samples of what they said. Another way is to give just a hint of what people say, using dashes to show they didn't finish or they were cut off, as in:

> "You know—" said his mom.
> "Yeah—" said Dave.
> "It's already so late—"
> "Wasting time—"
> "So close to home—"
> "Movers aren't coming 'til tomorrow afternoon—"
> "Make better time—"
> "The boy's exhausted—"
> Asa watched this dialogue pass between them, looking up from the highways of Colorado. (Brooks, 1992, *What hearts*, p. 188)

We can't be sure whether any of the previous dialogue overlapped, but the dashes are suggestive.

That example brings out an important point: In speech we often don't finish our sentences. Sometimes that's because we are interrupted, as in:

> "When the overall man got back in line I said, "Thank you, sir, I really tried to get—" But he popped me in the back of the head, hard, and said, "Next time don't be gone so long." (Curtis, 1999, *Bud, not Buddy*, p. 48)

But even when we're not interrupted, we speak in fragments, particularly if we're answering questions, and we count on context to make our utterances comprehensible.

SYNTACTIC VARIATION

Earlier I warned against trying too hard to be true to the sounds of real speech. At the same time, I stressed the fact that there is a lot of variation in language. You know that very well. When the phone rings and you answer it to a person you've never heard before, you can tell a great deal about that person from hearing just a few words. You can usually tell if it's an elderly person or a small child, a male or a female, someone from around your local area or someone from another area of the country (and depending on your experience, you might be able to guess what that area is), a native speaker of the language or a non-native (and, again, depending on your experience, you might be able to guess at the native language of the person). You can sometimes tell the race of the person, and often whether the person is highly educated or barely educated. You might feel quite sure you know this person is upper class or lower class. And, given the associations we have with certain combinations of geographical area, educational level, and financial–social class, you might even feel like you can guess at the ethnicity or religion of the person.

Your ear is trained. For our purposes in this chapter, it doesn't matter how it got trained, it did. Use that knowledge. If you have a 6-year-old in your story, that person should speak differently from the teen in the story, who should speak differently from the 40-year-old parent, who should speak differently from the 70-year-old grandparent. If there's a child in your story who just moved here from Thailand, that child should speak in a distinct manner, and a different manner from the child who just moved here from Atlanta, Georgia, and so on.

One of the most effective ways to introduce language variation into your text is through exploiting differences in syntax. Consider this example:

> "When you due?" Geneva asks.
> Ma looks at her fingers, her face calculating. "Probably March. I carry long."
> Geneva asks, "You seeing a doctor?"
> Ma looks at the five of us. "I've got plenty experience. Haven't needed a doctor yet. Always use midwives. You wouldn't happen to be a midwife, would you?" (Hesse, 1998, *Just juice*, p. 35)

Here one character, Geneva, omits auxiliary verbs from her questions. This is a syntactic characteristic that makes her distinct from certain other characters in the book. Ma, on the other hand, often omits the subject "I." Again, this syntactic pattern makes us able to recognize her dialogue immediately as belonging to her.

Another difference in syntax between speakers is that some people use fancier language in conversation than others. That is, they use longer sentences, with more embeddings (subordinate clauses). This difference often has no connection to sociolinguistic factors. That is, you can find both well-educated and poorly educated speakers who do this—both upper class and lower class speakers who do this. Instead, this trait is strongly related to personality, and, as such, can be exploited beautifully in fiction to help us understand a character. Consider this passage:

> "Louis, my son," he began in his deep, resonant voice, "this is the day we have long awaited—the day of your return to our sanctuary in the Red Rock Lakes. No one can imagine the extent of our joy or the depth of our emotion at seeing you again, you who have been absent from our midst for so long, in lands we know not of, in pursuits we can only guess at. How good it is to see your contenance again! We hope you have enjoyed good health during your long absence, in lands we know not of, in pursuits we can only guess at—"
>
> "You've said that once already," said his wife. "You're repeating yourself. Louis must be tired after his trip, no matter where he's been or what he's been up to." (White, 1970, *The trumpet of the swan*, pp. 68–69)

The "he" here is a father swan, whose pleasure at making announcements comes across perfectly. Notice how he uses a somewhat archaic phrasing in "in lands we know not of." Putting *not* after the main verb gives an archness that reinforces the overall impression of self-importance. And juxtaposing his exaggerated complexity with the mother swan's simplicity underscores once more.

CHOICES OF WHICH LEXICON TO EMPLOY

The last example also brings out an important point. The father swan uses the lexical items *awaited, midst, countenance*. These are not particularly difficult words. By high school, most native speakers of English in the United States, at least, will know these words. Yet they undoubtedly add to the impression of fanciness in the father swan's speech. Why?

Students, as high schoolers, use thousands of words in their daily interactions. Between talking to friends, older relatives, teachers, employers, coaches, and so on, high school students use a range of words that I've seen estimated at around 8,000 at the very least. That's their speaking lexicon. But their reading lexicon is far larger. It is certainly double that, and might even be as large as 40,000 or 50,000 words. Precise figures are hard to confirm, but the general statement is not: High schoolers command a vast reading lexicon. Words like *countenance* are from that reading lexicon. In fact, such a word is from the reading lexicon of all of us—we simply don't go around talking about people's countenances. When you insert a word from your reading lexicon into a direct quote, it affects the passage. It can make the passage seem fancy, as in the example with the father swan, where we understand him to be making a speech rather than simply having a conversation.

But another effect it can have is to make speech seem old. Many of the words of our grandparents, for example, feel fancy to us, even though they were part of the ordinary, daily lexicon of our grandparents when they were young. So to us, these fancy words get associated with oldness. And this association can be useful to the fiction writer. You might well want to write a story that has language in it that you cannot possibly hear. For example, let's say you set your story in a faraway time and place, as in:

> "Power," Jasper said.
> "I'll match your power act for act."
> "You challenge me?"
> "I challenge you."
> Vetch had dropped down to the ground, and now he came between them, grim of face. "Duels in sorcery are forbidden to us, and well you know it. Let this cease!" (LeGuin, 1968, *A wizard of Earthsea*, p. 57)

None of these words is unfamiliar. Yet by using *challenge* instead of *dare*, *forbidden* instead of *not allowed*, *cease* instead of *stop*—these choices from our reading lexicon inserted into direct quotes—the author impresses on us the distance in time and place between our world and the world of the story.

REFERENCES

Brooks, B. (1992). *What hearts*. New York: HarperCollins.
Cleary, B. (1970). *Runaway Ralph*. New York: William Morrow.
Cormier, R. (1977). *I am the cheese*. New York: Dell.
Creech, S. (1994). *Walk two moons*. New York: Scholastic.
Curtis, C. (1999). *Bud, not Buddy*. New York: Delacorte Press.
Ford, R. (1986). *The sportswriter*. New York: Vintage Books.
Gantos, J. (2000). *Joey Pigza loses control*. New York: Farrar, Straus & Giroux.
Hamilton, V. (1991). *Plain city*. New York: The Blue Sky Press.
Hesse, K. (1998). *Just juice*. New York: Scholastic.
Jacque, B. (1991). *Mariel of Redwall*. New York: Philomel.
Kindl, P. (1993). *Owl in love*. New York: Houghton Mifflin.
LeGuin, U. (1968). *A wizard of Earthsea*. New York: Parnassus.
Patterson, K. (1980). *Jacob have I loved*. New York: HarperCollins.
Raskin, E. (1978). *The westing game*. New York: E. P. Dutton.
Sacher, L. (1995). *Wayside School gets a little stranger*. New York: William Morrow.
Salisbury, G. (1994). *Under the blood-red sun*. New York: Delacorte Press.
Spinelli, J. (1982). *Space station seventh grade*. New York: Little, Brown.
Voigt, C. (1982). *Dicey's song*. New York: Atheneum.
White, E. B. (1970). *The trumpet of the swan*. New York: Harper & Row.
Wolff, V. E. (2001). *True believer*. New York: Atheneum.
Woodruff, E. (1997). *The orphan of Ellis Island*. New York: Scholastic.
Zindel, P. (1968). *The pigman*. New York: Bantam Starfire.

18

Applications of Corpus Linguistics in the English Language Classroom

Tony T. N. Hung

Corpus Linguistics is a branch of language study engaging in the systematic and extensive collection of real language data, both written and spoken, as a basis for linguistic analysis and description. Advances in computer technology in recent decades have made it possible for massive "corpora" or "databanks" of hundreds of millions of words to be collected, and for the data to be tagged and categorized, and retrieved with ease for various purposes.

Language corpora have become such an important tool for linguistic research, and especially for lexicography, that it is almost unthinkable nowadays to produce a dictionary or a descriptive grammar of a language which is not (to some extent at least) corpus-based: see, for example, the *Collins Cobuild Dictionary*, the *Oxford English Dictionary* (2nd ed.), the *Cambridge International English Dictionary*, the *Longman Dictionary of Contemporary English*, and the *Longman Grammar of Spoken and Written English*.

Given the essential nature of language as communication (and not just a formal system), the importance of authentic data from *language use* for research purposes is perhaps too evident to require detailed comment. Biber et al. (1998) provided a helpful introduction to the various uses of corpus linguistics for language research—in particular, for lexicography, grammar, discourse analysis, register variation, and English for Specific Purposes.

The increasing importance of corpus linguistics for practitioners of language research has not, however, been paralleled among practitioners of language teaching. In fact, it would be fair to say that most English language and language arts teachers today are not even aware of what language corpora can do, let alone make use of them in their own teaching. This is perhaps a symptom of a more general lack of interest among K–12 teachers in the findings of modern linguistic research and their potential relevance to language teaching (cf. Hung, 2003). In this chapter, I show how all English language arts and language teachers, including those with little or no background in linguistics, can benefit from the use of language corpora in the teaching of English. I do not refer to its usefulness for linguistic research as such (of the kind mentioned earlier by Biber et al.—see also McEnery & Wilson, 1996; Garside, Leech, & McEnery, 1997; and Sinclair, 1991), but only for English language teaching, particularly the teaching of grammar.

THE "FACTS" OF LANGUAGE

Before anyone can teach a language or teach about a language, they have to know at least the "facts" (i.e., the state of the language *as it is actually used today*). But where are the "facts" of grammar—as opposed to the theories—to be found? There was a time when self-appointed authorities, like the 18th-century grammarian Robert Lowth, used to lay down the law on what was grammatical or ungrammatical in the English language, even when it went against common usage or common sense. Lowth's most famous saying was that "It is not the language but the practice that is at fault"—in other words, the language itself was perfect but the users were not, thus giving the former an independent existence from, and a status above, the latter. Among his many precepts, which have since been repeated *ad nauseam* in countless prescriptive grammar books, are the following:

1. Don't split infinitives (e.g., "to constantly maintain that . . .").
2. Don't end sentences with prepositions (e.g., "This is the kind of nonsense I will not put up with"—a famous example which Sir Winston Churchill once parodied as "This is the kind of nonsense up with which I will not put").
3. Use the nominative form of pronouns (e.g., *I* or *he* rather than *me* or *him*) in *It was I/he* and *She is taller than I/he*, and so forth.

It seemed to matter little to prescriptive grammarians that most people then and now actually said or wrote "It was *him*" and "She is taller than *me*" and "You are someone I can count *on*," and so on, rather than the arbitrary, stilted forms that they advocated: After all, the grammar itself was supposed to be perfect, and the users to be corrupt or sloppy. We have, thankfully, come a long way since then. One of the most important lessons of modern linguistics in the 20th century was that the grammar of a language resides not in grammar books but in the *minds* of its *living speakers* (as reflected in their use of the language), and it is these speakers collectively who are the ultimate "authority" for the current state of the language. Regardless of what any grammar book may say, if the majority of educated speakers in the present day end sentences with prepositions or use *who* instead of *whom*, then that usage becomes "grammatical" and "acceptable" in standard English. This also accords with another basic tenet of modern linguistics, which is that all living languages are in a constant state of *change*—in its phonology, syntax, vocabulary, and discourse. It follows therefore that there are no "pure" or "original" forms of a language, only *early* or *later* forms, and whatever grammarians put forward as "correct" or "acceptable" are (at best) only correct or acceptable for a *particular point in time*, and not for *all time*.

Seen in this light, the importance of language corpora for teachers is evident: They provide readily accessible, comprehensive and up-to-date sources of data on the *current* state of the language, in all of its aspects (syntax, vocabulary, phonology, discourse). Here, right at their fingertips, is the concrete evidence that teachers and students will need to show how a particular word, expression, collocation, or grammatical construction in English is used by its educated users today, as recorded in extensive corpora of hundreds of millions of words gathered from contemporary sources such as newspapers, magazines, books, and radio and TV broadcasts. No longer will teachers and students have to rely on the dubious claims of centuries of prescriptive grammarians, whose main "authorities" were the age-old precepts of Latin grammar, older forms of English, and arbitrary conventions.

Take for example the use of interrogative *who* and *whom*. Most prescriptive grammars would tell you to use *whom* when the pronoun functions as the object in the clause (e.g., "Whom did you see?", "Whom did you invite to the party?", etc.). But for several decades now, increasing numbers of users of English have (understandably) shown a marked preference for *who* ("Who did you see?", "Who did you invite to the party?"). The trend alarmed even someone like H. W. Fowler, who was normally the most level-headed of prescriptivists: Notice the tone and choice of words in this entry from his *Modern English Usage* (first published in 1926, and still in print in a revised edition):

> This colloquialism [*who*] is indeed so common that it is *invading* printed matter. . . . But *who*'s *invasion* of the province of *whom* has not gone so far in . . . , and we may reasonably suspect such sentences . . . to be due to *carelessness* rather than a splendid *defiance of grammar*. [italics added]

"A splendid defiance of grammar"—as if grammar had an independent existence from, and authority over, the actual users of the language! We have no statistics on the relative frequency of *who* and *whom* in Fowler's time, but now we do. Here is a table from the *Longman Grammar of Spoken and Written English* (Biber et al., 1999, p. 214), which is based on an extensive corpus of spoken and written data:

Interrogative *who* and *whom*

[Number of tokens per million words in the Longman Corpus]

	who	*whom*
Conversation	1,000+	0
Fiction	350+	< 25
Newspapers	150+	< 25
Academic writing	50+	< 25

The foregoing figures show that the use of interrogative *whom* has virtually disappeared from conversational English, and that its occurrence in written English is very negligible and far below that of *who*, even in academic writing. (It would not be too far-fetched to predict that it will disappear completely from English usage in the not too distant future.) When the discerning teacher combines these facts of modern English with the common-sense observation that the use of *who* instead of *whom* is both simpler and more symmetrical (none of the other interrogative pronouns—*what, which,* etc.—exhibit any distinction between the nominative and accusative forms), there seems to be little justification for continuing to teach the use of *whom* as the "correct" form in interrogative contexts, regardless of what prescriptive grammars may have said. At best, teachers may want to say that it represents an old-fashioned, ultra-formal usage which is becoming increasingly rare.

LANGUAGE CORPORA AS A "WINDOW" ON MODERN USAGE

A corpus-based grammar like the *Longman Grammar of Spoken and Written English* is a convenient tool for looking up facts such as the above on the use of *who* and *whom*. But for the most comprehensive and systematic access to modern-day language data, teachers will need ready access to one or more of a number of large corpora available via the Internet today (usually by paid subscription), such as the Bank of English (Collins Cobuild), British National Corpus, International Corpus of English, Brown Corpus (for American English), Wellington Corpus (for New Zealand English), and so on. (See the References section for their respective Web sites.) The Bank of English corpus, for instance, contains more than 450 million words, and is constantly being expanded and updated; the data are taken from various written and spoken sources over the past 10 years, from Britain, America, and Australia, and are therefore reasonably comprehensive and international in character.

In the rest of this section, I provide a number of examples from the Bank of English to illustrate what teachers can learn from language corpora about the grammar of the English language today, which they might not do from a conventional textbook. But first, a general observation. One of the most striking things that one notices when engaging with real language data is the fact that there is much more **variation** in a language like English than most teachers would care to admit or allow. I am not referring to learners' errors, but to Standard English as produced by educated users, and appearing in newspapers, books, and broadcasts. Teachers ought to be fully aware of the existence of variation in any living language (in matters of pronunciation, vocabulary, as well as syntax), and to pass this on to their students, instead of giving them the false impression that language is monolithic and that there is only one correct form for everything and one correct answer to every question. Teachers have often voiced their concern that recognizing or "allowing" variations would further "confuse" the students. I believe that the exact reverse is true. If students are told that there is only one correct form (e.g., "*Whom* did you meet," "This is no different *from* that," "There were *fewer* people than I expected") but when they step out of the classroom into the real world, they constantly encounter alternative forms (e.g., "*Who* did you meet," "This is no different *than* that," "There were *less* people than I expected"), *then* they will be truly confused. An enlightened acceptance of variation—not of the "anything goes" mentality but of genuinely attested variants which a corpus of real language data can reveal—is a much sounder approach to teaching a living language than artificial conformity.

Example 1: *syllabuses* Versus *syllabi*

At the simplest and lowest level, language corpora allow us to check on the relative distribution of morphological variants in the English of today. Take the plural form of the word *syllabus*, for which two variants are given in most dictionaries (i.e., *syllabi* and *syllabuses*). Which is the preferred form among English users today? A quick check on the occurrences of both forms in the Bank of English shows the following number of tokens:

syllabuses: 29   *syllabi:* 1

Evidently the form *syllabuses* is heavily favored by present-day users over *syllabi*. Given this fact, and the fact that *syllabuses* is regular and therefore much easier to learn, there is every reason to give it higher priority than *syllabi*.

Example 2: *if I were* Versus *if I was*

Moving on to a syntactic structure, let us take another irregular form, *if I were*, which is one of the very few surviving forms of what used to be called the "subjunctive" in English. What about the regular form, *if I was*? One finds the following number of tokens for each form in the Bank of English:

> *if I were:* 345   *if I was:* 647

A cursory examination of the data shows that the great majority of the *if I was* tokens (over 75%) are used in the "subjunctive" sense, as opposed to the simple past tense use. Even after making those allowances, the data still show that *if I was* is now more frequently used than *if I were* in the subjunctive sense, and though the former may be more common in speech, the data come from both spoken and written English. I am not saying that teachers should not teach *if I were*, but if our students use *if I was*, I do not think they should be faulted, or else over half of English users today should also be faulted.

Example 3: *less* + Plural Noun

In most traditional grammars, the quantifier *less* is supposed to apply to singular mass nouns, as in *less money, less time*, and *fewer* to plural count nouns, as in *fewer people, fewer books*, etc. It is interesting to note, however, that *less* has begun to gain currency with plural count nouns as well as singular mass nouns. The Bank of English gives no less than 153 tokens of this use:

He says there are **less teachers** to choose from when jobs
in the trees scales down—because **less leaves** are being eaten and broken—
presumably because there were **less parasites** around to be transmitted
media of today where they're taking **less chances** and basically every film is
back into the state in return for **less expenditures** in attempting to try to
I think you find less and **less people** who will support things.
I did expect more food and **less people**. That I expected would be
It's better because you get **less ways** of getting stuck up or
spending less and therefore paying **less taxes** on income and property. So
This translates into **less benefits** or higher premiums.
these companies with 20 or **less employees** typically are paying low
Fewer people working, you've got **less taxes**. Fewer people working, you

and therefore they had **less calories** and fat, when in fact, the
What I want to do is give them **less taxes**, less regulation and less
This would mean even **less resources** available to schools.
afraid that later Koen will have **less opportunities** in life because of his
to the consultants, would produce **less accidents** because fewer pedestrians
scrip was weak, J.B Were could hold **less shares** back for its own clients.
by advisers which will result in **less funds** flowing into BT in the short
Mr Fitzgerald said. Less and **less people** are taking them up, and I
to supervision. "It results in **less people** in prisons," he said. All
Well, there's less and **less people** in the country. In the
usually get the same model with two **less doors**. We are offering them a real
country music's Mike Flowers, **less mavericks** and more mimics. They
and would cause **less problems** for the people of Virginia
Everything's just the same except **less people** are going to watch it. By
they might have had **less profits**, but their customers would
for next season. There will be **less clubs** in the Premier League by then
Lomu, 20, would probably have had **less games** than Matt Le Tissier has
In that way we would risk **less casualties** if they have grenades."
your whole attention and to give them **less results** in errors or
etc. etc.

Although it is true that about 400 tokens of *fewer* + plural nouns are also given in the corpus, the point remains that *less* is no longer "substandard," but is gaining currency among educated users today. Personally, I have no doubt that it will displace *fewer* completely in the not too distant future, if for no other reason than that it is both simpler and more symmetrical, given that the opposite of *less* is *more*, which applies equally to both kinds of nouns (i.e., *more people, more money*, and so on).

Example 4: *everyone* + Singular or Plural Pronoun

Mathematical logic is often invoked to settle arguments over grammar and usage—for example, a sentence like "I didn't say nothing" is said to mean "I said something" because (mathematically) two negatives supposedly make a positive, in contrast to its obvious intended meaning where the double negation serves to *reinforce* the negative meaning. But natural human language is not mathematics. A good example of how linguistic usage overrides mathematical logic is the use of a plural pronoun like *they, them*, or *their* to refer to the singular pronoun *everyone* or *everybody*. This practice has become increasingly common over the past 20 years or so, as a strategy for avoiding the use of the sexist pronouns *he, him, his, himself* to refer to *everyone/everybody*, or the unbearably clumsy *he or she, him or her, his or her, himself or herself*, etc. To more and more people, the use of the plural *they, them, their, themselves* seems like the most expedient and sensible solution to the problem. The following data consist of the first 20 entries from the Bank of English involving *everyone* followed by a pronoun. It shows that plural pronouns are preferred to singular in the majority of cases involving *everyone*. It is no use invoking mathematical logic (as some teachers do) and saying that there is a mismatch between singular and plural. The users of the language have declared their preference.

Ray suggests that everyone must ask **themselves** one central

it offers a chance for everyone to pull **themselves** together after

versus the British of course, everyone is out for *himself* in this game of

told her it would be a while. 'Is everyone behaving *herself*? And him?

The navy should destroy everyone who revealed *himself* as a traitor.

he discovered, was a business. Everyone was out to enrich *himself*, and

all that bullshit that everyone puts **themselves** through in order

and that everyone in Yugoslavia is arming *himself* as

but the other did not. For everyone who exalts *himself* shall be

Not only did everyone enjoy **themselves**, but over & dollar;

hand round the sauce in a bowl for everyone to help **themselves**.

why doesn't everyone go out and buy **themselves** a cheap

creating more hurt than good. Everyone must think for **themselves**, not

and everyone is falling over **themselves** to pay &

backer giving half that amount, everyone would be falling over **themselves**

has been watching everyone training and enjoying **themselves**

I thought we'd get a draw. Now everyone must pick **themselves** up.

She had little ways of making everyone feel better about **themselves**. If

I have been at the club. Everyone is enjoying **themselves**—including

Arthur makes the arrangements and everyone enjoys **themselves**.

Example 5A: *none* + Singular Verb

Still on the subject of number, a good deal of argument has been wasted on things like whether the pronoun *none* is singular or plural. A quick check in any modern corpus would show that users of English treat it as both, and there do not seem to be any identifiable variables that condition the choice of one or the other, as evidenced by the following entries from the Bank of English.

even-handed film. None of his characters **is** truly heinous—

would be highly improbable and none of the crew **is** implicated, says the

At their own request, none of the girls **is** being identified. But
supermodels like Naomi Campbell—none of the stars **is** black. The new
and make sure that none of my colleagues **is** gullible enough
composer Judith Weir. None of our composers **is** as adept as
A decade later, of course, none of our critics **is** volunteering to
in the next few years. None of these companies **is** wholly focused
On the present showing, none of those conditions **is** likely to be
the park itself is small and none of the buildings **is** unduly grand.
about 40 of the time. Likewise, none of these securities **is** subject to
and cross-check meaning. None of these activities **is** prerequisite
to be built at the airport. None of the streets **is** named on the map
Ravel's Bolero or Nutcracker but none of the composers **is** likely to be

Example 5B: *none* + Plural Verb

smuggling the food in on mules, and none of the men **are** starving. Despite
Well, at the moment, none of these organizations **are** doing
has been affected by a virus. None of her runners **are** likely to be
through their individuality. None of mine **are** like that. We've only
lay clients with a service second to none and its members **are** justifiably
in exactly the same way. None of my friends **are** girlie types
However, none of these symptoms **are** very specific
I'm beginning to be afraid, because none of my feelings **are** coming back.
a lover, a hunter, a fighter, and none of those instincts **are** given much
who are in need," she said. None of the proposals **are** definite just
some of whom would be Australians, none of whom **are** responsible for the
genre, isn't it strange that none of the above **are** fashions for men?
jobs unpaid. Clach made it clear none of their players **are** guilty of
with closure due to lack of cash. None of the staff **are** paid so the
be entitled to top billing. But none of the teams **are** likely to be
But they're not all on a manhunt. None of the girls **are** married, and only

Teachers who are aware of such facts of usage should be open-minded
enough to accept both from their students, rather than arbitrarily insisting
on one or the other.

Example 6A: *recommend that* + Finite Verb Form

A final example comes from another area of grammar which has been undergoing change. In traditional grammars, the verb form which follows such
verbs as *recommend, suggest*, etc. is supposed to be in the "subjunctive"

(e.g., "I recommend/suggest that she *return* the money immediately"), which in this case is identical to the nonfinite, uninflected form of the verb. However, the regular inflected form is now gaining acceptance, such that in the Bank of English there are about as many tokens of the inflected and the subjunctive forms. For example:

Mr Chapman would not recommend that Charles **puts** away his polo
substantial bonuses, I recommend that she **pays** pound 150 a month
Greater Manchester, which will recommend that Britain **does** not set up an
of Defence is today expected to recommend that Britain **joins** France and
non-binding resolution which would recommend that the President **does** not
Perez de Cuellar, is to recommend that the UN **adopts** sweeping new
Markmen's parades. We'd recommend that everyone **visits** the flea

Example 6B: *recommend that* + Nonfinite Verb Form ("Subjunctive")

500 billion target, he would recommend that the president **reject** the
Shamir has said he will recommend that his country **participate** in
we're not in a position to recommend that anybody **take** anything.
Wren says he, too, isn't ready to recommend that everyone **take** vitamin E
asked me whether or not I would recommend that she **start** using an anti-
as other regions. We recommend that the woman simply **incorporate**
particular family. Some theorists recommend that the therapist **assess**
urged Justice Ambrose to recommend that the Crown **pay** all parties'

All the examples given underline the importance for teachers to have constant access to extensive and systematic collections of real language data, to check on any aspects of modern English grammar and usage, and to update their own knowledge of present-day English and keep track of the changes that have been taking place in recent years. Corpus linguistics and modern surveys of grammatical usage are an essential source of information which helps teachers to decide on what is current and what is outdated in teaching the grammar and lexis of the language.

LANGUAGE CORPORA AS A RESOURCE FOR DESIGNING LANGUAGE-LEARNING TASKS

The main contribution of corpus linguistics to English language teaching (as opposed to linguistic research) is thus to provide the teacher with crucial evidence for the state of the language as it is used today. But corpus linguistics can also serve as an almost inexhaustible resource for teachers in constructing language-learning tasks. The readily accessible data will not only save teachers the time and trouble of making up their own sentences and texts, but have the important advantage of being *authentic* and up-to-date examples of language use.

There are various ways in which corpus data can be adapted for use in the classroom. For example, data on the use of a particularly difficult or unusual grammatical construction (such as "it is time that . . .") can first be presented to students in such a way as to help them notice the special features of the construction. A small sample of data such as the following would suffice for purposes of getting students to come up with their own generalizations about the special linguistic features entailed by this construction:

Example 7: *it is time that . . .*

> solution. Jaffe: I think it is time that voters **took** responsibility for
> school books. It is time that books taught at school **were**
> a minimum income in old age". It is time that Mr Smith **apologised** for
> of the European game. It is time that it **came** down from the clouds.
> sub-standard performance. It is time that comfort zone **was** removed and
> be in a tight spot. But maybe it is time that you **were** forced into a position
> of technical change, and it is time that sociologists again **attended** to
> tend to be too sweet, then it is time that you **discovered** just how good
> for good reading, but maybe it is time that one airline **learned** its lesson

From the foregoing data, most students will probably arrive at the generalization that the construction "it is time that . . ." entails the use of the past tense form of the verb in the dependent clause that follows. In this way, they can learn to discover grammatical rules inductively, rather than being told explicitly and without exercising any mental effort. Once students are used to this type of linguistic analysis, they can be taught to look up and analyze particular words or grammatical constructions in the data bank by themselves (assuming that the school has a subscription to the data bank that permits multiple users).

As a follow-up to analytic tasks such as the above, students can be given further sentences extracted from the corpus where they are asked to fill in the blank with the appropriate form of the verb given in parentheses:

Exercise

Fill in each of the blanks with the appropriate form of the verb in parentheses:

1. I think it is time that voters _____ (*take*) responsibility for their choices.

2. It is time that Mr. Smith ____ (*apologize*) for his behavior.

3. It is time that you ____ (*discover*) just how good you really are.

4. Maybe it is time that airlines ____ (*learn*) their lesson.

CONCLUSION

This chapter has provided some indications and examples of the ways in which language corpora can help teachers to update and expand their knowledge of the facts of modern English grammar and usage, and to construct language-learning materials which are authentic and which raise the students' consciousness to specific features of English grammar. In conclusion, it would be timely to remind ourselves that, however useful it may be, corpus linguistics is (when all is said and done) only a *tool*, and that ultimately it is the teacher's own linguistic sense, knowledge, and experience which will determine how wisely and productively this tool is used in the teaching of a language.

REFERENCES

Bank of English Web site: http://www.cobuild.collins.co.uk/boe_info.html

Biber, D., Conrad, S., & Reppen, R. (1998). *Corpus linguistics: Investigating language structure and use.* Cambridge, England: Cambridge University Press.

Biber, D., Johansson, S., Leech, G., Conrad, S., & Finegan, E. (1999). *Longman grammar of spoken and written English.* Harlow: Longman.

British National Corpus Web site: http://www.hcu.ox.ac.uk/BNC/index.html

Brown Corpus Web site: http://www.hd.uib.no/icame/brown/bcm.html

Cambridge International Dictionary of English. (1995). Cambridge, England: Cambridge University Press.

Fowler, H. W. (1965). *Modern English usage* (2nd ed., revised E. Gowers). Oxford, England: Oxford University Press.

Garside, R., Leech, G., & McEnery, A. (Eds.). (1997). *Corpus annotation.* Harlow: Longman.

Hung, T. T. N. (2003). How linguistics can contribute to the teaching of grammar. In C. Ward (Ed.), *Grammar in the language classroom: Changing approaches and practices.* Singapore: Regional Language Centre.

International Corpus of English Web site: http://www.ucl.ac.uk/english-usage/ice/

McEnery, T., & Wilson, A. (1996). *Corpus linguistics.* Edinburgh: Edinburgh University Press.

Oxford English Dictionary. (2nd ed.). (1989). Oxford, England: Oxford University Press.

Sinclair, J. (1991). *Corpus, concordance, collocation.* Oxford, England: Oxford University Press.

Wellington Corpus Web site: http://www.vuw.ac.nz/lals/wgtn_crps_spkn_NZE.htm

19

English *Gairaigo*: Learning About Language Structure From the Margins of Japanese

Anca M. Nemoianu

Baseball, the all-American game, was introduced to Japan in the middle of the 19th century by Horace Wilson, a young American history and English teacher. The Japanese quickly and enthusiastically adopted it. With it came the requisite vocabulary: *surii sutoraikku* 'three strikes', *hoomu ran* 'home run', and even *supotsu*—yes, the generic word 'sport', for team sports, did not exist in Japan until then. Just as the game of baseball was adapted to the Japanese cultural identity, so were the baseball-related words adapted to the Japanese sound system, along with a very large repertoire of other English *Gairaigo* (i.e., foreign) words. And the presence and status of English in Japanese have grown considerably ever since.

The more general linguistic phenomenon known as *Japangurisshu*—Japanese English—holds a particular fascination with young Japanese speakers, its avid users, as well as with many English speakers, who collect "samples" and share them with the public at large on their Web sites.[1] In this chapter I propose that *Japangurisshu* be considered a potentially valuable resource in the K–12 language arts curriculum: The systematic investigation of this body of language can and will shed light on crucial aspects of linguistic form and meaning in much the same way in which the study of *haiku* has proved to be a successful approach to poetry in many language arts classrooms. Both have qualities of simplicity and transparency; both satisfy the human desire to reach far, into unfamiliar territories. With very little knowl-

---

[1]www.engrish.com is a continuously updated repository of commercial uses of English in Japanese. They invariably contain errors of spelling, word choice, or grammar—hence the somewhat deprecatory label, which highlights the stereotypically incorrect pronunciation of the word *English* by Japanese speakers.

edge about the structure of Japanese, a lot can be learned about specific language facts—from aspects of the sound system to word formation principles, from language change to functions—by examining the fate of English words as they migrate into Japanese and are organically adapted to the host language. What *Japangurisshu*, and more narrowly English *Gairaigo*, offers the K–12 language arts curriculum is a sizable sample of a natural language, created at the intersection of two very different languages, on which students can apply inductive techniques of discovery in order to reach an understanding of linguistic concepts outside ready-made textbook descriptions and prescriptions.

In this chapter I outline one way of bringing students closer to the study of language and helping them reflect on the structure and meaning of English with the help of an unknown language—all of this without leaving English, the medium they are most comfortable with, too far away. The unknown language is Japanese, but just a small and nonthreatening part of the language—English *Gairaigo*, the rich repertoire of English borrowings, adapted in various degrees to Japanese.

WHY DELVE INTO JAPANESE TO LEARN ABOUT ENGLISH?

Traveling afar in order to make sense of what is going on at home is by no means a novel pedagogical approach. Let us look back at the 18th-century English grammar school approach, when Latin grammar was taught in order to "discipline" the schoolchildren's native language. Come to think of it, for 6-year-old children, memorizing the endings of countless nouns and verbs must have seemed an awesome adventure, whose purpose they did not know and seldom questioned. Imagine a child looking at a string of words for a noun that, by its ending, signals its function—much like a contemporary child electronically searching for a way out of a maze filled with dangerous traps in a video game. Later in life, the former will not be entirely shocked by the notion of subject in an English sentence the way many students are nowadays. The teaching of Latin grammar had the expected consequence of developing the analytical tools and the vocabulary for examining the structure of English even when some grammatical concepts hardly applied to the English vernacular.

Far be it from me, however, to advocate the return to the teaching of Latin grammar in first grade. The assumption behind my proposal of using *Japangurisshu* as a resource in the K–12 language arts curriculum is that one of the most appropriate venues for teaching language structure, at any level of analysis, from sound to meaning, is at the intersection with another language. The learning of another language provides the context and the rationale for introducing the vocabulary and the tools for language analysis.

The structure of another language can also provide the vehicle for understanding the structure of English, simply by comparison and contrast. This is no negligible benefit and, I believe, should be paid due attention.

Given the realities of the K–12 curriculum, what many students in secondary school bring to a typical language arts class is a rudimentary knowledge of a foreign language: a few conversational formulas learned within the ambitious context of acquiring communicative competence, where grammar receives at best secondary status. Rarely does a whole group of students share the same foreign or native language (in the case of non-native speakers of English), which can make any contrastive references pointless, or at least confusing. There are, however, alternative approaches that combine the familiarity of English with the novelty of another natural language.

As an ever expanding global language—the language of the Internet, of international business, bureaucracy, and diplomatic negotiations—English is leaving an imprint on many languages of the world, and they in turn shape it so as to fit the new molds. Japanese, a language genealogically unrelated to English and typologically quite different from it, is a fascinating example of a generous host language to a large number of English words. The examination of the relatively large repertoire of *Japangurisshu*—Japanese English—can and will facilitate the teaching of some otherwise arid linguistic concepts, which can then be compared or contrasted to English and other languages the students may speak.

The examination of *Japangurisshu* is a highly entertaining way of effecting the necessary departure from English without going too far away into threatening unfamiliar territories: by looking at Japanese words and wondering what English words they hide behind their Japanese masks; by reading English texts that are sometimes incomprehensible to the English speaker and trying to figure out their intended meanings; and finally, by considering the reasons behind the fascination of the Japanese with a language so different from their own.

ENGLISH *GAIRAIGO* AS LINGUISTIC CORPUS

Throughout its history, Japanese has been a most hospitable language. A non-Indoeuropean language whose genealogy is still debated,[2] Japanese added massively to its indigenous vocabulary (*yamato-kotoba*). First, in the eighth century, Chinese was introduced as a more "masculine" language, more suited to bureaucratic life. To this day, many of the Chinese words in Japanese (*kango*) are no longer considered *gairaigo*, words of foreign origin, although technically they are. In the subsequent centuries of relative (and

---

[2]Genealogically, Japanese, a non-Indoeuropean language, has been considered an isolate, unrelated to any other language; or a member of the Southeast Asian family of languages; or a member of the Ural-Altaic family, together with Korean.

sometimes absolute) isolation, Japanese still managed to borrow words: *pan*, 'bread' is a prime example, borrowed from Portuguese during the 16th century, the Catholic missionary century—a less basic word in a culture where bread is not a staple food, which explains its late entrance into the language. But both country and language opened up to foreign influence again only in the middle of the 19th century, when words from the three major European powers they emulated in different ways—France, Germany, England—were borrowed in large numbers to give a proper linguistic cast to Japan's newfound modernity of West-European inspiration.

English, however, took over as the principal source language after WWII, during the American occupation, and has continued in this role to this day. The impact of American English has been so powerful and so freely accepted by the Japanese that these days older people get English tutors to teach them those English words that have found a home in Japanese and without which they cannot communicate with the younger generations or understand most of the highly imaginative Japanese advertising. Nowadays there are English borrowings in most of the languages of the world just as there are countless loan words in English. But in Japanese they amount to a phenomenon, not just because of their large numbers, but also and most importantly because of the highly creative ways of change and adaptation to the host language, and because of the overall status of English in Japanese everyday life.

Loan words adapt to the sound and word-structure rules of the host language. As they are often borrowed because the host language has no words for new concepts and referents, their meanings remain the same as in the source language; just as often, though, the original meanings drift into new meanings and novel semantic fields. This is true of loan words in all languages. In Japanese, however, English borrowings, the *Gairaigo* of *Japangurisshu*, often undergo further structural change (e.g., in *hangaa-sutoraiki* 'hunger strike', both parts of the compound word are shortened further, to *han-suto*), and many non-English words get formed with the help of English elements, giving rise to pseudo-loans, or *wasei-eigo* (e.g., *oobaa-dokutaa* 'over-doctor' = a PhD without a job). All in all, English *Gairaigo*—organically integrated in the language, and fluently and unselfconsciously used in spoken and written Japanese—is a much livelier linguistic phenomenon than one would expect, one worth examining more closely by both teacher educators and their students, future K–12 teachers.

THREE MINI-LESSONS IN LINGUISTIC ANALYSIS

An entire *Japangurisshu* module can be developed for the K–12 language arts curriculum; it can be narrowed or expanded depending on the age of the students and the goals of a specific class. The module will consist of several units, each focused on a different linguistic aspect, and each linked to a different language situation. For instance, a unit on sound differences between English and Japanese can be triggered by the speech of a character in a work of literature or in a movie; a unit on word formation can be related to the creation of new words in, say, teenagers' slang or advertising. In each unit the starting point consists of a minimum of necessary facts about Japanese. Then, with a handful of *Gairaigo* examples in which the English source is obvious, students and teacher together establish patterns of linguistic change which are later confirmed and refined by analysis of further examples. The observations about the ways in which English is adapted to Japanese can then be used for analyses of similar linguistic phenomena in English. Thus, we start with English, move empirically to English in Japanese, and then go back for a more informed look at English.

In the process, several goals are accomplished: linguistic facts about Japanese itself are inferred analytically; students become aware of similar patterns at work in English; and general linguistic principles become evident on the basis of data from two genealogically and typologically[3] different languages. In other words, the investigation of the *Gairaigo* corpus helps develop a language awareness based in specifics but capable of reaching out to English and other languages.

Gairaigo data are available from small, specialized lexicons. Most of the examples here are from Akira Miura's *English in Japanese: A Selection of Useful Loanwords* (1998), which contains several hundred loan and pseudo-loan words. The advantage of using one lexicon is the consistency of the romanization system, since each lexicon uses variations of the Hepburn romanization (*Hebon-shiki roomanji*) developed in 1886 by James Curtis Hepburn, an American missionary doctor who compiled the first Japanese–English dictionary. The lexicon is arranged in alphabetical order. Each entry contains the romanized[4] version, the *katakana*[5] version, the English source word, meaning and usage notes, examples of sentences using the words, and, where available, the indigenous synonymous word. Here is an example of such an entry, modified so that it appears without the *katakana* version and the accent, and with the examples only in the English translation:

---

[3]While English is typologically an analytical language (i.e., grammatical function is signaled through the basic Subject-Verb-Object word order), Japanese is a so-called agglutinative language, where the grammatical function of subject or object is marked by "postpositions," and the basic word order is Subject-Object-Verb; for example, *watakushi wa utsukushii hana wo miru* = I + postposition for Subject + beautiful + flower + postposition for Object + see = "I see a beautiful flower."

[4]The romanization system used in Miura (1998) is a modified Hepburn system, which uses the doubling of vowels to indicate long vowel sounds. I maintained that convention, but eliminated the marking of the accent for the sake of simplicity.

[5]Japanese writing system used for foreign words.

Raberu (<label)

Labels on bottles, jars, cans, etc., are *raberu*, which comes from English *label*, although an older form *retteru*, derived from Dutch *letter*, is also used to refer to the same object.

1. Please take this medicine after reading the label carefully.
   Raberu also refers to the label at the center of a phonograph record. In this case, *retteru* is never used.
2. If you read the label on the record, you'll know who's singing.
   Raberu has another version, *reeberu*, which is closer to the original English pronunciation, but is not used as often. *Raberu* is an example of spelling pronunciation. (p. 125)

The remainder of this chapter includes several examples of language discovery units, built around the English *Gairaigo* corpus, which will illuminate linguistic facts about sounds (phonology), word structure (morphology), and meaning of words (lexical semantics).

ENGLISH>ENGRISH: A LESSON IN PHONOLOGY

A few pronunciation pointers have to be provided before the phonological discovery process could begin. They have to do with some basic differences between the English and Japanese sound systems. First, Japanese has only five vowel sounds: /a/ as in "ah," /e/ as in "eh," /i/ as in "ee," /o/ as in "oh," and /u/ as in "oo." Thus, the rendition of the much richer English vowel system is bound to be very approximate. Second, as can be seen from the entry quoted earlier, in Japanese all syllables must end with a vowel (*ra-be-ru*), not with a consonant, with the exception of the consonant sound [n] (e.g., *min-chi* 'mince'). Third, all syllables must begin with one consonant sound, rather than a consonant sound cluster, such as [sl] or [kr] (e.g., *ko-roo-ru* 'crawl, only in swimming'). The Japanese word for 'baseball' exemplifies both: *besuboru* has four consonant+vowel syllables, thus avoiding the final consonant /s/ and the final consonant [l]. It also exemplifies, together with *raberu* and *korooru*, a further feature of the Japanese phonological system, one most English speakers are familiar with, and which will be the very focus of the sample lesson in phonology I am presenting here. It can be easily inferred by the students after examining several adaptations of English words to the Japanese sound system.

The phonological unit can start with a series of *Gairaigo*, as in the two lists below, preceded by pairs of English words with related sounds:

led/red	**van/ban**
light/right	**rove/robe**
sarada 'salad'	*ebento* 'event'
rain 'line'	*Barentain-Dee* 'Valentine's Day'
guriru 'grill'	*doraibaa* 'screw*driver*'
guriin-beruto 'green belt'	*saabu* 'serve'
ereki-gitaa 'electric guitar'	*reshiibu* 'receive'
roon 'loan'	*raito-ban* 'light van'
bureki 'brake'	*beniya-ita* 'veneer'
sukeeru 'scale'	*seebu* 'serve'

The boldfaced pairs of words at the head of each list highlight the sound distinction English makes between the consonant sounds /l/and /r/ on the one hand and /v/ and /b/ on the other—in English they are **phonemes**, that is, basic, contrasting sounds. After all, the words in those pairs differ only by one such sound—they are minimally contrastive.

What is happening to these two minimal pairs of phonemes in *Japan-gurisshu*? From the way they are spoken in Japanese, it is clear that Japanese speakers cannot hear either of these two pairs of sounds as contrastive: [l] and [r] are heard as almost one sound, and so are [v] and [b]. They are phonetic variants, or **allophones**, of two basic sounds, one closer to the English phoneme /r/, the other closer to the English /b/, neither one pronounced exactly like the English phonemes /r/ and /b/. That is why the romanized version of the English words adapted to Japanese has "r" any time the English word has a /l/ or /r/ phoneme in it, and "b" any time the English word has a /v/ or /b/ phoneme in it, irrespective of their position in the word, **in free variation**.

The rest of the sound changes is predictable, on the basis of the minimal introductory information about the Japanese sound system. As expected, therefore, because of the nature of the Japanese syllable structure, all the consonant clusters in English (e.g., *scale, brake, green*), with the exception of the one ending in /n/ (*ebento*), are broken by a Japanese vowel sound, usually /u/ or /o/; and a vowel sound is added to all final consonant sounds, except /n/ (*Barentain, rain*). Also it can be noticed that although most of the *Gairaigo* words are based on the pronunciation of the English source words, some are based on the English spelling: for instance, *sarada* (instead of *serada*, which would be closer to the pronunciation of the first vowel sound in the English 'salad'). *Besuboru*, the example from the very beginning of this chapter, also has a partially spelling-based variant, *besubaru*.

The *Gairaigo* examples clarify a basic phonological concept—the relationship between phonemes and allophones—one that is not readily accessible on the basis of English examples alone. In a multicultural classroom, with students from several cultural-linguistic backgrounds, other phonemic/ allophonic distinctions can be pointed out, for example, English (/f/ and /p/) vs. Korean (/p/) or English allophones, such as the /t/ sounds in 'ton' and 'stone' and 'kitty'. Students become aware of the reasons behind pronunciation difficulties in some of their friends and neighbors or in characters from books or movies; they become aware of the *patterned* ways in which these "errors" occur, and this awareness will transfer into their understanding of dialects and registers.

MAKARONI-UESUTAN: A LESSON IN MORPHOLOGY

Moving now from words as sequences of sounds to their internal structure, that is, from phonology to morphology, students can start out again by examining a set of English *Gairaigo* in order to see some morphological mechanisms at work. For indeed, after undergoing phonological adaptation to the Japanese sound and syllable system, many of the English words are further changed. Some of the word formation mechanisms in English precede the list of structurally changed *Gairaigo* words.

fab <**fab**ulous
sci-fi <**sci**ence fiction
brunch <**br**eakfast+**unch**
father-in-law

omu-raisu 'omelet rice' vs. *omuretsu* 'omelet'

moga 'modern girl' vs. *modan gaaru*

mobireeji 'campside for car owners' vs. *automobiru bireeji* 'automobile village'

pan-suto 'panty hose' vs. *pantii-sutokkingu* lit. 'panty stocking'

bodii-biru 'body building' vs. *bodii-birudingu*

kaateru 'motel' vs. *kaa hoteru* 'car hotel'

han-suto 'hunger strike' vs. *hangaa-sutoraiki*

ero-guro-nansensu 'erotic, grotesque, nonsense' vs. *erotiku, gurotesku, nansensu*

engeeji-ringu 'engagement ring' vs. *engeejimento-ringu*

shinpa 'sympathizer' vs. *shinpasaizaa*

peepaa-toraberaa 'paper traveler'

DPE 'development, printing, enlarging'

In the boldfaced examples at the top we have some ways of forming new words in English, entirely with English words. What is happening in the *Gairaigo* words? In a word like *shinpa*, which has a much narrower meaning than the English word, that is, 'sympathizer of the Communist Party', we notice (aside from the phonological change of /s/ to /sh/) the shortening of the English word, similar to the process in the creation of the English word *fab*.

This word formation process—the dropping of several syllables—is called **clipping**. Clipping is also present in all the other *Gairaigo* words, but not just clipping alone. In several of the compound words, one or both words are shortened: In *omu-raisu* only the first word is clipped, while in *pan-suto* both words in the compound are, as in the English *sci-fi*. But **compounding** (see *father-in-law* in English) does not necessarily entail clipping, as we can see in the interesting *Gairaigo* word *peepa-toraberaa*, a non-English word formed of two English words, meaning, a possessor of a passport who has never taken a trip abroad.

There are many such "pseudo-loans" in *Japangurisshu*, compound words coined in Japanese out of English (and other foreign) words. The very word in the title of this section is a pseudo-loan: 'macaroni western', for what in English we call 'spaghetti western'. *Ero-guro-nansensu* is another such pseudo-loan compound formed of three English words—'erotic, grotesque, nonsense', the first two clipped, referring to a decadent period in Japanese history at the end of the 1920s and the beginning of the 1930s. Finally, in *moga*, for instance, we find both clipping and the fusing of the two clipped words, a process called **blending**, as in the English word *brunch*.

Most languages increase their vocabularies by borrowing words from other languages, but also by applying various morphological processes, such as clipping, blending and compounding, to indigenous material. In contemporary English one of the most productive word coining mechanisms is the simple **abbreviation** (e.g., TV, ID, etc., but also in the Japanese *DPE*, an abbreviation of English words, which appears only in Japanese photo shops). The examples in this unit show morphological change applied to loan words. Clipping is probably the most productive of these changes, not surprising, given the length of the borrowed words once the Japanese syllabic structure has been applied to them.

With these empirically derived facts about morphology, the stage is prepared for a more thorough discussion of English word formation principles, of the most productive ones in the students' slang, of the status of newly coined words in more formal writing, etc. With an understanding of word formation principles in English, students could coin words for situations and actions that do not have English labels and gather them in their own lexicons of "necessary words."

PEEPAA DORAIBAA: A LESSON IN LEXICAL SEMANTICS

Languages augment their vocabularies all the time. There is always need for words to express new meanings. Additional meanings are often attached to already existing words (see for instance metaphoric extension, whereby a word that applies to a referent will be used to another area of experience, as in 'bland food' and 'bland ideas'). Also, new words are coined within a language out of indigenous forms. But what happens to the meaning of words that are borrowed from other languages, either as entire words, loan words, or as parts of newly formed words in the host language, or pseudo-loans?

enjin-kii lit. 'engine key'—ignition key

doraibu-mappu lit. 'drive map'—road map

peepaa doraibaa lit. 'paper driver'—owner of a driving license who does not drive

suupaa-sutoa lit. 'super-store'—self-service retail store (not a grocery store)

toppu-redii lit. 'top lady'—First Lady and the most prominent woman in a field

tan 'tongue'—only animal tongue used for food

sukurappu 'scrap'—only as clippings from newspapers, mainly in *sukurappu-bukku*

hiyaringu 'hearing'—only as one of the skills taught in a foreign language class

burookun 'broken'—only about imperfectly spoken language

sadoru 'saddle'—only for bicycle

In the first five examples borrowed English words are turned into compound words that do not exist in the source language, novel lexical creations, known as **pseudo-loans**. In the last five examples, the English *Gairaigo*, phonologically adapted to Japanese, have meanings that are much narrower than the original words. In almost all cases there are no indigenous words that the borrowed words are replacing. Thus, Japanese already has a word for 'a saddle for a horse', *kura*, and the word could have been used by metaphoric extension to the saddle of a bicycle or motorcycle; but instead, Japanese speakers opted for another word, and English *Gairaigo*, to denote the latter. Some of the pseudo-loans were formed with English words, which had already been borrowed by Japanese, and were already known by many speakers; that is why *enjin-kii* won over *igunisshon-kii* ('ignition key'). For others, like *raibu-hausu* ('live house', a coffee-shop with live music), there is no easy explanation. Odd as these pseudo-loans may sound to English speakers, they are now Japanese words, fully incorporated into the Japanese system, meant to be understood by the Japanese. They are no longer English words. They are no more recognizable to English speakers than, say, the word 'very' can be identified by the French as their very own word 'vrai' (true).

Issues of borrowing in order to fill lexical gaps can be discussed further, with examples from contemporary English. Another topic that can be raised at this point is the fate of borrowed words that are synonymous with indigenous words. A well-known example from English is the series of meat–animal doublets (e.g., pork/pig), with synonymous words of French and Anglo-Saxon origin, which illustrates the "division of labor" that takes place spontaneously between words that have identical meaning but different origins. And a natural extension of this topic is work with a **Thesaurus**, which is said to be a repository of synonyms. To what extent can we talk about perfect synonyms, words that have identical meanings?

ENGLISH IN JAPANESE OR LANGUAGE AS STATUS SYMBOL

A recent Japanese TV commercial for Kikkoman Soy Sauce features three cartoon bodybuilders with fish heads, like the plastic fish containers for soy sauce that are in every Japanese child's lunch box, singing, "Show me! Show you!" This is one instance of *Japangurisshu*, or English in Japanese—a true phenomenon in the contemporary linguistic landscape, reflected both in the huge impact of English on Japanese and in the utter fascination it holds on some English speakers, who collect such examples and comment on their quaintness. It just happens that in the example at hand, "Show you!" is not simply an unacceptable use of the imperative in English, not just another "weird" use of English in a commercial setting. It is rather the English sound rendition of the Japanese word for 'soy sauce', which is homophonic with the odd English imperative; it is, therefore, not just a simple error, but an apparent error that serves as a cross-linguistic pun, all too fitting in a tradition where punning has a long poetic tradition.

Let us take another example: the loan word *fantajikku* 'dreamlike', based on the English word *fantastic*. Japanese already has a word for 'dreamlike', the indigenous word *gensooteki*. Why did they borrow the English word then? The answer that is usually given in such instances—of which *fantajikku* is not alone—is the English word sounds "more modern." English *Gairaigo* words lend their users a certain cachet, a mark of distinction. English in commercial ads, adjusted to Japanese, and often incomprehensible to either Japanese or English speakers, is seen as part of the artistic design; the information the ad communicates is always in Japanese. In general, *Japangurisshu*, pervasive as it is in contemporary Japanese, is a status symbol. To a large extent, the function of much of *Japangurisshu* is not communicative, but aesthetic, having to do with the aesthetics of commercial design. But the linguistic phenomenon is real, and although some of the borrowed words and pseudo-loans may drop out of the language as the areas they apply to drop out of fashion, many will stay and become part and parcel of Japanese.

By way of conclusion, let me repeat that English *Gairaigo* words in *Japangurisshu* represent a rich source of accessible and entertaining language data on the basis of which students can learn what happens to sounds and words and meaning, in systematic ways, when they travel far from home—a fun-filled way of approaching the workings of language at many levels, from sound and word to meaning and function, without leaving the comfort of English too far behind.

RESOURCES FOR ENGLISH IN JAPANESE

Miura, A. (1979). *English loanwords in Japanese: A selection*. Tokyo, Japan, and Rutland, VT: Charles E. Tuttle.

Miura, A. (1998). *English in Japanese: A selection of useful loanwords*. New York and Tokyo: Weatherhill.

www.engrish.com (with additional links to other relevant web pages).

20

Opening Dictionaries
to Investigation

Anne Curzan

"When *I* use a word," states Humpty Dumpty in Lewis Carroll's (1941) *Through the Looking-Glass*, "it means just what I choose it to mean—neither more nor less" (p. 123). Alice, puzzled, wonders if he really can make words mean so many different things. Was Humpty Dumpty himself allowed "to be master" when it came to meaning? The question may seem absurd to many speakers of Modern English, who "know better": Words mean what the dictionary says they mean, not what Humpty Dumpty says they mean.

This statement, that dictionaries are the final arbiters on meaning, while certainly more reasonable than Humpty Dumpty's, is still not completely right. First of all, which dictionary are we talking about with the phrase "the dictionary"? Second, if lots of young people start using, for example, *dog* to mean 'friend,' but the dictionary in which they look does not record that meaning, does that mean that *dog* does not mean 'friend'? And if I, in this chapter, create a word on the spot, like *dictionarylike*, and we all understand what I mean by that word, but it is not in the dictionary, is it not a word? Although dictionaries certainly provide an enormous amount of valuable information about what and how words mean, they cannot tell the whole story—and they cannot contain all words and all meanings. That is where speakers and their knowledge of language come in. Speakers will always be ahead of their dictionaries, and although dictionaries can be authoritative, they are not the sole or final authority.

This chapter focuses on dictionaries—and the practice of lexicography more generally—as a valuable resource in the K–12 language arts curriculum, far beyond their standard use as an authority on questions of meaning and spelling. In fact, the status of "the dictionary" as a linguistic authority is where the investigation can begin. Is it a prescriptive or descriptive resource? This chapter then describes some of the ways in which dictionaries can be incorporated into the curriculum as a subject of study, to enhance investigations of the lexicon, word meaning, and language change as well as to encourage discussions of language and power.

The chapter works from the premise that it is critical for students at every level of the educational system—from college students preparing to be teachers to the K–12 students whom they may teach—to examine the sources of linguistic authority on which they rely, from grammar books and style guides to dictionaries, in order to rethink what we can and do mean by "right" and "wrong," "correct" and "grammatical," "standard" and "non-standard," when it comes to language. For this reason, the question of where linguistic authority resides in the construction of "standard" or "good" or "correct" usage can be a useful place to begin, as the dictionary is clearly a central source of linguistic authority for most English language users. The sometimes conflicting goals of dictionary makers and users raises important questions about prescriptive and descriptive approaches to language and how dictionary definitions work. This chapter suggests ways in which students can examine the creation and content of dictionaries, both historically and currently, particularly in light of their own expectations of what a dictionary should contain.

Readers must from here on suspend any disbelief they may bring to this chapter's argument that dictionaries can be fascinating and remain open to being persuaded otherwise. While Samuel Johnson described the lexicographer as a "harmless drudge," the ambition of lexicographers to record as much of the entirety of a language as possible is far from modest and their accomplishments toward these ends are astounding. When we retrain the lens from the finished product to the process of creating dictionaries and to the layers of decisions that must be made for every word entry, we can no longer take their presence or their form for granted, and this perspective opens rich new areas for investigation and exploration.

BACKGROUND ON ENGLISH LEXICOGRAPHY

Lexicography—the theory and practice of creating dictionaries—is both a profession and a field of study. Although most dictionary users rarely if ever think twice about the publisher of their dictionary, the structure of its entries, the content of its front matter, the choices for illustrations, and the other many details of any dictionary's format, professional lexicographers painstakingly make decisions about each and every one of the entries, from edition to edition, and are highly aware of the differences across dictionaries and the motivations for these differences.

One of the most comprehensive texts on the practice of lexicography is Sidney Landau's (2001) *Dictionaries: The Art and Craft of Lexicography* (2nd edition), a text which not only unpacks the various components of the standard dictionary (e.g., definitions, usage labels) but also usefully differentiates among different kinds of dictionaries (e.g., abridged vs. college dictionaries). Landau also tackles some of the fascinating ethical issues involved in dictionary making, such as copyright (including the litigious battle over who owns the name *Webster's*) and plagiarism; as Landau writes, "The history of English lexicography usually consists of a recital of successive and often successful acts of piracy" (p. 43), and in the 20th century, lexicographers stopped publicly acknowledging their debt to other dictionaries.[1]

The concise history of lexicography that follows this opening remark in Landau's book can be supplemented by Jonathon Green's (1996) more detailed account in *Chasing the Sun: Dictionary Makers and the Dictionaries They Made*. Part of the history of the making of the *Oxford English Dictionary* (*OED*), a work that most lexicographers view as the most impressive lexicographic feat in modern history, hit the *New York Times* bestseller list with the publication of Simon Winchester's (1998) *The Professor and the Madman*, which tells the (somewhat sensationalized) story of Dr. William Chester Minor, an insane asylum resident who was also the biggest single contributor of quotations to the *OED*. In framing Samuel Johnson's stunning achievement with his dictionary in 1755, Winchester describes Shakespeare writing his plays without a dictionary, a description that usefully highlights the relatively recent development of the English dictionary and emphasizes the ambition, ingenuity, and determination that allowed the *OED* to be completed over four decades at the turn of the 20th century.[2] (See Bailey, 1987 and Davis, 1999 for more useful background information on lexicography.)

---

[1]Landau (2001) adds that a truly "new" dictionary, that radically departed from those that preceded it would not be desirable: "The pressures of the marketplace dictate that every dictionary be 'new.' A really new dictionary would be a dreadful piece of work, missing innumerable basic words and senses, replete with absurdities and unspeakable errors, studded with biases and interlarded with irrelevant provincialisms. Fortunately, very few dictionaries are really new, and none of the general, staff-written, commercial dictionaries published by major dictionary houses are" (p. 43).

[2]For a wonderful biography of James A. H. Murray, the original editor of the *OED*, as well as a detailed history of the making of the *OED*, see K. M. Elisabeth Murray's *Caught in the Web of Words*. A recent edited collection on the *OED*, *Lexicography and the OED*, provides a range of interesting papers on the history, reception, coverage, and editorial decisions involved in the making of the *OED*. There is also a range of works addressing other historical dictionaries, such as Samuel Johnson's dictionary (e.g., Sledd & Kolb 1955), Webster's *Third* (e.g., Morton, 1994), and many more.

One of the important questions that the history of English dictionaries raises is whether dictionaries are descriptive or prescriptive resources. Many lexicographers themselves have had a fraught relationship with this question. In an often quoted section of the preface to his dictionary, Samuel Johnson describes his original desire to "fix" or permanently stabilize the language through the dictionary and his subsequent realization that language change (which he saw as decay) was inevitable and could not be stopped by a dictionary, no matter how comprehensive or authoritative. Many lexicographers view the project of a dictionary as a descriptive one: to record the language as it is used. But almost every editorial decision has the potential to be read prescriptively: the ordering of pronunciations and definitions; the usage labels attached to certain words (e.g., *slang, offensive*); the inclusion and exclusion of certain meanings and words. And throughout the history of English lexicography, changing value systems in the social world that lexicographers inhabit have raised different questions of proscription, from the exclusion of "bad words" in the Victorian era (Noah Webster did not include these in his American dictionary of 1828 and most of them were not included in the first edition of the *OED*) to the handling of inclusion of "politically incorrect" words at the end of the 20th century.

No matter the goals of lexicographers, users of English dictionaries seem to seek prescriptive authority. As Green (1996) notes: "Survey after survey records that dictionary users, in America at any rate, want their dictionaries to lay down the lexical law. The last thing, apparently, they desire is to use their own judgment" (p. 455). Green describes the "act of faith" by almost all dictionary users that their dictionaries are, somehow, beyond the subjectivity that characterizes other forms of published writing. Although speakers' own judgment may be that a word means something different from the definition provided by a dictionary, the dictionary is taken as an authority that can put speakers' own use into question, no matter if the preface may describe the editors' goals of recording speakers' actual usage rather prescribing correct usage. In the face of language change, the dictionary seems a stable authority for determining what a word "really means," even if we as speakers are all using it to mean something else. Very interesting recent work in sociolinguistics has addressed speakers' desire for authority in language and their natural tendency toward what Deborah Cameron (1995) calls "verbal hygiene," or the regulating of other people's language. It is a natural part of speech communities, she argues, for some speakers to try to regulate the language of others. In English, verbal hygiene takes the form of, among other things, grammar books, style guides, newspaper columns on usage, and dictionaries—no matter the intentions of their creators. And dictionary users have been known to become quite upset if they feel lexicographers have abdicated that responsibility—the controversy over Webster's Third being a prime example. Speakers trust dictionaries to tell them if a semantic change has "really happened," if a word is standard or slang—in other words, if a word or a meaning is legitimate, rather than a "misuse" by "lazy," "uneducated," or otherwise "unworthy" speakers.

Semantic change, or the process of words' meanings changing over time, is a natural part of ongoing language change. Most linguistics textbooks outline four major types of semantic change: generalization or broadening (i.e., a word's meaning becoming broader, such as *aroma*, which used to mean 'the smell of spices'); specialization or narrowing (i.e., a word's meaning becoming narrower, such as *girl*, which used to mean 'child,' and *meat*, which used to mean 'food'); amelioration (i.e., a word's meaning becoming "better," such as the word *awesome*); pejoration or deterioration (i.e., a word's meaning becoming "worse," such as *silly*, which used to mean 'nice,' or *wench*, which used to mean 'child' and then 'girl,' before acquiring a set of more negative meanings).[3] Words can change their denotations (or what we might think of as literal meanings) and their connotations (or the associations that words carry for speakers). Speakers are also wonderfully creative with their language, creating new words all the time, through processes such as compounding, affixation (adding prefixes and suffixes), blending (merging two words such as *netiquette* from *net* and *etiquette*), clipping (e.g., *limo* from *limousine*), as well as borrowing words from other languages and dialects. Slang is one of the most creative areas of the lexicon, and an area that K–12 students know particularly well. The next section looks specifically at how instructors can engage this knowledge to talk about language change, the definition of words, and the authority of dictionaries.

DICTIONARIES IN THE K–12 LANGUAGE ARTS CURRICULUM

In a survey of 400 fifth- and sixth-grade teachers, Erin McKean (2000) found that nearly half the teachers reported using dictionaries to teach "traditional" dictionary skills (e.g., looking up words) and many of them employed dictionary games as well. She then adds: "When asked what obstacles kept them from doing more dictionary activities with their classes, 67% percent [*sic*] said that they wished they had more ideas for activities or lessons, 58% wanted more class time, and 20% wanted more dictionaries" (p. 85). This chapter cannot, unfortunately, create more class time for K–12

---

[3]Other types of semantic change include strengthening, weakening, metaphoric and metonymic transfer, and "semantic shift" (often used as a label for shifts of meaning that seem hard to categorize in retrospect).

teachers or more money to purchase dictionaries. But the following sections do provide new ideas for activities with dictionaries in the K–12 classroom, to begin to fill that gap, and the final section suggests a few dictionaries that instructors may want to consider purchasing should their budgets allow for it. Given the reading skills required to use dictionaries, these activities will be best suited for upper level primary school and all secondary school instructors and students. (For more details about ways to incorporate dictionaries into the college curriculum, see Curzan, 2000).

Who's in Charge Here? The first step in asking students to think more critically and more interestingly about dictionaries, is to step back from the phrase "look it up in the dictionary." Who writes the dictionary? Who wrote the dictionary the students are using? Who published it? When was it published? Does that matter? Would the editors of this dictionary know all the words that they use? Should their slang be in it? Instructors can and should ask students to read the front matter of the dictionary and see if they agree with all the editorial decisions that have been made. For example, do the pronunciations that have been included include their pronunciations? If the students are from any nonstandard English-speaking part of the country, the answer is probably no. Would they change that if they could? How do they feel about only having "standard" forms in the dictionary? What about the ordering of meanings under any given word? Should the oldest come first or the most common? Should out-of-date meanings still be in the dictionary, even if no one knows that the word used to have that meaning? These questions emphasize for students both how many decisions go into a dictionary as well as how these decisions are human and fallible.

How Does One Look up a Word? Teaching basic dictionary skills is clearly a critical component of using dictionaries in the K–12 classroom. McKean (2000) summarizes two of the most common devices primary school teachers employ, in addition to individual student's use of dictionaries: dictionary races in which students try to look up words as quickly as possible; and scavenger hunts in which students look for particular kinds of words or labels (e.g., words of Latin origin or words that are labeled as "scientific"). The use of the dictionary quickly becomes naturalized for students, and for secondary school students, it can be an interesting exercise to write a narrative, explaining step by step to someone who has never looked up a word in a dictionary how to do so (i.e., a version of the "how to make a peanut butter and jelly sandwich" exercise). This exercise allows students to take nothing about the dictionary for granted. For example, which dictionary should this person use? How are the words organized? What if there are multiple entries for a word? How should this person interpret all the various kinds of information that follow the headword in the entry? What if the person does not know a word in the definition?[4] What if there is an abbreviation the person does not understand?

Should "Doh!" Be in the Dictionary? In fact, one can put any relatively new slang word into that question and it works just as well; I have often used this example (a Homer Simpsonism, for anyone not familiar with it) because it appears in an article from the *Star Tribune* on June 15, 2001, about words newly included in the online version of the *OED* ("Doh!"). Another article in the *New York Times* describes the lexicographical debate over the possible inclusion of *yada yada yada* (Brockman, 1999). The debate over whether new words should be included in new editions of long-standing dictionaries is happening in dictionary offices around the country, and it can effectively be recreated in our classrooms. The critical question is whether the new word will "make it"—that is, is the word only a fad that will pass or is it a genuine addition to the English vocabulary that will continue to be used consistently? The word *jiggy*, which became popular with the Will Smith song in the mid-1990s, seems to have faded from use. Will *yada yada yada*, not created by *Seinfeld* but certainly brought to new prominence by it, survive the end of the sitcom? One way that lexicographers try to answer such questions is by tracking usage in print sources, such as newspapers and magazines (see Landau, 2001 for more details). If instructors have access to Lexis-Nexis in their schools, the *New York Times* online, or any other electronic newspaper or magazine database, these are wonderful resources for tracking the use of words in the media. If not, instructors can structure the exercise as more of a scavenger hunt. If students think that one of the slang or newer words that they know and use should be included in a dictionary, they must find evidence for its use in print sources, be that books they read or newspapers or magazines.

What if We Made Our Own Dictionary? McKean (2000) notes that one of the more popular classroom dictionary exercises is the creation of class dictionaries. John M. Sirmans (cited in Glowka et al., 2000), describing his involvement in the professional lexicography project "Among the New Words," states that the project gave him and the others involved "a brief glimpse of action on the front lines where 99.99% of the non-English-majoring population actually manipulates language on a daily basis for profit and enjoyment and occasionally coins words and meanings that will be held sacred by future English major" (p. 102), as well as a new appreciation for the work of editors at every level, proof readers, and everyone else involved in creating dictio-

---

[4]One of the fundamental principles of comprehensive dictionaries is that every word used in a definition must also be included as a headword. It is, as one can imagine, a time-consuming editorial process to confirm that the policy has been followed.

naries. The class lexicography project does not have to be professionally published to be equally instructive. If the students are working with a standard classroom dictionary, the project can be framed as a supplement, including words that the students use that are not included as well as new meanings to words already included.

In writing their own dictionary entries, students must study the format of published dictionaries in order to figure out how to mold their knowledge of a word's meanings and usage into that format. If the classroom or library is equipped with multiple dictionaries, students can compare formats, to see which they prefer for their own dictionary. Then when defining their own words, they must address questions such as: What part (or parts) of speech is the word? How would they define it? This second question can lead to the design of surveys, which students then administer to other speakers and compare results in order to come to a consensus definition. They must also make sure that any word they use in the definition is used in the dictionary—either the published one or their own. Should there be cross-references? Synonyms? The act of creating definitions makes real for students how difficult it is to pin down meaning, to separate different meanings into a discrete list, and to capture connotations. It becomes clearer how much dictionaries can capture as well as what they cannot.

In rewriting entries in a published dictionary, students should also consider whether the meanings should be reordered and where the new meaning they would like to add should fit. For example, the word *peruse* has undergone a drastic shift in meaning within this past generation of speakers. Most dictionaries record the word's meaning as 'to read closely'; most speakers under the age of 35 or 40 seem to use the word to mean 'to skim' or 'to scan.' Students can survey speakers of their parents' age, grandparents' age, older siblings' age, etc. With these results in hand, they can debate, what does the word now mean? How would they redefine it in their dictionary? Obviously, this kind of discussion returns to important issues of any dictionary's authority (versus the authority of speakers' actual usage) and the nature of language change.

How Should Dictionaries Handle Slang and "Bad" Words? This question can be raised in relation to published dictionaries and/or supplemental class dictionaries. When slang and taboo words are included in the dictionary, who labels them and how? Students should look at published dictionaries to see what usage labels the editors choose to use. Then they should look up slang and taboo words in multiple dictionaries. How do editors handle the words differently? Do they agree with the definitions and usage labels attached to these words? And when does slang stop being slang? Jonathan Swift, at the beginning of the 18th century, deemed words such as *bamboozle* and *uppish* so slangy and colloquial that they should be ex-

punged from the language (quoted in Green, 1996, p. 253); the fourth edition of the *American Heritage College Dictionary* (2002) labels both as "informal." Should, for example, *cool* meaning 'good' be labeled as "slang," "informal," or nothing at all? What about *fried* meaning 'drugged out' or 'tired out'? If instructors feel it appropriate for the level of their students, it can also be very interesting to discuss why taboo words might get left out of dictionaries for various levels of students. What exactly are we as speakers afraid will happen if bad words are included in a dictionary? One could argue that authorizing such words by putting them in the dictionary makes them even less "exciting" than they might be otherwise.

Did the Word Girl Really Used to Mean 'Child'? Many of the foregoing examples highlight the fact that language change is happening around us all the time, be that with words like *peruse* or slang creations like *doh*. It is important for students to realize that this kind of change has happened throughout the history of the English language and it is not a sign of decay. To examine more recent changes, students can look at a dictionary published before the 1990s and see that, for example, words like *web*, *dot*, and *network* have taken on new meanings since then. They can look back at earlier dictionaries to see when they can find the meaning 'good' for *awesome*. The *OED*, with its comprehensive historical scope, is obviously the best resource for tracking semantic change, but it may be too dense for many secondary school students and may well not be available to many if not most instructors. If it is available, instructors may want to excerpt the chronology of meanings outlined in the *OED* for interesting words (rather than asking students to unpack the complexities of the entire entry) and look with students at how the words have changed over time. What kind of semantic change is involved, for example, in the shift of the word *corn* from any grain to maize specifically, or of the word *starve* from 'die' to 'die from hunger' to sometimes describing the state of extreme hunger? The *Random House Historical Dictionary of American Slang* also provides detailed histories of words categorized as slang.

What Do You Mean Dictionaries Haven't Always Looked This Way? In addition to telling students about the creation of dictionaries before computers, instructors with internet access can also now show students what is usually cited as the first English dictionary: Robert Cawdrey's (1604) *A Table Alphabetical*, which is publicly available online. In print, it is a very thin volume. It was, as all English dictionaries would be for the next 100 years, a dictionary of "hard words"; after all, everyone knew the easy words so why put them in the dictionary? In the online version, students can examine the very short definitions, which stand in stark contrast to modern dictionaries, and all the material they might think is missing (e.g., pronunciation, part of speech); they can also, if they look carefully, see that the alphabetical ordering is not always perfect! Cawdrey's dictionary can also serve as an effective reminder of how much language changes: *ocean*, *alien*, and *library* are all included as hard words, as they were still relatively new to the language in 1604. There are also new dictionaries that call into question the now "traditional" format of dictionaries. For example, three relatively recent feminist dictionaries take quite different approaches to the defining of words: *A Feminist Dictionary* (Kramarae & Treichler, 1985) is selective in the words that it includes and often opts for relevant quotations under entries as opposed to definitions; *Womanwords* (Mills, 1989), takes a more narrative approach, describing in significant detail the history and usage of many "gendered" words; and *Websters' First New Intergalactic Wickedary of the English Language* (Daly, 1987) comprises three word-webs in which both familiar and unfamiliar words are redefined by websters, or female weavers of words.

What Other Kinds of Dictionaries Are Available? In addition to general-purpose dictionaries (what most speakers think of when they say "the dictionary"), there are what Landau calls "special-purpose dictionaries" (ranging from etymological to pronouncing dictionaries, dialect to slang dictionaries, dictionaries of idioms and neologisms, and everything in between) and "special-field dictionaries," which would encompass most dictionaries of academic fields. John Ray, a botanist by training, is often credited with creating the first dialect dictionary of notable scope: *A Collection of Words Not Generally Used*, published first in 1674 (cf. Görlach, 1999). There have been several impressive dialect projects since, most notably the *English Dialect Dictionary* (1898–1905) by Joseph Wright and the *Dictionary of American Regional English*, still underway at the University of Wisconsin (the newest volume, IV: P-Sk, was just published on December 15, 2002). Frederic Cassidy, who was Chief Editor of *DARE* until his death in 2000 and envisioned *DARE* as both complementing and surpassing the *EDD*, is also known for his work in creating the *Dictionary of Jamaican English*. The *Dictionary of South African English* (Branford & Branford, 1991) records the words and meanings specific to that variety of English. Clarence Major's (1994) *Juba to Jive* records African American slang, and Geneva Smitherman's (2000) *Black Talk* aims to record the unique features of what she calls "Black Language," which is not synonymous with African-American slang. All of these dictionaries record and lend their lexicographic authority to regional and ethnic dialects of American English as well as world varieties of English. Students who are native speakers of any of these varieties are generally interested in seeing how their dialects get recorded, and they are in a position to affirm or question the editors' definitions. Students who are not native speakers of these varieties can learn a lot about dialect variation in

American English and variation among World Englishes by examining both the entries in these dictionaries and the prefaces, in which the editors talk candidly about the motivations for these dictionaries in terms of authorizing varieties of English that are not considered "Standard English," about giving these varieties the legitimacy that comes with having a dictionary.

CONCLUSION

Dictionaries are very powerful language resources. They contain enormous amounts of information from which speakers can learn about the meaning and usage of words. They also possess the power to legitimize and delegitimize words, dialects, and the speakers who use them. Behind every dictionary is a story of its creation and the people who created it (both those who edited that particular dictionary and their many predecessors who established what an English dictionary looks like and what goes in it); and as students come to understand what "the dictionary" is better, they themselves become more authorized and informed users, both of the dictionary and of the language. Students realize that dictionaries are, in fact, a relatively new invention in the history of the English language and that not all dictionaries are created equal. In the process, they can also learn a great deal about how words mean, how words change, and how they can investigate the ways in which words are being used and recorded all around them.

REFERENCES

Bailey, R. W. (Ed.). (1987). *Dictionaries of English: Prospects for the record of our language.* Ann Arbor: University of Michigan Press.

Branford, J., with Branford, W. (Eds.). (1991). *Dictionary of South African English* (2nd ed.). Cape Town: Oxford University Press.

Brockman, E. S. (1999, August 22). In the dictionary game, yada yada yada is satisficing to some, not others. *The New York Times*, 4.7.

Cameron, D. (1995). *Verbal hygiene.* London and New York: Routledge.

Carroll, L. (1941). *Through the looking-glass, and what Alice found there.* Mount Vernon, NY: Peter Pauper Press.

Cassidy, F. G. (Ed.). (1985). *Dictionary of American regional English.* Cambridge, MA: Belknap.

Cawdrey, R. (1604). *A table alphabetical.* Available online at: <http://www.library.utoronto.ca/utel/ret/cawdrey/cawdrey0.html>

Curzan, A. (2000). Lexicography and questions of authority in the college classroom. *Dictionaries, 21,* 90–99.

Daly, Mary, in cahoots with Jane Caputi. (1987). *Websters' first new intergalactic wickedary of the English language.* New York: HarperCollins.

Davis, H. (1999). Typography, lexicography, and the development of the idea of 'standard English.' In T. Bex & R. J. Watts (Eds.), *Standard English: The widening debate* (pp. 69–88). London and New York: Routledge.

Doh! It's not just in Homer's dictionary. (2001, June 15). *Star Tribune*, A19.

Glowka, W., Hendrix, K. C., Lester, B. K., Scott, E., & Sirmans, J. M. (2000). *Among the new words* as an editing project in a methods of research class. *Dictionaries, 21*, 100–108.

Görlach, M. (1999). Regional and social variation. In R. Lass (Ed.), *The Cambridge history of the English Language, Vol. III (1476–1776)* (pp. 459–538). Cambridge, England: Cambridge University Press.

Green, J. (1996). *Chasing the sun: Dictionary makers and the dictionaries they made*. New York: Henry Holt.

Kramarae, C., & Treichler, P. A. (1985). *A feminist dictionary*. London: Pandora Press.

Landau, S. I. (2001). *Dictionaries: The art and craft of lexicography* (2nd ed.). Cambridge, England: Cambridge University Press.

Lighter, J. E. (Ed.). (1994). *Random House historical dictionary of American slang*. New York: Random House.

Major, C. (Ed.). (1994). *Juba to jive: A dictionary of African-American slang*. New York: Penguin.

McKean, E. (2000). Dictionary activities in the elementary classroom: News for lexicographers. *Dictionaries, 21*, 81–89.

Mills, J. (1989). *Womanwords*. London: Virago Press.

Middle English Compendium (including the *Middle English Dictionary*). Available online at: <http://www.hti.umich.edu/mec/>

Morton, H. C. (1994). *The story of Webster's Third: Philip Gove's controversial dictionary and its critics*. Cambridge and New York: Cambridge University Press.

Oxford English Dictionary. (1989). (2nd ed.). Oxford, England: Clarendon.

Sledd, J. H., & Kolb, G. J. (1955). *Dr. Johnson's dictionary: Essays in the biography of a book*. Chicago: University of Chicago Press.

Smitherman, G. (2000). *Black talk: Words and phrases from the hood to the amen corner* (Revised ed.). Boston: Houghton Mifflin.

Winchester, S. (1998). *The professor and the madman: A tale of murder, insanity, and the making of the Oxford English dictionary*. New York: Harper Collins.

About the Authors

Jean Ann is Assistant Professor of Linguistics at SUNY Oswego. She teaches courses in both the T.E.S.O.L. and Linguistics Programs. Her research and writing interests include formal vs. functional approaches to sign language phonology, linguistics in the teaching and learning of second languages, and the connection between language and social justice.

John Baugh is Professor of Psychology, Anthropology, Education, and English at Washington University in St. Louis and holds the inaugural Margaret Bush Wilson professorship in Arts and Sciences. He also serves as Director of African and American Studies. His books include *Beyond Ebonics: Linguistic Pride and Racial Prejudice. Out of the Mouths of Slaves: African American Language and Educational Malpractice* and *Black Street Speech: Its History, Structure and Survival*, as well as numerous edited volumes, articles, and book chapters.

Robert Bayley is Professor of Bicultural-Bilingual Studies at the University of Texas at San Antonio. He specializes in sociolinguistics and second language acquisition. He is co-author of *Sociolinguistic Variation in ASL* (Gallaudet University Press, 2001) and *Language as Cultural Practice* (Lawrence Erlbaum Associates, 2002).

Susan Meredith Burt teaches linguistics at Illinois State University; her research interests include language choice and language shift, intercultural pragmatics, and politeness theories. Her papers have appeared in journals such as *Journal of Pragmatics, Multilingua, Pragmatics,* and *Journal of Multilingual and Multicultural Development.*

Anne Curzan is Associate Professor of English at the University of Michigan. She teaches courses in introductory and advanced English linguistics, history of English, language and gender, and other fields of English language study, as well as pedagogy. Her research interests include history of English, historical sociolinguistics, lexicography, language and gender, and pedagogy. She is the author of *Gender Shifts in the History of English* (Cambridge University Press, forthcoming) and co-author of *First Day to Final Grade: A Graduate Student's Guide to Teaching* (University of Michigan Press, 2000).

Kristin Denham is Associate Professor of linguistics in the English Department at Western Washington University. She teaches introductory linguistics courses, descriptive grammar, the history of English, as well as courses that examine orality, literacy, and dialect (including Native American language, literature, and translation; and the use of dialect in writing). Her research interests include syntax (especially *wh*-question formation) as well as orality and literacy, grammar and writing, and applications of linguistics in K–12 education. She is chair of the Committee on Language in the School Curriculum of the Linguistic Society of America and is Co-Editor of *Syntax in the Schools*, the quarterly journal of the Assembly for the Teaching of English Grammar (ATEG).

Patricia A. Dunn is Associate Professor of English at Illinois State University in Normal. She teaches courses on Rhetoric, Composition, and Issues of Grammar in the Teaching of Writing in High School and Middle School. She has published several articles and two books: *Learning Re-abled: The LD Controversy and Composition Studies* (1995) and *Talking, Sketching, Moving: Multiple Literacies in the Teaching of Writing* (2001), both from Boynton/Cook Heinemann.

Kirk Hazen is Assistant Professor of Linguistics in the English Department at West Virginia University. He has been awarded an Outstanding Teacher Award and an Outstanding Researcher Award from the Eberly College of Arts and Sciences at WVU. Specializing in language variation and change, Professor Hazen conducts research on U.S. dialects, including African-American and Appalachian varieties of English. He is the director of the West Virginia Dialect Project, (former) chair of the Linguistic Society of America's Language in the School Curriculum committee, and member of the American Dialect Society's Committee on Teaching.

Janet Higgins is currently a professor in the Department of International Communication at Okinawa University in Japan. She has taught EFL/ESL and worked as a teacher trainer in Britain, Hong Kong, Japan, Malaysia, Spain, and the Sultanate of Oman. She is a practical assessor for the University of Cambridge (UCLES) Diploma in Teaching English Language to Adults (DELTA) examination scheme, and has carried out assessments in Abu Dhabi, Britain, Japan, Korea, Malaysia, and the Sultanate of Oman. Her current research interests concern critical discourse analysis and the media.

Tony T. N. Hung is Head of the Language Centre, and Director of the Centre for the Advancement of English for Professionals, at the Hong Kong Baptist University. He has published on New Englishes (especially Hong Kong and Singapore English), the teaching of grammar and pronunciation, syntax-phonology interaction, and Chinese linguistics.

Jin Sook Lee is Assistant Professor in the Department of Education, at the University of California, Santa Barbara. She teaches courses on second/foreign language learning, bilingualism, and bilingual education. Her research interests include the development of pragmatic competence in language learners, codeswitching among bilinguals, and heritage language maintenance.

Kenneth Lindblom is Assistant Professor of English at Illinois State University. He teaches courses in rhetoric, composition, and English education and co-founded the Graduate Certificate Program in the Teaching of Writing in High School and Middle School. Among other journals and collections his essays on language and the teaching of writing have appeared in *English Journal, Journal of Pragmatics,* and *Rhetoric Review.*

Anne Lobeck is Professor of linguistics in the English Department at Western Washington University. Her publications include articles on syntactic theory, language and gender, and linguistics and education, and she is author of two books: a college grammar textbook, *Discovering Grammar: An Introduction to English Sentence Structure*, and a book on syntactic theory, *Ellipsis: Functional Heads, Licensing and Identification* (both published by Oxford University Press). She teaches courses in syntactic theory, language and gender, linguistics and literary theory, the history of English, and grammar and the teaching of writing, and is Co-Editor of *Syntax in the Schools*, the quarterly journal of the Assembly for the Teaching of English Grammar (ATEG).

Patricia MacGregor-Mendoza is Associate Professor of Spanish and Linguistics at New Mexico State University. Her research interests include the education of linguistic minorities, the language use and language attitudes of bilingual communities, language policy and first and second language acquisition.

Lynn Mancini (née Messing)'s dissertation studied hearing people's signing during English conversations. She chaired an international, interdisciplinary workshop on the relationships among speech, sign, and gesture, and Oxford University Press has published a book she co-edited on that subject. She currently teaches computer networking and can be reached at mancini @college.dtcc.edu.

Donna Jo Napoli is Professor of Linguistics at Swarthmore College and has taught courses in syntax, phonetics, phonology, morphology, historical and comparative linguistics, Romance studies, structure of Japanese, structure of American Sign Language, poetics, poetry workshops, dialogue, fiction writing workshops, writing for ESL students, and mathematical and linguistic analysis of folk dance. She has authored and edited numerous books, ranging from syntax to semantics to phonology (including historical) to psycholinguistics. She has published numerous other articles on syntax, morphology, the structure of Italian, and the structure of American Sign Language. She has also published over forty fiction books for children, from picture books up through young adult novels, many of which have won awards. She has also contributed poems to six anthologies and been co-editor of four and has written several essays about children's literature.

Anca M. Nemoianu teaches linguistics in the English department of the Catholic University of America in Washington, D.C. Her students are undergraduate English education majors and graduate students of literature, and her current research interests reflect these pedagogical realities: ways of making linguistic analysis more palatable to students by integrating their interests into the curriculum and using academic service learning as a way of giving the study of linguistics relevance in the students' everyday lives; and linguistic markers by which fiction writers shift narrative perspective. Her article on teaching language change that is happening "in front of our eyes" appeared in Rebecca Wheeler (Ed.), *Language Alive in the Classroom* (Praeger, 1999).

Bruce Long Peng is Assistant Professor of Linguistics at SUNY Oswego. He teaches courses in educational research, linguistics, and English as a second language. His research and writing interests include second language sound systems, formal phonological structure and theory such as Optimality Theory, language teaching methodologies, and linguistics in the schools.

Kathryn Remlinger is Associate Professor of English at Grand Valley State University in Allendale, Michigan. She teaches a variety of linguistics courses including sociolinguistics, language and gender, and the history of the English language. Her research interests include classroom discourse; language, gender and sexuality; and language variation and change.

Sandra R. Schecter is Associate Professor of Education and Women's Studies at York University in Toronto, where she teaches courses in language pedagogy, communication, and research methods. An ethnolinguist, she has published on language socialization, language education, and language policy and planning. She is co-author of *Language as Cultural Practice* (Lawrence Erlbaum Associates, 2002) and *Becoming a Language Educator* (Lawrence Erlbaum Associates, 1998).

Alicia Beckford Wassink is Assistant Professor in the Department of Linguistics at the University of Washington, and a Visiting Research Fellow at the University of the West Indies, Mona Campus, in Kingston, Jamaica. Her research lies in the areas of language ideology, Jamaican Creole phonology, and acoustic phonetics.

Rebecca S. Wheeler is Assistant Professor of Linguistics at Christopher Newport University. She is former editor of *Syntax in the Schools*, the quarterly journal of the Assembly for the Teaching of English Grammar (ATEG), and of the two volumes, *Language Alive in the Classroom* and *The Workings of Language: From Prescriptions to Perspectives* (Praeger, 1999). Wheeler's teaching and research focus on reducing the achievement gap through the use of codeswitching, a linguistically informed approach to language varieties. She has just been appointed to the Committee on Language in the School Curriculum of the Linguistic Society of America.

Hua Yang has a Master's Degree in Education from University of Wisconsin, Oshkosh, and teaches English as a Second Language at Tippler Middle School. Her interests include Applied Linguistics and language shift. She hopes this research will awaken interest in her native language, Hmong, and encourage Hmong speakers to appreciate the beauty of their language.

Author Index

Subject Index